THE DREAM & THE HOPE

THE HISTORIC RISE OF
KETANJI BROWN JACKSON
TO THE NATION'S HIGHEST COURT

THE DREAM & THE HOPE

THE HISTORIC RISE OF
KETANJI BROWN JACKSON
TO THE NATION'S HIGHEST COURT

GAREN THOMAS & LORI ROZSA

HARPER
An Imprint of HarperCollinsPublishers

HarperCollins Children's Books, a division of HarperCollins
Publishers, 195 Broadway, New York, NY 10007

HarperCollins Publishers, Macken House, 39/40 Mayor
Street Upper, Dublin 1, D01 C9W8, Ireland

ISBN 978-0-06-331144-2

Typography by Kathy H. Lam
25 26 27 28 29 LBC 5 4 3 2 1
First Edition

For Phoenix and Pharrah. Though sometimes sad or scary, our history's also full of promise and hope. . . . May all your hopes and dreams come true. —G. T.

To my daughter Lillian, whose knowledge of the law and shared admiration for Justice Jackson helped and encouraged me from day one. —L. R.

CONTENTS

I

WHAT'S IN A NAME?

IT WAS SEPTEMBER 14, 1970—a balmy day tinged with silver in Washington, DC. Ellery Brown had given birth to a daughter "on the other side of [the] high water mark of the [Civil Rights] Movement, just two years after Congress [had] enacted two Civil Rights Acts and the Voting Rights Act." John and Ellery Brown, both public school teachers, had wanted to give their daughter a special, meaningful name—an African one. One that expressed "both pride in their heritage and hope for the future," and the relentless, stubborn survival of Black Americans.

Ellery had asked her sister Carolynn, who was serving in the Peace Corps in Liberia in west Africa, for a list of suggestions for them to choose from. She came back with "Ketanji Onyika," which they'd never heard before. They were told it meant "lovely one" in an African dialect (though they have never been able to figure out which one), and Ellery was intrigued by how it sounded. This was how their beautiful little girl, Ketanji Onyika Brown, got her name.

Exactly forty-nine years earlier, on the same day in 1921, Constance Baker Motley was born in the United States to Caribbean immigrant parents. She grew up to be the first Black woman to argue a case before the Supreme Court of the United States (SCOTUS).

In 1962, she won the young Black student James Meredith the right to study at the University of Mississippi. It was one of several universities still leaning on their state's racist policies that refused Black people the same opportunities white people enjoyed. In this case, the opportunity James Meredith sought was a college education. And Constance Baker Motley led the way.

Twelve years earlier, in 1950, Motley had written a legal complaint against the Board of Education in Topeka, Kansas, on behalf of thirteen Black parents. This included lead plaintiff Oliver Brown, whose daughter Linda had to travel twenty-four blocks, past schools for only white kids, to get to the nearest one for Black children. Motley argued that it was unfair for children of color to have to go to extraordinary lengths to receive an education, usually one that was lesser in quality than the schooling white children enjoyed. Her efforts resulted in the landmark 1954 *Brown v. Board of Education* Supreme Court decision. It declared the nation's "separate but equal" policies unconstitutional. These were policies that severely limited Black people's access to education, as well as fair and quality housing, real estate, banking, public transportation, hotels, public restrooms, gas stations, restaurants, cinema seating, theater access, jobs, even something as basic and necessary as water fountains.

The fabric of American life was built on this type of racism—where towns and cities were designed to benefit one race of people over another, and where Black people's ability to read and learn was deliberately held back. This is called structural and institutional racism. The United States of America had been founded with this in place. Reading and learning are the keys to understanding the difference between right and wrong, to voting, and to finding freedom and success in life. So keeping Black people back allowed others to believe that they were better than Black people. It allowed them to own more than Black people, to earn more than them, and even to force them to work for little or no pay. These are the types of American policies Black people have spent centuries fighting. But the issue of school segregation was one battle Constance Baker Motley was slowly but surely winning.

Still, that decision of the nation's highest court hadn't changed everyone's minds. Certain people (including politicians), states, and institutions like the University of Mississippi continued to block Black people's equal access to these basic human needs, often through terrorism and violence. That is why James Meredith's lawsuit was so important. Even today, there are people in law, education, law enforcement, government, and politics fighting to overturn the progress won by people like Constance and go back to the old structures and policies designed to uplift white people at the expense of Black people and other minorities. But there are those who keep pushing back and fighting against that kind of evil oppression—those are the people whose names we will recognize in the future as belonging to heroes. . . .

In 1945, after her second year at Columbia Law School in New York, Constance Baker Motley began working as a clerk (a person who assists a judge in writing first drafts of legal papers, researching the law, and performing other tasks) for another giant in United States history: Thurgood Marshall. In 1967, he became the first Black person to sit on the US Supreme Court as an associate justice. Constance had joined his Legal Defense Fund and went on to successfully end the policy in Birmingham, Alabama, of reserving restaurant lunch counters for "whites only," as well as to defeat other racist restaurant polices in Memphis, Tennessee. She even won freedom from prison for Dr.

Martin Luther King, Jr., after one of the many times he had stood up, boycotted, or marched against racial injustices on display prominently and proudly in the South.

For instance, in the Southern states, the practice of forcing Black people to sit in the back of buses so white people could sit in the front still existed, as did making them give up their seats on public transportation so white people could sit down. And the unsafe conditions Black sanitation workers faced were so bad they had to fight for the right to form a union. Through the union they could negotiate with their employers with one voice in order to win things like better pay and safer work conditions for all.

To be clear, the North was not without its own dark, deep-rooted structural and institutional racism and injustices, such as denying Black people the opportunity to rent apartments. Or preventing them from buying homes, except in lower-income or less safe industrial areas the government could then choose to run highways through. Or structuring policy, laws, and neighborhoods so many Black people could only afford to attend underfunded schools or those with poorer instruction. Or turning a blind eye in schools where Black children were treated unjustly by teachers who would punish them excessively, or who might expect less from them, refusing to put real effort into educating them. Or where school administrators or law enforcement might target Black children for punishment. Or where Black people were not getting the same job opportunities or were being passed over for advancement. These behaviors and policies weren't the rule everywhere in the North, but they were widespread and common enough. The North just did a better job hiding its tactics, so discrimination there wasn't as obvious. Even today, across the country, people are building toxic AI (artificial intelligence) data centers, often in Black neighborhoods, which negatively impact Black people's health and livelihoods more than others' by polluting the air and environment around them.

Like Ketanji's, Constance Motley's social activism and battles for righteousness started early, all the way back in her elementary school days. She stood up for causes she believed in, even as a young girl. She joined youth councils and set an example among her classmates never to settle for second best. She was a force behind the scenes—a Black woman and, at times, an unsung hero in the Civil Rights Movement and the courts. Until later, when she emerged from the shadows and became a New York state senator, then Manhattan Borough president, and was finally appointed to the United States District Court for the southern district of New York in 1966. She was the first Black woman ever to become a federal judge.

Motley's legacy looms large. She paved a path for people to demand equality for all in the United States. And it was especially meaningful for young Black girls who hadn't yet seen themselves in places of power, especially not in the law. Hers is one of those names worth remembering. A true pioneer and force, Judge Constance Baker Motley left an incredible, permanent mark on American history—and on one young girl in particular named Ketanji, who also shared her birthday.

II
FAMILY HISTORY

JOHN AND ELLERY BROWN BOTH started their careers as public school teachers in Washington, DC, and got married on August 17, 1968, in Miami-Dade County. They welcomed their lovely daughter, Ketanji Onyika Brown, into a rapidly changing, politically chaotic, wide and wonderful world filled with hope and promise. At several points in history, such progress had seemed very far off—almost like a pipe dream. But the Browns, and Black people as a group, had kept the faith that there would be better days, and a "change [was] gonna come."

The family moved to Florida and lived in a married students' housing complex at the University of Miami Law School. Ellery was pulling "double duty" in her job as a public school science teacher—the family's lone breadwinner—and homemaker. Before first light on any given weekday,

Johnny would rouse his only daughter, Ketanji, and help her get ready for nursery school at Jackson's Toddle Inn (a Black-owned business) and, later, for kindergarten. He'd drive forty minutes to the Brownsville area to drop her off, then circle back to the University of Miami Coral Gables campus to attend his own law classes. Ellery would collect her on her way home from teaching science at Rockway Junior High.

By then Ketanji had been reading for over a year—since before she was two years old. Her mother thought, "If she could speak, she can read," and made sure that happened, providing her with all sorts of reading resources at home. She put labels on the various objects in Ketanji's room—alphabet and word cards everywhere she looked. These instincts and efforts of Ellery's helped Ketanji learn to sound out words, which she found exciting. Ketanji was talkative, friendly, and outgoing. "She had a lot of thoughts and ideas she liked to put down in writing," remarked Mrs. Brown, who believed her daughter being so sharp-witted was due to her being able to read and write.

Everyone in the household was committed to education in some capacity. Mr. Brown would sit at the dining room or kitchen table, reading his law books while Ketanji marveled at him from across the table. As he dug into his textbooks on contracts, torts, and constitutional law, she used crayons to doodle in her coloring books, stacked high before her. He led by example and became her first "professional role model."

The Browns were also intent on teaching Ketanji all about Black history: "The race-based experiences of African Americans in this country through the ages," she now calls it. It's the additional education that Black parents insist on giving their children outside the classroom. It's the kind of education often deliberately kept out of schools, but the kind necessary to turn Black and mixed-race children into thriving adults, and more importantly, keep them alive.

At the tender age of four, Ketanji would repeat what she knew to whoever would listen! She'd tell them that "on December 1, 1955, Ms. Rosa Parks said 'no' when she was asked to give up her seat on a bus in Montgomery." She'd already learned about Dr. Martin Luther King, Jr., and how he had spent eight lonely days in a Birmingham, Alabama, jail cell. She could also spot a "young John Lewis from almost any angle in those grainy photographs of a crowded bridge in Selma taken on that Bloody Sunday." And she knew that four beautiful little girls "not much older than myself" were murdered just because they were Black, when a bomb made of at least fifteen sticks of dynamite planted by members of the Ku Klux Klan exploded. It tore apart the Sixteenth Street Baptist Church where the girls, who were in the basement restroom, had just attended Sunday school. Cynthia Wesley, Carole Robertson, and Addie

Mae Collins were fourteen years old. Denise McNair was eleven. These are sad and uncomfortable facts for a child to hear, but Ketanji's parents "never lied" to her. They needed her to know the truth—all the truth—if she was going to be "prepared for life in America."

One such story of truth, change, and hope centers around the life of a man named John Green (or "Greene"), an ancestor of Ketanji's, who sailed to the US from Trinidad. The oral history (later written down in a two-page document and shared at family reunions) suggests that he was born free and was cautioned not to get off his schooner in Charleston, South Carolina. It was the largest slave port in the United States and most of the people brought to America in chains passed through there. But he was independent, a man with his own mind, and he got off his ship despite the warning.

Unfortunately, he was abducted, trafficked, and sold into slavery on the Sharp plantation. The government's written record finds evidence of a John Green, who met an enslaved woman named Ella on John P. Sharp's plantation. They married around 1875 after the Civil War ended and had children of their own. Whether this is the same John Green from Trinidad, or a descendant of his, is hard to prove. Ketanji's family history also states that after American slavery was abolished, John Green assisted his three brothers (it's believed one was named Peter and another Anderson) and a sister (possibly named Callie) in getting to America, where they too could embark on their own pursuits of the so-called American Dream of freedom, opportunity, and equality.

It is not particularly easy for Black Americans to trace their histories and find their family roots. The "wall of slavery" tends to get in the way. When their ancestors were brought by force to America to do unpaid, often grueling labor their whole lives, the details of their family lineage (background), customs, history, and identity were cut off on purpose by slaveholders. Even if people could trace their family trees as far back as a slave ship, their connections to their homelands and families on the Mother Continent were lost. Under slavery, children were often sold and separated from their families forever, their family trees permanently broken. Far too often, poor or no records were kept about those who were enslaved. They were considered property, not people. (Unless they were already free, Black people were not identified by name in the United States census—the record the government keeps of all its citizens—until after the Civil War.)

Over the decades, many records have been lost or ravaged by fire. On top of that, census takers often didn't bother to understand or spell Black people's names correctly, or identify their places of birth accurately. Sometimes they even misidentified people's races! Black people's lives didn't matter much to census takers, and their histories were not only deliberately erased but also stolen from them by sloppy and indifferent record-keeping. All hope is not lost, however. There are people working today on restoring the records and helping Black people piece together their pasts.

For all these reasons, oral histories matter a great deal, especially within Black America. Stories passed down through the generations can be closer to the truth than things written down and interpreted by outsiders. Ketanji's family's oral history gave historians great leads for places to begin searching for clues and official documents on John Green. Family history is important—it gives children a sense of who they are and why they matter. Genealogy (the study of the links between past and present family members) was originally rooted in racism and nativism (putting the interests of native-born people above those of immigrants). It was used as a way to divide people along racial and class lines. But today it is used to fill us with a sense of belonging and pride, which is another reason why it was so evil to strip an entire people of that ability.

Ketanji's ancestors, the John and Ella Green who met on the Sharp plantation, were the great-grandparents of Ellery Ross (Ketanji's mother), who grew up only nine miles from a particularly beautiful spot on a beach in Miami.

The ocean waters off the coast were dazzling—the sun brought the azure out in the blues and the emerald out in the greens, the low waves capped with curls of white foam. The seashore stretched for miles—soft, fine sand dotted with seashells and bits of coral, shaded in spots by palm trees. From every angle, it was as pretty as a postcard.

It was also for white people only. All seventy-two miles of shoreline in Miami-Dade County were "restricted," off-limits to anyone who wasn't white.

So the seven Black people—five men and two women—who waded into the water at Haulover Beach on a warm May day in 1945 expected to be arrested, as others had been before them. Supporters gathered on the sand to watch the group and keep an eye on the sheriff, who'd shown up.

The waders weren't frolicking or swimming. They were not there to have fun. They just stood there in the surf, waiting. A Black lawyer named Lawson Thomas watched from nearby. He had helped organize this "wade-in," the first public protest in Miami over segregated beaches. Thomas had a wad of cash in his pocket, ready to pay their bail.

To all their surprise, the sheriff decided not to arrest anyone. He and city officials knew that such an incident could become a public rallying cry for people demanding equal access to the beaches, which could threaten the area's booming tourist industry.

Thomas went on to become the first Black judge appointed in the American South since the late 1800s. He and the brave swimmers who challenged the "whites only" beach rule had succeeded in one of the first nonviolent civil rights protests in America. City officials finally agreed to allow Black people to go to the beach, but not the same beaches that white people used. The only "colored beach" was on a small island that was hard to get to—it had to be accessed by boat.

Like so much else in American public life at the time, the beach was separate but *un*equal. Yet in the Black community, the victory was huge. It showed what a nonviolent protest could accomplish. More than a decade later, lunch counter sit-ins became a signature protest for people fighting for civil rights, especially young people.

Three months after the wade-in, two people from different families, Ellery Ross and Johnny Brown (Ketanji's parents), were born only two weeks apart. World War II had just ended, and many people in America hoped that a global conflict that was fought to save freedom and democracy would mean freedom and democracy could at last be enjoyed by everyone in the country. Black soldiers who had fought in the war wanted a "Double V": victory abroad against fascism—a political system led by a dictator who exercises near complete control over the population—and victory at home against racism.

Black people had helped create Miami. Nearly half the votes to make Miami a city in 1896 came from Black men. Black workers, many of them from the Bahamas, helped build the mansions, hotels, and city offices that still stand today. But such hopes and dreams were short-lived, because instead of equality, the Jim Crow era of separate and unequal access to opportunities and experiences gained a stranglehold in much of the country. It was designed to hold Black people back and was especially effective in Southern states like Florida.

The term "Jim Crow" originated with a struggling white actor named Thomas Dartmouth Rice, who performed a traveling musical act in the 1800s dressed as a character he called Jim Crow. He painted his face black (called blackface) and spoke with an exaggerated, unschooled Southern accent that was meant to imitate, insult, and make fun of Black people. These minstrel shows gained popularity, and therefore even after the end of the Civil War, the vilification and dehumanization of Black people continued.

Although slavery was outlawed, agriculture was still the most important part of the economy in Southern states, and white farm owners needed cheap labor to continue to make the profits they had grown accustomed to under slavery. They wanted Black people to work for them as sharecroppers for little or no pay, continuing to exploit their labor and basic survival needs.

Sharecropping did little for the Black families who did most of the work on the farms. They had a house to live in, but they usually didn't own it. They could buy from the landowner what they needed to plant, grow, and harvest the crops, but at interest rates so high that they rarely made a profit. And the profits they did make had to be shared with the landowner, who was almost always a white farmer.

Those practices made it nearly impossible for Black farmers to get ahead, to acquire land, or to build wealth for their children and grandchildren. No matter how hard they worked, Jim Crow laws and practices made escaping poverty unattainable for generations of Black Americans.

And once Jim Crow had kicked in, a Black citizen attempting to vote was very dangerous in Florida (and most of the Southern United States). There were white politicians who wanted to prevent it from happening, so they did whatever they could. This included turning a blind eye to violence, intimidation, and even murder committed against the brave people who were fighting to exercise their right to vote.

States that were determined to suppress the Black vote also held one-party primaries called "white primaries," because only white people belonged to the political party in power. Florida had such a law, but the Supreme Court overturned it in 1945, declaring it unconstitutional. (In 1940, only about 5 percent of Black citizens in Florida were registered to vote, and by 1947, that number had increased to about 15 percent due largely to that ruling.) It would take a series of Supreme Court decisions and, finally, acts of Congress to remove most of the barriers to the ballot box for Black citizens.

America's Jim Crow era lasted for a hundred years after the Civil War. Unfortunately, the country is currently trending toward reversing the gains fought for and won by activists in the 1950s, '60s, and '70s, taking the country back to a time of unchecked voter suppression and intimidation. For instance, in 2022, a federal judge ruled that only the US attorney general, and not individuals, can file lawsuits claiming voting rules are racially discriminatory. And in Alabama, the state legislature mapped out districts in a way that only had one district with Black people in the majority, which would have ensured that no matter how most people of color voted, the state would always have more Republican congresspeople than Democrat ones. (That's called gerrymandering.)

Ellery Ross's father, Horace Ross, Sr., and her mother, Euzera, had moved from Georgia to a one-bedroom shiplap house in Miami, south Florida, hoping the situation there would be better. But life was not much easier for them in their new home. Horace had never finished school, and worked with his father, Jim, digging wells, then as a driver, and later as a landscaper. Euzera was a nurse's aide. Their youngest son, Ellery's brother Calvin Ross, recalled how their father would come home at the end of a long day of working outside dripping with sweat, but would keep his children on task with their homework and chores. The four siblings had childhoods full of hard work—their father had them labor alongside him at his landscaping jobs in the summer. But they also lived lives full of inspiration. Their parents were to be admired for their commitment to making a better life and a better world for their children.

City laws dictated where Black people could live. In the 1930s, many lived in a neighborhood called Colored Town, later named Overtown, a small area near Miami's business district that held most of Miami's Black population. Conditions were terrible—25,000 people were crowded into a 350-acre section of the city. The housing was mostly small, dilapidated shacks that lacked electricity or running water.

Following the Great Depression (1929–1939), a decade-long financial crisis that put millions of Americans out of work, President Franklin Delano Roosevelt created an agency called the Public Works Administration. It built the first public housing in the Southern United States near Overtown. It was called Liberty City and had been built specifically for Black families. It immediately became a magnet for middle-income Black families who wanted a better place to live than run-down Overtown. John and Ellery's families lived on the same street there.

White families did not welcome the housing development—they built walls between Liberty City and their all-white neighborhoods. Ellery and Johnny still couldn't attend the better-equipped schools where the white children got to go, or sit in the same restaurants, or go to the same beaches, and had to be segregated on buses. Their parents would never make as much money as their white counterparts, and their opportunities for better jobs were almost nonexistent. So as soon as they were old enough, Ellery and Johnny left Miami. They went to colleges out of state, both choosing historically Black colleges.

Historically Black colleges and universities, or HBCUs, are higher-education schools that were established to educate Black students when few existing universities in the country would admit them because of segregation and racism. They were essential pathways for students to achieve higher learning and they continue to succeed in providing excellent educational experiences and the promise of future employment opportunities for their graduates.

Ellery went to the Tuskegee Institute in Alabama. Johnny, who had won a full scholarship to any HBCU of his choosing, delayed attending school by a year in order to work washing dishes and busing tables so he could pay for all his other college expenses (like books, clothes, and everything other than tuition) without having to ask his parents for help. He ultimately attended Kentucky State, but soon decided he wanted to transfer to North Carolina Central University, where many fine Black scholars had gone. Johnny needed help typing up his transfer application during the winter break, and ran into childhood friend Calvin Ross on the basketball court. Calvin told him his sister Ellery could help him with the typing. She did, and in the process the two began to fall in love. Johnny transferred to NC Central, where he pledged the fraternity Omega Psi Phi (ΩΨΦ).

Both John and Ellery joined protests and marches for civil rights at their schools. They were fully engaged in the fight for justice for all Americans in general and Black Americans in particular. And this is where little Ketanji comes in.

III

GROWING UP

WHEN KETANJI WAS TWO, JOHN and Ellery took a trip to Ghana, Sierra Leone, Côte d'Ivoire, and Liberia. They left Ketanji, who was too young to travel for that long, in Miami with her mother's parents, Horace and Euzera, who still lived in Ellery's childhood home. Ketanji even slept in her mother's old bedroom. Her grandparents doted on her, dressed her up, gave her sweets, and brought her to the Bethel Apostolic Temple church on Sundays. From a young age, Ketanji felt a sense of belonging there, surrounded by people whose skin was the same color as hers. And as she got older, she realized that the musical score of her Sundays was filled with hymns about redemption and staying the course through tough times, with the promise of better to come on the other side.

Grandma Euzera considered Ketanji a "blessed child,"

who was always going to be okay, no matter what she faced in life. Ketanji was precocious and people delighted in hearing her speak, confident as she was in her language skills while still a toddler. Meanwhile, her parents found a new sense of identity and connection to their ancestors during their travels. At the end of their trip, Ellery called Ketanji to let her know they were on their way to get her, but Ketanji didn't want to go home. She wanted to stay with her grandmother!

After a few years in Washington, Johnny decided to leave his job as a public high school history teacher and instead go into law. Ellery suggested he consider applying to the University of Miami School of Law. It was closer to their extended family on her mom's side and would allow Ketanji to maintain the tight bond she felt with her relatives. Johnny was accepted there, to the class of 1977— one of the first Black people to attend the university after it was desegregated in the 1960s. The family returned to the deep South, to a Miami that had changed dramatically since Johnny and Ellery had left for college. Jim Crow laws had been overturned at last. And while racism persisted in many aspects of life, it was now possible for them to pursue professional careers and raise their family in a safe and prosperous neighborhood.

Every day Ketanji's father set a positive example for her—with his hard work, studying, and discipline. Just the fact that he was a student affected Ketanji greatly, and positively. She witnessed the value and importance of education and understood it was something she could achieve too. Her parents made sure to set her up to win by putting her in the best school districts and environments that encouraged learning. Watching her father study law made her love the law and want to pursue it as a profession, like he had.

Everything Ketanji did, she took seriously and put her heart and soul into. She set her own goal to be the best at everything she tried. She read a lot, including for enjoyment, and her family's house was always filled with books. She could rarely be found without one in hand, whether riding in the car or eating supper.

Ketanji's grandfather Thomas Brown died before she was born. But she did grow up with her dad's mother, Mama Queenie, who her dad said was "simply the sweetest woman God ever made," and her mom's parents, Horace and Euzera Ross, who played prominent roles in her life. And even though structural racism prevented them from being able to receive more formal educations, they worked hard in their manual labor jobs. They wanted their kids and grandkids to have it better than they had and be able to excel in their chosen professions. Their strong work ethics rubbed off on their children and their children's children, including Ketanji, and eventually her brother, Ketajh, nearly nine years younger than her.

By the time she was in first grade at George Washington Carver Elementary School (named after the famous Black inventor), which was a fully integrated school, Ketanji was a great reader and began channeling her love of words and stories into a new skill: performance. She and her close friend and neighbor Sunny Schleifer, who was Jewish, often got to be scene partners in the school's Library Week performances, where students performed passages from the books they read. They nicknamed themselves the Two Giggling Girls, as though they were an official, professional performance act. They both got parts in a production of *Charlotte's Web*, based on the popular children's book by E. B. White. Ketanji was cast as Charlotte, the spider who spins words into her webs that describe her friend, a delightful, kind pig named Wilbur, played by Sunny.

One thing Ketanji wanted with her whole heart was a part in her elementary school production of *The Wizard of Oz*. And at age seven, she got her wish. She was cast as the Wicked Witch of the West, and loved the cackling and singing and melting she got to do in the role. Sunny played the head Munchkin. These two friends would bring their love of the theater home with them and put on performances for their parents, cobbling costumes together from their moms' wardrobes.

Sunny was a wonderful, supportive, and loyal friend. In fact, she noticed some things that Ketanji didn't, including something that could have affected Ketanji negatively. Sunny saw how one particular teacher at their school would mistreat the Black children. He'd send them to the principal's office if they forgot their homework or laughed with friends, but he wouldn't punish white kids when they did the same thing. It hurt Sunny when she witnessed the racist mistreatment Black children experienced at such a young age. She loved her friend and understood how wrong it was to treat people differently just because their skin color wasn't the same as hers.

One afternoon, the two were playing together outside next to their building unsupervised, which was normal back then. A neighborhood girl joined them, and after a little while, the three returned to the little girl's home to play with her kitchenette. It didn't occur to Ketanji to tell her mother where she was going—or ask if she could go. Time flies when you're having fun, and when Ketanji finally looked out the window, it was nightfall.

Ketanji hurried home, and when her mother saw her, she was very angry. She was sick with worry because she hadn't known where Ketanji had gone. But she was especially afraid because a Black child alone in the South, in a recently integrated world, was a prime target for someone who might want to take their hatred of Black people out on her. She could have been kidnapped or killed and might never have been found. Ketanji, unaware of the race-related reasons why her mother felt so powerless and upset, burst into tears and apologized. She promised never to repeat her mistake.

Ketanji's childhood was rich in creative arts, music, and reading. She wrote her own book of poetry entitled *Dandelion Fluff* and, starting at seven years old, studied piano at the Miami Oratorio Society with its founder, Victor Kelly. Kelly created the society to bring "cultural and spiritual fulfillment to the community through classical and spiritual music."

Her mother also enrolled Ketanji in swimming lessons. Until recently, segregation had denied Black people access to pools or beaches where they might have grown comfortable in the water and learned to swim. In fact, the stereotype that Black people cannot swim has its roots in those racists policies: How can someone learn to swim if that person has restricted access to the water? Now, with the laws changed, Ellery was determined to take advantage of the door that had been newly opened to Black people and equip her daughter with this very important life skill.

The summer before third grade, at a pool party hosted by a teacher friend of her mother's, Ketanji floated calmly on her back with her eyes closed in the still blue water near the pool's edge. She was confident in her swimming skills and knew she was only an arm's length away from the side. However, when she opened her eyes, she had drifted toward the deep end. In a split second, she panicked, and instead of keeping her head and swimming to the side of the pool, she sank to the bottom, the water choking her as she dropped like a stone to the floor.

Her mother noticed Ketanji was nowhere to be seen and hurried to the pool's edge. Before she could leap in, another teacher, Bob Losyk, dove in fully dressed and brought Ketanji to the surface. Her father patted her back, helping her cough up the water she'd swallowed. It was all very confusing to Ketanji and so unlike her to second-guess her abilities in anything. She would carry this "swimming" lesson with her from then on: that even in the face of fear, she was going to keep her head up, stay afloat, and trust in herself. Sinking would never be an option again.

Ketanji entered the Miami-Dade County Youth Fair & Exposition public speaking contest. Her mother had her recite the inspirational poem "For My People," written by Margaret Walker, the first Black person to win the Yale Younger Poets Prize. "For My People" is an anthem honoring Black people—a tribute to their resilience, hope, and spirit in overcoming the past in triumph.

"For my people everywhere singing their slave songs repeatedly . . . For the boys and girls who grew in spite of these things . . . Let a new earth rise. Let another world be born. . . . Let a second generation full of courage issue forth. . . . Let a beauty full of healing and a strength of final clenching be the pulsing in our spirits and our blood. . . ."

Ketanji's voice rose, punctuated with conviction as she performed before her largest audience to date. She had them enrapt, on the edges of their seats, just by using her words. It was a wonderful feeling. She won the competition as well as the purple rosette—a distinction even better than first place—impressing the audience and the judges with her confident stage presence and passionate delivery.

Now at a new school, Ketanji noticed Sunset Elementary was not very diverse. Here, she was enrolled in the school's gifted program, which was almost exclusively white. Ketanji was not aware of this, but the history of gifted and talented programs in America is a troubling one. They operate under the premise that "gifted" children, those whose IQs (intelligence quotients) are above a certain number, should be given more and specialized attention at school. They're to be offered more academically challenging schoolwork so they won't get bored and can therefore reach their academic potential. They are also given access to more artistic and creative opportunities.

On the surface, that sounds great. However, gifted programs were born out of a fear of integration after the *Brown v. Board of Education* Supreme Court decision. The state of Virginia chose to close its public schools for years rather than integrate. At the same time, there was the phenomenon of "white flight," where white families nationwide left cities and settled in the suburbs in order to avoid having to share public spaces, neighborhoods, schools, and other facilities with Black families. Meanwhile, many white educators and legislators crafted new criteria and benchmarks that students would have to meet in order to attend their schools or be in certain classrooms. The problem with this is that IQ tests are not culturally neutral—that means one's cultural background can influence how high one might score on the test. And from early on, the tests were deliberately misinterpreted to favor white people over others, dishonestly categorizing whites as more intelligent.

Southern states quickly began adopting IQ-based gifted and talented programs. In 1959, Virginia was the first to start using the Education Testing Service National Guidance Testing Program (or ETS, which currently administers exams like the Scholastic Aptitude Test, or SATs).

A closer look at the misuse of IQ tests takes us back to 1924, when the state of Virginia passed the Virginia Sterilization Act (Eugenical Sterilization Act). Eugenics is the practice of making sure only people with "desirable" traits and features are allowed to reproduce and have children. This is supposed to improve the human race, but in reality, it's an excuse for keeping the white race "pure" by not allowing people of different races to have children together.

The law allowed the state to perform operations on institutionalized people, leaving them unable to have children of their own if the state found them to (1) be "feeble-minded," (2) have low IQs, or (3) have the potential to commit a crime in the future.

A white woman named Carrie Buck had been committed to the Virginia State Colony for Epileptics and Feeble-Minded, even though she was neither feebleminded nor epileptic. While there, she was forcibly sterilized (that means she did not agree to have an operation that would make her unable to have kids). She'd already had a child with mental challenges and her mother had been diagnosed as having similar struggles with processing information. So the superintendent of the colony, Albert S. Priddy, chose her and a few others for sterilization in order to gain broader national support for the practice.

Carrie Buck sued Priddy, who died in 1925, so the defendant in the lawsuit was changed to Hendron Bell, the new superintendent. Carrie Buck lost her case and appealed the ruling all the way to the Supreme Court, where the justices upheld the *Buck v. Bell* ruling in 1927. Over the years, more than 70,000 Americans across different states were forcibly or unknowingly sterilized as a result of the Supreme Court's decision. Each state used different unethical (morally wrong) reasons for wanting certain people not to be able to have biological kids.

A woman in Mississippi, future civil rights leader Fannie Lou Hamer, went in for an operation to have a tumor removed from her womb. Instead, a white doctor took out her entire womb on purpose so she could not have any more children! Mississippi wanted to reduce the number of poor Black people and encouraged these types of assaults on Black women's bodies. Fannie Lou coined the term "Mississippi appendectomy" to mean the practice of telling a woman she was going in for one procedure (the removal of her appendix organ), while having doctors secretly perform sterilization on her instead.

This practice was a disgusting violation that was used to target people of color, mainly Black, Native American, and Puerto Rican women. Somewhere between 25 and 50 percent of Native American women were sterilized between 1970 and 1976, and the rate was even higher for the women in Puerto Rico.

A similar thing happened to mentally challenged sisters Minnie Lee and Mary Alice Relf in Alabama. The Montgomery Community Action family planning service began "birth control" experiments on low-income, mainly Black citizens, and forcibly sterilized them instead.

IQ and mental ability tests have been used to do some awful things to people. Even though eugenics is a despicable practice and outlawed in most states today, and Virginia's governor formally apologized for the practice in 2002, the

Buck v. Bell decision has never been overturned. In effect, it remains the law of the land in the United States. There are many, many times when the Supreme Court does not get its decisions right. And sometimes it takes a generation or more for the court to overturn its prior terrible rulings, if in fact it ever does.

Not only are gifted programs problematic and discriminatory because they tend to exclude Black and Latino students due to the flawed IQ test and other selection criteria, but they are also based on a program that was initially formed to study, enhance, and support the academic achievement of Black, lower-income, and disadvantaged students! The irony of this cannot be overstated.

After the *Brown v. Board of Education* decision, many educators wondered how they might effectively teach Black students, since Black children had been historically disadvantaged in their access to quality education or positive learning environments. In 1956, the New York City Board of Education launched the Demonstration Guidance Project in two New York City junior high public schools. The aim was "to identify and upgrade potential college students from" disadvantaged backgrounds, where they had "limited cultural opportunities."

The first group was made up of eighty-seven Black kids, thirty-six Puerto Ricans, a single Asian student, and twenty-four others. They were each assigned a psychologist and social worker to help them with home life and other things that could cause them worry or stress. They were exposed to a rich menu of cultural activities, like visiting museums or science labs, taking a trip to see Congress or the president in Washington, DC, attending symphonies and plays, or going to the ballet. They spent more time in English class to encourage reading. And not to be forgotten was class size. Today, as the number of students assigned to a single teacher in public schools balloons, the evidence is clear: Students do monumentally better when there are fewer of them in each class.

It should not come as a surprise, then, that IQs and reading levels among these kids rose dramatically, and nearly 70 percent graduated, compared to 47 percent outside the program. Students went on to attend colleges like Dartmouth, Amherst, Columbia, Barnard, Vassar, Antioch, Radcliffe, New York University, and New York State Teachers Colleges. The results were incredible.

Educators across the country took notice. They were highly impressed . . . but shamefully, this experiment's initial goals of helping disadvantaged youths were abandoned. Just like how the television show *Sesame Street* pivoted away from its initial focus in 1969 of appealing to "the four-year-old inner-city black youngster" as part of President Lyndon Johnson's Great Society agenda (which had a goal of eliminating racial injustices and poverty), educators shifted their focus too. Instead, school districts applied these Demonstration Guidance Project practices and techniques toward giving already privileged and predominantly white students more advantages through the new "gifted" programs. Unfortunately, Black and other kids of color were left out and left behind once more.

Ketanji had very involved, present parents who were educators at heart. They had the awareness and time to expose her to experiences outside the classroom that would benefit her. All those note cards, lessons in reading, participation in recitals, educational toys, reference books, written works on their shelves about the Black experience with all its joy and sadness, along with her natural talents, kept Ketanji in lockstep with her white peers. It's what got her into those gifted programs that were essentially designed to keep Black kids out. Not only that, all those things also helped put her in a league of her own. But her parents made sure that she remained grounded. Being in a gifted program didn't make her better than other kids; it only meant that she had been blessed with more opportunities than many others had gotten. And even though she might feel out of place surrounded by mostly white children, they wanted her always to remember to love to learn.

Ketanji's third-grade teacher had difficulty pronouncing her name. She'd mess it up every day, unable for some reason to memorize and pronounce it correctly. As innocent as that might seem, her butchering of the child's name resulted in peals of giggles from her classmates. It ended up being yet another instance of making Ketanji seem different, like she didn't belong. Some of her classmates would also trip over the pronunciation. But Ketanji had a soothing, optimistic, and forgiving nature. Instead of making her teacher feel bad for her daily nervous fumble at roll call, Ketanji approached her one day before recess and told her just to call her Kay. Her teacher was relieved, and Ketanji had succeeded in taking on the burden of making this person comfortable—an adult who was for all intents and purposes harming her self-esteem.

One Sunday, when Ketanji was at her grandmother Euzera's home, she went to wash her hands in the kitchen before eating. Her grandparents lived in a tiny green three-bedroom house in which they'd raised five kids, with a kitchen barely big enough to contain two people at once. Ketanji turned on the faucet and nothing came out. The sink, with its green Formica countertops, was broken. She noticed someone had left a message on a napkin inside the sink, which read something along the lines of: "brok sink, wate for repare." Ketanji couldn't believe someone couldn't spell these simple words correctly. She retrieved her mother to show her the note, then laughed as she pointed out the errors.

But instead of laughing, her mother was furious. How could Ketanji make fun of someone, especially for this? She held Ketanji's upper arm tightly and leaned her face close to hers. She asked Ketanji who she thought wrote the note. Ketanji was dumbstruck—she had no idea. Her mother told her that, even though Ketanji was getting so many opportunities in her life, she had no business thinking she was "all that." She might have learned to spell, but that didn't make her one bit better than anyone else. She was never to laugh at someone who couldn't spell or read. Ellery wasn't done: "I thought I raised you better than this." She hoped Euzera hadn't heard Ketanji laughing, "because that would really hurt her feelings."

Ketanji was a people pleaser and it was especially important to her to make her parents proud. In this instance, she had not. Her grandmother had written the note. Euzera was a hard worker. Her husband, Horace, had had a stroke, so she was also his caregiver. She'd managed to navigate living in a country that historically had been hostile to her people and raised a fine family in the process. She just hadn't had an opportunity to receive the kind of formal education Ketanji had.

Ketanji was humiliated, her mother was disappointed in her, and she had unknowingly mocked her own loving, amazing grandmother. Ketanji snatched her arm away and ran outside in a flood of tears. She sobbed the rest of the afternoon, leaning up against the chain-link fence, refusing to go back in. It wasn't until much later, as night fell, that she returned and approached her grandmother, mortified by how insensitive she'd been and also by her mother's disapproval. She apologized. "I'm really sorry for how I acted, Grandma."

Whether her grandmother knew what she was referring to is unclear, but she forgave her nonetheless and gave her a huge, warm hug to reassure her. Ketanji learned a big lesson in that moment: not to look down on others and to be kind. She had already been given so much in life. She must never forget that so many others had not been nearly as fortunate. Her mother had always told her never to throw her blessings back in God's face. And it was her grandmother who'd been the one to call her a "blessed child." That took on a whole new meaning now. And Ketanji was forever humbled.

Ketanji did not have siblings yet and often had to entertain herself. The truth was, she liked her alone time. It allowed her to hear her own thoughts clearly and be honest about how she felt about things or what she wanted in life. In public or at school, in her mostly white surroundings, she had to take on more of a role—put on a face—as the inoffensive, high-achieving, perfect child. And that could be exhausting.

So at home, alone in the safety of her own thoughts, she'd play by herself in an area behind the apartments for married students on the University of Miami campus, where her family lived. She nicknamed this courtyard Circle Square, because there was a giant red circle painted inside the concrete slabs on the ground. Sometimes she'd have tea parties with stuffed animals, or listen to the soundtrack from *The Wiz*, the all-Black 1978 movie version of the play based on the film *The Wizard of Oz* and filled with images and ideas important in Black culture, with a musical score by the legendary composer and producer Quincy Jones. Sometimes she'd read, or play with Wildlife Treasury cards, or put on skits starring TV characters from kids' programs she was allowed to watch (like *Sesame Street* or *The Electric Company*). Her parents made it a point to steer her toward shows that had diverse casts, to make sure she always kept ties to her identity as a Black American.

When Ketanji reached sixth grade, she spent time after school as both a crossing guard and as a teacher's helper at the church preschool across the street. She watched over the young children there, including her brother, Ketajh, who'd come into the world in June 1979. Her mother had volunteered her for the position, wanting to make certain her brother was in the presence of someone she trusted. Beyond that, her parents were much more lax with her brother, who was much more adventurous than Ketanji and was allowed to watch programs her parents would have forbidden her from ever viewing. The television landscape had changed a lot since Ketanji was little, and now there were more diverse shows featuring positive depictions of Black people. So her parents weren't as worried her brother would fall victim to Hollywood's negative portrayal of Black people . . . or its total erasure of them.

Ketanji was self-motivated. Her mother said, "I cannot remember a time where we had to say, 'Do your homework.'" In fact, sometimes her parents thought she did more work than was even necessary. Ketanji credited her mother with her determined work ethic: "She made sure that my brother and I were always learning," she said. "I was raised in a household with a very strong maternal influence—my mother is all of 5 feet 2, but she is a towering presence."

Ketanji's uncle Calvin Ross, who once served as chief of police of Miami and Florida A&M University, said it was clear that "from an early age, she was extremely focused on her desires to follow her dreams in the legal profession." They knew that "whatever she did, she was going to land on her feet."

His older brother, Harold Ross, a Vietnam staff sergeant and Bronze Star recipient, believed that "she always showed tenacity." And that "she was a leader—and a very studious one at that." Her father would say something similar:

"Ketanji had already made up her . . . mind in junior high school" about wanting to do law. "That was her goal and she never wavered from it one iota." In fact, she was almost twelve years old and reading a Black magazine (*Black Enterprise*, *Ebony*, or *Essence*) when she stumbled across a piece on Constance Baker Motley. She was drawn in by the fact that they shared a birthday—and skin color—and Ketanji began to envision her life mirroring Constance's somehow.

In time, her father, Johnny Brown, got a job as chief attorney for the Miami-Dade County school board and the family would move to a wealthy, leafy, predominantly Jewish suburb of Miami called Cutler Bay. Her mom became the principal at a public magnet high school and college, the New World School of the Arts in Miami. Johnny and Ellery had grown up in Florida during the height of segregation, and unfair laws meant to hold them back made them want to understand those laws and change them. That's where Ketanji got it from—she understood that the law was "an instrument of change."

Ketanji's parents made sure their daughter's path to greatness was clear—that she wouldn't face the same obstacles that they had. Ketanji recognized that her parents "experienced firsthand the spirit-crushing limitations that legal segregation by race imposes while they were growing up in South Florida." But even if there were still going to be roadblocks, she knew, "If I worked hard and believed in myself, I could do anything or be anything I wanted to be."

Ketanji met Stephen Rosenthal in seventh-grade civics/history class inside a portable overflow classroom at Palmetto Junior High. (The school's population had outgrown its buildings.) He sat on the right side of the room and she sat on the left. She came over at some point sporting her trademark bright, beaming smile, and was so friendly and outgoing that they became fast friends, bonding over schoolwork and class discussions.

Stephen was new to the school, like Ketanji. And his relatives had also had to face and overcome unimaginable circumstances before getting where they were in America today. His father's grandparents had fled Nazi Germany in the 1930s, and his mother's had left Ukraine due to the rise in hate against Jewish people there (now called anti-Semitism). Adolf Hitler had risen to power and become leader of the Nazi (National Socialist German Workers') Party (which used to be called the DAP or German Workers' Party) in 1921. In 1939, he invaded Poland, hoping to conquer all of Europe for the benefit of the "Aryan" (white) "master race." That was the start of World War II. He planned to round up all the Jews on the continent in concentration camps and kill them. This event in history is called the Holocaust.

Hitler was obsessed with "racial purity" and didn't want

Jewish or Black people "polluting" the white race by having children with white people (called Rassenschande or Blutschande in Germany and miscegenation when referring to Black and white couples in the United States). By 1937 any mixed-race or half Black people in Germany were forcibly sterilized so they could never have biological children of their own. Sinti and Romani people were also considered "genetically inferior" and were sterilized or killed. Gay men and trans people were prosecuted as well, sent to camps, and/or sterilized. Less than a decade after the United States Supreme Court *Buck v. Bell* ruling, Nazi Germany, led by Hitler, would apply the same forced eugenics and sterilization tactics across Europe that it had learned from America. Black prisoners of war were either killed or treated worse than white ones by the German Gestapo (police). By the end of the war in 1945, over six million Jewish people had been murdered by Nazis.

Both Stephen and Ketanji were in Miss Roxanne Lombroia's English class (the schoolkids used to call her "Foxy Roxy"). Miss Lombroia often wore skirts with a tight belt, resembling a leading lady from 1950s Hollywood. But what made her so memorable was that she was a phenomenal English teacher, who had the children diagram sentences. They were made to diagram often, and it truly taught them how to write—and write well. Students learned how sentences fit together, which parts worked well with others, and how they could move words around and string them together to make an even more effective, powerful, or eloquent turn of phrase. Stephen credited his own admirable wordsmith skills and those of an even better writer, Ketanji, to having had "that educational base from Roxanne Lombroia."

Ketanji and Stephen, who for fun she sometimes called "Stevie Nicks" (the legendary solo artist, producer, songwriter, and lead singer of Fleetwood Mac), were both part of the gifted program in junior high, taught by Dr. Houchen. The group met in a room off the library. In the summer of 1984, Ketanji, Stephen, and the rest of the group went on a trip to Washington, DC. One of their excursions was to Georgetown, where the kids stopped in a store called Commander Salamander. Inside, employees sold funky and new-wave clothing and whatever else was on trend, while blasting music from their personal collections from the DJ booth. Thursdays through Saturdays, the store stayed open until midnight! Lots of pink. Neon. Culture Club. Duran Duran. Prince. Anything that screamed '80s, pop, or punk rock, you could find there. Ketanji loved that world. She had always been into pop culture, so visiting a place like Commander Salamander was almost like something out of a dream.

On another leg of the trip, the kids got to meet one of their congresspeople, Dante Fascell, and got their picture taken with him while standing on the steps near the Capitol. The Supreme Court Building stood only a few hundred feet away.

Ketanji put herself out there to try to be at the top of anything she set her mind to, even if doing so was scary. That determination required that she possess a certain confidence, which, if it were anyone else, could have rubbed others the wrong way, especially her competitors. But because Ketanji had always been so nice and warm, no one seemed to mind. It was yet another unique and admirable quality of hers. Ketanji was driven and had very good and distinctive penmanship that hasn't changed since junior high. (Except she no longer uses pink ink in her pens or peppers her words with hearts.)

While Ketanji excelled at school, schoolwork didn't consume her life. She had lots of friends. She'd often hang out with her friends Debbie, Buffy, Cheryl, Jennifer, or Denise Lewin, and they'd go to The Falls, an upscale mall, or to the movies. She was also very into music. Denise, who along with Ketanji was one of only three Black girls in the school's honors and Advanced Placement classes in high school, said, "We'd go to pool parties. We'd spend a lot of time at each other's houses, just hanging out. . . . Ketanji wasn't as big on [going to] the beach as I was, but we'd go now and then [too]." But Ketanji was still in the minority. And there was only one Black boy on the honors track.

Even though she was just an eighth grader, the high school debate teacher, Fran Berger, noticed what a natural leader and speaker Ketanji was. Fran, a legendary mentor in the high school debate world, was a short, stout, politically conservative woman with dyed blondish hair styled in a puffy updo, who usually dressed in leggings and bright silk blouses. She had brought kids from the senior high school debate and forensics team to the junior high to present to the eighth graders. Right away, Fran imagined how Ketanji could fit on the team: She was a free thinker, spirited, rational, levelheaded, and able to make cogent, convincing points. Fran wanted her to participate on the high school debate team, which was exciting to Ketanji, so she dove headfirst into those waters! And Ketanji quickly became one of Coach Berger's favorite pupils on the whole team.

Mrs. Brown knew from the outset that it would be a perfect fit: "We as parents could never win in an argument or anything with her because her debate expertise [kicked] in even before she was on the debate team."

So Ketanji started working with Berger's nationally recognized speech and debate team. She'd get up earlier than her classmates and walk half a mile from the junior high building to the Miami Palmetto Senior High School. Stephen thought the fact that she was hanging out with high school kids was really cool.

Ketanji was elected "vice-mayor" of their school and for their 1985 junior high graduation, the school put together a newspaper with a special section on standout students. She was featured as "Best Girl" and shared "Most Likely to Succeed" with Stephen.

IV

UP FOR DEBATE

THEN CAME HIGH SCHOOL. KETANJI shone brightly there as well. She was elected class president in her sophomore, junior, and senior years at Miami Palmetto Senior High School! And it was a large school—her graduating class had 800 students.

It was also one of the best public schools in the Miami area, with other grads who went on to noteworthy accomplishments, including former US surgeon general Vivek Murthy, who graduated in 1994.

Her election as class leader was a testament to her popularity. She also did the morning announcements over the intercom, so everybody knew her voice, even if they didn't know her personally.

Her classmate and fellow debate team member Nathaniel

Persily called her a "star in the making" who "could write and give a speech that would leave the audience clapping . . . she could do a dramatic play or a humorous one and she was outstanding in all those things." He recounted how when she did dramatic interpretations, both the judges and audience members were "literally . . . crying . . . because she was so good." On the flip side, she left those same "people dying with laughter when she did the humorous ones." Most important, he believed her to be "the same person today as she was at Palmetto when we were both thirteen." Kind, funny, smart, unaffected, an "incredibly polished speaker" without ego, and "the most morally centered person" he'd ever met. "You look at this gold-plated résumé that she has, and you would think that she's been trying to climb a particular ladder to get to the next rung. But she's never been that kind of person." His long-lasting view of Ketanji is that she is "incredibly humble" and "very generous, giving, self-deprecating—you know, the least arrogant person I've ever met." But as much as Ketanji would like to have been without an ego—she definitely wanted to win. And to be remembered.

Ketanji developed a very useful habit during her debate competition years. Every time she walked into a new classroom throughout her storied speech and debate career, she'd enter with her customary resolute step, exuding confidence and a big smile with her head held high and her back straight. She was just over five feet tall, but she seemed taller to her friends because of the way she carried herself.

Ketanji knew that a confident posture helped to convince the judges watching from the front row that she knew what she was talking about. She was always prepared, well-rested, and ready to win.

But she knew that she had another obstacle to overcome that had nothing to do with her confidence, or with how brilliant her public speaking was, or how sharp and on point her speeches and comebacks or rejoinders were. She was Black, and the judges and competitors were almost always white. Therefore, she walked with purpose to the chalkboard at the front of the room, and with a smile, briefly turned her back to the judges and wrote on the board:

K-e-t-a-n-j-i

She'd put the chalk down and then turn back to face the judges, still smiling. She'd spell her name out loud, and then pronounce it, clear as a bell.

"She would always just articulate it really clearly," said Stephen, who was also on the team, and had watched her introduce herself like that dozens of times. "It was a simple, 'Hello, my name is Ketanji Brown, K-e-t-a-n-j-i.'" He noted that she was a dark-complexioned "Black young woman, a teenager. And she had an unusual name. And so she had to immediately convey to the person who's going to be literally judging her who she is right off the bat." The memory of her third-grade teacher routinely messing up her name might have compelled her to suit up in this preemptive armor. Now, by writing it down, spelling it out, and saying it out loud, no one had any excuse for not getting her name right.

Her forthrightness and charm won over many judges from the start. It was another sign of the good communicator Ketanji was learning to be: She was presenting herself and the facts clearly, removing the guesswork about her name that might have given the judges pause. She took command of the room.

"She was very poised and trying to eliminate the distance or . . . the perceived otherness right off the bat. . . . She had to confront who she was every time she entered a room," Stephen recalled.

It always worked, and if she ever got tired of having to do it, she didn't let it show.

Ketanji recalled many years later, "Whether it was running for class president, or becoming a champion orator, or even applying to Harvard after my public high school guidance counselor 'helpfully' suggested that I not set my sights so high, I recall distinctly not being fazed by the slings and arrows of implicit, or even explicit, bias, and making the conscious decision to push forward nonetheless." Despite her guidance counselor's advice, not only did Ketanji apply to Harvard, she applied Early Action! (That's when you apply to a school before the regular application deadlines, though you don't automatically have to go if you're accepted.) In one of her supplemental essays in her application, she wrote that she wanted to go to Harvard to help her "fulfill my fantasy of becoming the first Black, female Supreme Court justice to appear on a Broadway stage." She dreamed big and didn't let little ignorant comments stand in her way.

Her speech and debate coach, Fran Berger, always told her students they were a team, and to approach their competitions with confidence but not arrogance. A skillful competitive speaker makes an impression by being confident, not cocky. There's a fine line between the two. And that line makes all the difference between being someone who you want to listen to and work with, and someone you might listen to but won't respect much. Ketanji excelled at walking that line.

Of all the activities Ketanji participated in growing up, and "despite the obstacles," she considered her "high school experience as a competitive speaker" to be "the one activity that best prepared me for future success in law and in life." Not only did she learn how to reason and write, she also "gained the self-confidence that can sometimes be quite difficult for women and minorities to develop at an early age."

And she did so at a time when she could often be made

to feel like an outsider and an "other." There wasn't a large variety of foundation makeup or pantyhose for Black people then, and Ketanji looked more gray than brown when wearing the color closest to hers. Finding hair care products was a matter of trial and error—mostly error—because there were barely any options in local stores for Black hair in its many forms. She was also the only Black person on the debate team, and she felt it. But she pushed away any isolation she might have felt and didn't let on that it bothered her.

As talented as Ketanji was, there was a drama teacher who would not give her a chance at a role in a school play. The play featured a white family and Ketanji is Black. The teacher denied her a part, even though Ketanji had given one of the strongest auditions. Such attitudes toward casting were not uncommon among drama teachers back then, and it would take a strong child of tremendous character not to let that rejection from adults affect or demoralize her. "If you don't talk about it, you never deal with it," Jackson said later at a student panel about issues of race and prejudice at her school.

Students participated in a seminar and watched the 1981 Peabody and Emmy Award–winning Alex Grasshoff ABC Afterschool Special *The Wave* (based on a real thought experiment conducted by Ron Jones in his 1967 World History class), which originally aired in prime time. In it, students were brainwashed into blindly following made-up rules for a new disciplined youth society called the Wave. They were made to believe that those who joined were better than everyone else. In the end, the teacher in the TV show revealed that the kids had been sucked into following the Nazi movement and its leader, Adolf Hitler. Some children were horrified they could be that gullible; others were disappointed the Wave wasn't real because they finally felt important—like they belonged to something.

After the screening, the Palmetto students spoke about instances of prejudice they'd experienced. Stephen mentioned that he had experienced anti-Semitism, such as when he'd seen swastikas drawn in bathrooms. The swastika is a symbol that was used on the flag of Nazi Germany beginning in 1920. The flag was designed by Adolf Hitler, who combined the three colors of the German Imperial flag (red, black, and white) on it.

Ketanji brought up her experience with the drama teacher who'd refused to cast her. But the teacher wasn't moved by her concerns and defended his decision. His dismissiveness and discriminatory behavior was all the more hurtful because of Ketanji's passion for theater and her obvious gifts in the dramatic arts. By that time, she had already competed in and won competitions around the country for her dramatic presentations.

Remarkably, she has said, "I cannot recall a single time in my childhood in which I cared about the slights and misperceptions and underestimations that came my way." That is what forced her to become a fighter. She said, "What I do remember is often thinking, 'Hmm, well, I'll show them.'"

In October of 1987, the United States secretary of the interior Donald Hodel came to visit Miami. After he finished giving a brief speech, the students had the chance to ask questions. Ketanji was among them. She wanted him to explain why the Interior Department was allowing offshore oil drilling, even though it was endangering Florida's coral reefs. Coral reefs are structures made by hundreds of thousands of animals called coral polyps. The reefs are home to some of the most varied and numerous fish in the sea, who are in turn eaten by and support the existence of animals like sea turtles, marine mammals, birds, and invertebrates. Deepwater reefs supply homes and food to countless other forms of marine life too. If the reefs die, so do many animals, several of which could go extinct.

Ketanji told him "oil and water don't mix." But according to the editor of the school newspaper, David Eckstein, "He didn't really answer the question," and instead dodged the issue. Still, in that moment, Ketanji had once again stuck up for her beliefs.

The school's population was 73 percent white, 16 percent Black, and 11 percent Hispanic, and the students "do not frequently mix," Ketanji told the *Miami Herald* in 1988. As a high school senior, she joined a Jewish group as well as a Latino student organization, leading discussions with her classmates about how to encourage more communication among Miami Palmetto Senior High School's racial and ethnic groups.

Denise, whose parents were Jamaican immigrants, and Ketanji were bused to school—meaning they lived either outside the school district or much farther from their school than their white classmates. They both felt like outsiders in their predominantly white universe and quickly became best friends due to that familiar common ground. Denise noted, "We were in different spaces from a lot of our classmates." The two girls were well aware that they didn't come from money and had to work harder to be taken seriously. "I was driving a 12-year-old Caprice Classic in my senior year, and I was fortunate to have that, and our classmates were in new Camaros." At least one of their friends had a swimming pool and guest quarters on their property. It would have been easy to be jealous or feel less than in that kind of situation. Instead, it didn't matter. Their goals were set higher than money—they had their eyes on justice.

When Ketanji or Denise, suspected of being shoplifters,

were followed around stores while their white peers were not, it would have been easy for them to become bitter or angry at how they were being targeted. But Ketanji's mother and grandmother wouldn't let Ketanji take on a problem that belonged to someone else. The store attendants' racism was their own burden, not hers. Ellery would remind Ketanji to "guard your spirit." So she did. Ketanji chose to look forward, toward the dreams she could make come true. She focused on working hard and continuing to better herself, while leaving those people with small minds in the rearview.

When it came to debate, even rivals from other schools couldn't help but praise and recognize Ketanji's talent. Jeff Livingston, from South Carolina, competed against her in regional and national public speaking and debate competitions. He called her "legendary" and the same person today that she was in the '80s: "the way she pauses, collects her thoughts and then deliver[s] beautifully. You saw that at seventeen."

David O. Markus, whose team usually lost to hers, found her to be "smart, friendly, engaging, [and] dynamic." In fact, he said, "She is the absolute best."

Ketanji learned Fran Berger's lessons well. It helped that her personality suited the requirements of speech and debate. She was naturally quick-witted and insightful. But even more important than her natural gifts, Ketanji was a hard worker with a lot of self-discipline. She somehow always had a sense of what was working for the audience or judges or fellow students who were watching her. "It's not just what you say that leaves an impact, it's also how you say it," Ketanji said, "and how you get your message through to the people you are trying to convince."

Putting in the preparation time has been a hallmark of her success since she was a first grader, and it really paid off when she got to high school. She clarified that "while other kids were hanging out late going to parties, I was either writing or rehearsing my speech, or sleeping ahead of a 5 a.m. Saturday morning tournament wake-up call." Her self-discipline and sacrifice served her well and have "carried through at every stage thereafter, which, if I'm being honest, has made me kind of boring, but has also allowed me to have opportunities that my grandparents could not have even dreamed about."

Preparing for these events required many hours of study and practice—in front of a mirror, and in front of friends. "She'd do the thing over and over again, whatever it was she was working on," Stephen said.

Ketanji devoured books of all kinds, and she loved poetry. One of her favorite poems refers to the discipline it takes to succeed. It's called "The Ladder of St. Augustine," by Henry Wadsworth Longfellow:

The heights by great men reached and kept
Were not attained by sudden flight,
But they, while their companions slept,
Were toiling upward in the night.

Ketanji worked hard day and night, but it didn't feel like work when she was concentratig on something she loved. And she loved to perform. Speech and debate required a wide range of skills, and Ketanji's specialties were (1) oratory, where contestants write and deliver original speeches, and (2) interpretation, where they perform dramatic or humorous parts from existing material.

That category of competition combined two of her favorite things: theater and performing. But even when she reached eighteen and was a senior in high school with a lot of speech experience—and a lot of wins already to her name—she still got butterflies before a competition.

Walking into a room to face a panel of adults she'd never seen before was intimidating enough as a young person. Oftentimes it was in a strange city, in a state she'd never been to before. She and her speech and debate team arrived by Greyhound bus if the competition was in Florida, or by airplane if it was outside the state.

Even getting there was an effort. The debate team held fundraisers to earn money for trips to competitions around the country. Coach Berger expected the whole team to help with fundraisers—selling "bagel baskets, Mother's Day presents, candy bars, roses—anything that would sell at a good profit," Iris Katz, another teacher and Fran's best friend, said. Fran would sometimes buy suits for boys if they couldn't afford one, or airline tickets for those whose families were struggling. Ketanji was an enthusiastic salesperson, and helped organize some of the events.

Tournament travel was fun—staying in hotels, seeing new places, and sharing the experiences with her closest friends on the team, all under the tutelage of Coach Berger. But it was also stressful, like any competition can be.

In February 1987, over Presidents' Day weekend, Ketanji, Stephen, and the debate team went to Harvard University. It was very exciting to be able to travel all the way to Boston to a tournament with people from across the country. It was the first time either of them had been to Boston, and they stayed at the Sheraton Commander Hotel near campus and Boston Common.

The team assembled before they headed to the Academic Resources Center. The winter ground was covered with white specks, and being from Miami, Stephen bent down to pick up some of the snow. Ketanji reacted swiftly and exclaimed, "Stephen, put that down! Don't eat that. That's salt!" Stephen had mistaken road salt, used to melt ice on sidewalks and streets, for snow. Such was their inexperience with Boston winters, though they'd get a full, immersive education on New England weather in barely a year's time. . . .

Ketanji came in first again in dramatic interpretation at this tournament, having recited a selection from the Pulitzer Prize and Tony Award–winning Black playwright August Wilson's work *Fences*. Being one of very few Black students on the debate circuit, she had yet to encounter anyone else celebrating, honoring, and showcasing Black history to the mostly white crowds. It was important to her to highlight Black cultural giants like Wilson, Nikki Giovanni, and Ntozake Shange.

Ketanji kept on winning. Stephen said she was "like a living legend in the speech and debate community." He and their friends still remember when she gave soaring recitations of scenes from such plays as *Agnes of God* or "pee-in-your-pants" renditions of Neil Simon's *Fools*, in which a schoolteacher must break the curse of stupidity that's infected a whole village by educating a doctor's daughter before he is struck stupid too. It was such a winning performance that other kids copied her selection and performance in later debates, but with much less success. She "had this beaming, energetic, friendly personality and natural charisma" that made people sit up and listen.

She won first place in oratory at the Sixth Annual William Faulkner Invitational High School Forensics Tournament in Mississippi for an essay she wrote and presented called "It's About Time," a humorous look at how people spend their time.

"I, for one, am a classic example of wasting time due to my lack of organization," she wrote for the competition—though she was, in fact, a very organized teenager. As a result of wasting time, she said, "I wind up struggling to finish a physics lab at 1:30 in the morning and wondering where my time went."

Ketanji won the biggest high school debate prize her senior year—the oratory title at the National Catholic Forensic League Championships. She made the final round in another category too—humorous interpretation. She performed a ten-minute scene from Jane Wagner's one-woman play *The Search for Signs of Intelligent Life in the Universe*, which Lily Tomlin originated on Broadway. Ketanji's performance as "Trudy the bag lady" had the audience laughing at lines like: "I worry that if peanut oil comes from peanuts, and olive oil comes from olives, where does baby oil come from?" Said with perfect comedic timing, she looked directly at the audience for a moment as the joke landed.

In the scene, she snorts and wipes her nose with her hand in exaggerated gestures, she points at the audience, and she snaps seamlessly in and out of the various characters. She chose a role that is just as challenging for adult actors to deliver as it is for kids. But eighteen-year-old Ketanji, who'd rehearsed the part until she had every gesture and word timed perfectly, won over the audience.

Outside of debate, Ketanji and her friends did normal high school things. They attended performances where her mom worked at New World School of the Arts, and even went to a toga party. On Sundays, Ketanji attended church with her family. But in general, her get-togethers with friends always had a purpose. They'd come to her house to make flowers for the homecoming float; she'd go to theirs for debate prep. Sometimes she'd have friends over to her house and they'd try cooking different dishes to see what tasted best. But their favorite was her mother's tuna casserole.

Ketanji sometimes liked to go the extra mile for her friends, and for Stephen's eighteenth birthday, she coordinated with his mother to throw him a surprise party!

The two maintained a close friendship. She and Stephen would help each other with their homework, or Ketanji would counsel Stephen on how he might approach things with a girlfriend. They leaned on each other the way friends do, and their bond has endured.

Ketanji's classmates knew she was a good choice for class president because, among other attributes, her sense of responsibility meant that the planning for high school reunions was in good hands. Ketanji would get the job done long after they'd all left Palmetto High. She took that responsibility to heart.

As student body president her senior year, Ketanji was charged with planning the prom. Although she was popular and had lots of friends, her relationships were, on the whole, platonic. She didn't date at her mostly white school—the boys didn't ask her out. The same went for her best friend, Denise. That kind of thing can have a lasting impact on someone's self-esteem, especially since it was hard to know if boys' lack of interest was due mainly to her being of a different race. (Being smart didn't help matters either.)

"Both Denise and I were painfully aware that at Palmetto, nobody courted the brainy Black girls, at least not in a romantic sense," Ketanji said.

For as much enjoyment and fulfillment Ketanji had in those days, and for all the lifelong friends she made and keeps to this day, she still remembers what she calls "the peculiar loneliness of being unchosen nerdy Black girls in high school."

But a ray of sunshine broke through one Saturday as the debate team boarded a tournament-bound bus, when her friend and teammate Ben Greenberg asked her whom she was going to prom with. She confessed that she didn't have a date. A junior when she was a senior, he remembers her as being "incredibly smart, hardworking, super honest, and one of the nicest people." So Ben was shocked—she'd done so much to make sure the prom was going to be nice for so many others that Ketanji not going didn't seem right. He suggested he take her himself: "Why don't we go together?" He didn't think twice about asking her—he hadn't felt threatened by either her skin color or her brains.

It was nice that she didn't have to dumb herself down just for a date, or morph into someone white, if that were even possible. If a girl has to make herself small or stupid to attract a boy and get his attention, then that's not the boy she wants. It was an act of friendship and kindness that might not have seemed like a big deal to Ben, but it was an important one for Ketanji.

There had been a large discussion on the prom committee about what the theme should be, and the kids chose the song "Forever Young," by Alphaville. Ketanji's classmate David Kujawa remembered her laughing, saying, "We can't pick that song. We're not gonna be forever young. We have to be honest with ourselves, we're gonna get old." She was fine, though, if the group still wanted it. She took on leadership roles, but David believed "she was like one of those leaders . . . that didn't . . . make you feel like they were leading, [even when] they were. . . ." Though she was outvoted on the song, she took it with good grace. Now she has to hear it at every high school reunion.

"She likes to get people to smile and she likes to entertain a bit with her wit," he said. She made certain that people's voices were heard and that they'd come to an agreement where nobody was too disappointed. He remembered her once saying, "You know, not everybody's gonna be happy, but at least everybody can't be too upset." David felt they could "always count on her to kind of shepherd a group of people through to a decision . . . that people felt overall pretty good about." And she did it by being inclusive and respectful of other people's opinions.

Richard Rosenthal, Stephen Rosenthal's brother, was two years behind Ketanji and Stephen at Palmetto High, but he was close to her and remains so. "I was a sophomore and Ketanji was a senior. In our Latin American history class, I sat in the seat next to hers. But on this particular day, her chair was empty," he said. Then Principal Bucholtz "came on the PA system and announced that [four students in] our senior class had just been accepted to Harvard College that day—a huge achievement for our large, and often under-funded, public high school."

Just as Ketanji opened the door and entered the class-room, the principal called out her name. "The entire class immediately leapt to its feet, exploded in applause, and ran over to Ketanji to embrace her. It was one of the most genuine, heartwarming moments I have ever seen. Every student was so happy for Ketanji and so proud of her accomplishment. Nobody was jealous, nobody was resentful . . . and nobody was at all surprised. Because she was Ketanji."

When she told the news to her grandmother Euzera, who had begun treatments for breast cancer, she was thrilled, believing Ketanji had gotten into Howard University. When Ketanji clarified that she would be attending Harvard, not Howard, Euzera reassured her: "I'm sure Harvard is a perfectly good school too."

As graduation neared, senior yearbooks came out. Ketanji had written that she wanted "to go into law and eventually have a judicial appointment." She was voted into the Hall of Fame along with Stephen, and was voted "most likely to succeed," "most talented," and got an honorable mention in drama at the *Miami Herald* newspaper's Silver Knight Awards. She wrote lovely things in classmates' yearbooks and received the same love from them. Soon she, Stephen, and a few others from their year were headed off to the same college—Harvard, to be exact. The very school her guidance counselor had discouraged her from applying to, telling her not to set her "sights so high."

Well, she showed them.

V

PERSEVERE

KETANJI AND HER PARENTS DROVE all day and night, twenty-two hours from their life in Miami to Harvard in Cambridge, Massachusetts. Cambridge at the end of summer is glorious—sunny, warm, scenic, fragrant, inviting. Kids skateboard in the pit at Harvard Square. Pedestrians line the sidewalks eating ice cream, window-shopping, or just enjoying the bright outdoors. Ketanji had grown up in Miami, Florida—a place of nearly year-round warmth and outdoor activities, and Harvard seemed like it was full of similar possibilities. Harvard College has a wide, expansive central campus yard, home to stately freshman dorms, impressive lecture halls, towering churches, and majestic libraries. Ketanji was filled with anticipation—her future was in her hands. She would be on her own for the first time in her life. All her choices would be hers to make: the classes she selected, the friends she made. Everything would be new, except for the school itself.

The school, originally called New College, was founded on October 28, 1636 (only sixteen years after the Pilgrims came to America), by a legislative act of the Great and General Court of Massachusetts with an initial fund of £400 (pounds). That money was earmarked for the construction of its first building, where Puritan clergy (all men) could be trained and not have to rely on the arrivals of other immigrant pastors to replace the first group when they died. The Pilgrims were Puritan colonialist immigrants: white, English Protestants who wanted to practice their religion freely, without having to participate in the Church of England's ceremonies that were not directly tied to the teachings of the Holy Bible.

Reverend John Harvard, the son of a landowning English butcher, left England with his second wife, Ann (née Sadler), after nearly his entire family had died of the plague. He was the sole heir to all the Harvard family's wealth and property, and he immigrated to Charlestown, Massachusetts, on August 1, 1637. Sadly he soon died of tuberculosis the following year, on September 14 (Ketanji's birthday), roughly two months shy of his thirty-first birthday, and not long after the school had broken ground on its first campus building.

He didn't have children, so on his deathbed he left half his estate, £779 (pounds), 17s (shillings), 2d (pence/pennies), and his whole personal library of 400 classical and religious theological books to the new college. It was the largest gift anyone had made to the college, so the Massachusetts General Court renamed it in his honor on March 13, 1639. With that, Harvard College was born.

In 1642, the graduation year of the first Harvard class, a London pamphlet entitled "An Account of the Foundation of the Colleges at Cambridge in New England," expressed the reasons for establishing the college:

> After God had carried us safely to New England, and we had builded our houses, provided necessaries for our livelihood, reared convenient places for God's worship, and settled the city government; one of the next things we longed for and looked after was to advance learning . . . dreading to leave an illiterate ministry to the churches, when our present ministers shall lie in the dust. And as we were thinking . . . it pleased God to stir up the heart of Mr. John Harvard (minister of Charlestown), a godly gentleman, and a lover of learning, living among us, to give the one-half of his estate. . . . The college . . . is called according to the name of the first founder, Harvard College.

Harvard was the first college established in the American colonies and over time erected or acquired many buildings, including "Indian College." Finished in 1656, it was funded by a London-based Christian missionary charity to "re-educate" Native Americans and turn them into missionaries who would spread the Puritan religion to other Native people. Ironically, these re-education missions did not respect the rights of Native Americans to worship their own gods or live by their own rules on their own land—the entire reason why the pilgrims had left England in the first place. Indian College did not attract many students and was closed in 1693. Matthews Hall now stands in its place.

The Brown family drove their beige Cadillac into Harvard Yard through its main entrance, Johnston Gate—a rite of passage for freshman students. Just inside the decorative wrought-iron structure, there stands the famous bronze statue of John Harvard, cast by French artist Daniel Chester French. Students rub its feet for good luck. But the statue is a lie. Three, in fact. At its base the plaque refers to John Harvard as the founder of the college. He is not. It says the college was established in 1638. It wasn't. And it says the statue is of John Harvard. It isn't. No one knows what John Harvard looks like—the statue is of French's model, Sherman Hoar, who posed for French in 1884.

Ketanji was assigned to live in a dorm called Hollis Hall, named for the benefactor Thomas Hall II of London. It was small and worn with age, yet steeped in history (it was built in 1763). She and her parents carried her belongings—suitcases, boxes, and milk crates filled with cassette music tapes, books she loved, movie posters, art supplies, an Apple Macintosh computer, and clothes—up three dark, dank flights of stairs. They then went back down, taking trip after trip in and out of the building, until all her possessions were piled up outside her double room. She retrieved her room key and unlocked the door—and discovered the space was bigger than she'd anticipated. Her roommate had not yet arrived, so she decided which bed she wanted and hopped onto it—a first taste of the type of choices she'd now get to make.

Move-in day comes filled with mixed emotions. Ketanji and her mom continued unpacking while her dad moved the car. Soon her roommate arrived with her parents, but unlike Ketanji, she wasn't very social or talkative. She was perfectly pleasant, but arranged her belongings mostly in silence. Their personalities didn't line up immediately, but that can happen. Everyone needed time to warm up to their new circumstances and settle in, in their own way, in their own time.

Ketanji's spirits remained high, even that afternoon, when her parents got ready to head back to Miami. Her father teared up and hugged her. Her mother held her close for a long while. She told Ketanji they'd given her all the tools she needed to find happiness and success at the school, and that she would always be praying for her.

Not many days later, Ketanji left one of her classes and walked toward her dorm. Cambridge in fall can get very cold and dreary—as though the overcast skies from Cambridge, England, come over to the States to spend the holidays. Even though she had visited briefly in winter as part of her debate team, this chilly, unrelenting Harvard wasn't what she'd been introduced to then. The air outside at dusk was crisp—different from the more humid, warm breezes of home. Home. It was all that she could think of. She missed everything about it. She grieved that her grandmother Euzera might not be there when she finally got to go back for break. Like Dorothy from *The Wiz* (and *The Wizard of Oz*), she wished she were home. The lyrics from the musical sum it up best: *When I think of home / I think of a place / Where there's love overflowing / I wish I was home / I wish I was back there / With the things I been knowing.*

Ketanji had gone to a public high school and found that so many students at Harvard had gone to private schools or Harvard summer school to get a leg up. They were polished. They were different. They had money. Many seemed stuck-up. They arrived knowing all about Harvard and what to do when they got there—what clubs to join, classes to take, and faculty to impress. That wasn't her or how she operated in life—she wasn't shallow, or scheming, or fake. Or nearly as "prepped." She was always just herself.

Homesickness is a powerful, overwhelming feeling. As is impostor syndrome. That's when you feel like an impostor (a faker, like the cloth weavers in Hans Christian Andersen's "The Emperor's New Clothes," weaving webs of lies), and doubt your abilities, skills, and successes, believing you do not measure up or belong where you are. Similar to that statue of John Harvard, Ketanji too felt like a lie, with thoughts in her head telling her she was pretending to be something she wasn't. As if Charlotte from *Charlotte's Web* had lied to Wilbur and never had any spider skills to spin silk into shimmery words to save his life. Ketanji felt out of place, almost unwelcome, surrounded by buildings named for men she didn't know, most of whose histories she hadn't yet learned.

But had she known whose names were on the buildings, or who had given the school money to build, it would not likely have reassured her. Over a third of the money donated to Harvard in the first half of the nineteenth century came from five men who profited in some form or fashion off the inhumane American chattel slave trade.

Between roughly 1525 and 1867, a total of 10.7 million Africans, mostly from the west coast of the continent, were shackled and chained to ship floors, then transported across the Atlantic Ocean to the Americas to work in bondage against their will. Of those, roughly 388,000 were shipped directly to North America.

1. Peter Chardon Brooks insured merchant slave ships on the New England–Caribbean route—a business that made him New England's wealthiest man.

2. Benjamin Bussey sold crops—cotton, coffee, and sugar—that relied on the use of slave labor. His $320,000 estate was to be divided among Harvard's schools of divinity, law, and agriculture.

3. Abbott Lawrence Lowell and his family ran factories that produced yarn or fabric out of American South cotton, exploiting the labor of Black people both before and after the Civil War. He provided the school $100,000 in two installments (one after his death), which were used to establish the Lawrence Scientific School (now the Graduate School of Applied Science).

4. As part of the "triangular trade" between Europe, Africa, and the Americas, John McLean sent wood and food to the Caribbean and brought slave-grown sugar to the United States and Europe. He helped finance Massachusetts General Hospital's department for the insane, later renamed McLean Hospital.

5. James Perkins traded, sold, bought, and transported the enslaved in Saint-Domingue (now Haiti), where in its

heyday, 40,000 Black humans, including children, were trafficked yearly to keep up with the enormous losses of human life caused by the harsh conditions on sugar plantations. (Haitians revolted against slavery in 1791 and won their independence from France in 1804, which scared President Thomas Jefferson. He upheld US slavery and worked to prevent any similar uprisings in the States. In 1825, France demanded the Haitians pay 150 million francs to the French slaveholders for their "losses," which, over 122 years with interest, amounted to roughly $30 billion, leaving Haiti one of the poorest countries in the world today.) Upon his death, Perkins bequeathed $20,000 for the Perkins Professorship of Astronomy and Mathematics. Meanwhile, his descendants and relatives continued to donate vast sums to the school for the next century, one such relation being the first president of Radcliffe College (Harvard College's sister school for women, organized in 1879), Elizabeth Cary Agassiz.

Presidents, faculty, and staff of Harvard enslaved over seventy people. No one can escape the ghosts and shadows of slavers, slavery profiteers, and racialists there, as their names pepper the buildings where one eats, sleeps, studies, invents, creates, and performs—looming over every facet of student life: Winthrop (House), Perkins (Hall and/ or Room), McLean (Hospital), Atkins (Reference Room), Greenleaf (House), Agassiz (Museum, Theater, or House),

Holmes (Hall), Warren (Research Center), Eliot (House), Lowell (House), and others.

Although the school finally opened its doors to men of color in 1847, the first Black man admitted, Beverly Garnett Williams, died before he could go. It wasn't until Richard Theodore Greener was admitted nearly two decades later that a Black man would graduate from the school. But Harvard's celebration of the contributions of people of color to both the school and American life remained lacking. That was true even though (due to the echoes of slavery and America's foundational resistance to Black people accessing wealth, health, and social advancement) what so many Black alums could not offer by way of money, they certainly made up for in other ways.

For example, W. E. B. Du Bois, author and champion of civil rights, attended the college and was also the first Black American Harvard PhD. Charles Hamilton Houston (the first general counsel of the NAACP and first Black person on the *Harvard Law Review* editorial board), William Henry Hastie, Jr. (America's first Black federal judge, appellate judge, and governor of the Virgin Islands), and William Thaddeus Coleman, Jr. (the first Black person to clerk for a Supreme Court justice) were Harvard-educated lawyers whose work laid the groundwork for the landmark Supreme Court *Brown v. Board of Education* decision, which declared the practice of "separate but equal" unconstitutional. Yet none of their names are engraved in plaques on the facades of the buildings on Harvard's campus.

On top of that, Radcliffe College (originally the Society for the Collegiate Instruction of Women, or the "Harvard Annex"), first admitted a Black woman (Alberta Virginia Scott) in 1894. Over the next decades, the institution refused to grant Black women scholarships or housing, and only fifteen were allowed to attend before 1920. Eva Beatrice Dykes and Caroline Bond Day, who wanted to do advanced degree work there and had already graduated from HBCUs (Howard and Atlanta University, respectively), were forced to repeat their undergraduate degrees at Radcliffe, because the school did not respect the educations they got at their alma maters.

Regardless, in 1921, while at Harvard, Eva Beatrice Dykes became the first Black woman in the United States to earn a PhD. She did important work analyzing the attitudes of eighteenth- and nineteenth-century white writers toward slavery and Black Americans, and at the same time she recovered long-lost works of Black creatives. Caroline Bond Day, who had studied under Du Bois at Atlanta U, got her master's degree in 1930. She surveyed her biracial (mixed-race) friends, friends of friends, acquaintances, and network for a study that ended up challenging the racist notions of white Harvard scholars like Pulitzer Prize winner Charles Warren, who held views suggesting Black and mixed-race people were inferior to white people (again, this is called eugenics). Her conclusion—that people of color are not inferior—was rooted in science and evidence. Yet, as noted above, Warren, with his wrongheaded, anti-Black, racist views, has a research center named after him at Harvard. Day, however, who proved him wrong, does not. Does money matter more than merit or morals? Or positive social impact?

Harvard grads like Du Bois, Day, and Dykes, who fought discrimination, paved the way for Ketanji to find a place at Harvard-Radcliffe, the name on the degree women received back then. Houston, Hastie, and Coleman, along with Ketanji's hero Constance Baker Motley, made "separate but equal" a thing of the past, at least legally, so Ketanji could expect equal access to facilities and opportunities when she arrived. That was, as long as the gatekeepers and teachers believed it to be in the past too.

As Ketanji walked through the Yard, feeling like an outsider and longing to be surrounded by the familiar comforts of home, a Black woman she didn't know headed toward her. She came from the opposite direction on the sidewalk and must have seen the look on Ketanji's face on someone else before—she immediately recognized the way she was walking, her posture, the thoughts behind her eyes. It was like she could see past her skin and peer inside her heart, and understand how Ketanji was feeling: the insecurity, sadness, and doubt. Right as they came upon each other, the woman looked at Ketanji and leaned over as they crossed. She spoke directly to her: "Persevere," she said.

The woman kept going, didn't stop or turn to see if her word had landed on Ketanji—but she trusted that it had. Because, like so many other Black people who have found themselves in spaces where they are the minority, whether that's due to their race alone or with the added burden of gender or a lack of wealth tacked on, she had lived through that doubt and come out the other side stronger. She had faith in Ketanji at a time when Ketanji's confidence had wavered. It was only one word—a demand, not a question. And in that moment, Ketanji knew she was not alone. Others had come before her and felt the same things and made it through. Others like her had found the strength to change the way others saw them and the way they saw themselves. Others had graduated, even conquered this school. If they could do it, maybe she could too. . . .

But Ketanji's sorrow didn't go away. September 14, 1988—Ketanji's birthday was cooler, barely 70 degrees at its warmest. She was dressed in a scarf and hat and carrying books with her through the Yard, heading for the steps of the famous Widener Library. There would be no big celebration filled with family and friends. No joy and laughter and cooking and cake. She shivered from the cold weather and reception she was feeling, waves of sadness washing over her.

Harry Elkins Widener, a Harvard graduate from Philadelphia, Pennsylvania, was twenty-seven years old when he boarded the famed "unsinkable" ship *Titanic* in Cherbourg, France, on April 10, 1912. He and his wealthy parents, George D. and Eleanor Elkins Widener, traveled in first-class cabins across the Atlantic headed for New York City. Harry was bringing rare books he'd collected on his trip back with him. Twenty minutes before midnight, on April 14, 1912, the ship hit an iceberg. Captain Edward Smith insisted women and children be given priority access to the lifeboats, of which there were too few, and Harry and his father stayed aboard.

Hours later, the ship split apart and sank to the bottom of the ocean 400 miles off the coast of Newfoundland, Canada. Eleanor was rescued from lifeboat No. 4, but her husband and son died. As she grieved her losses, she fulfilled her son's wish to donate his book collection, including 3,500 rare books, to Harvard, and she provided $2 million to fund Harvard's construction of the massive Harry Elkins Widener Memorial Library. It contains 57 miles of shelves with ten levels of open stacks and is home to over 3 million books. When it opened on June 24, 1915, United States senator Henry Cabot Lodge dubbed it a "noble gift to learning" that "comes to us with the shadow of a great sorrow resting on it."

Ketanji sat down on Widener's grand steps, buried her head in her papers, and began to cry. She was lonely and homesick, a fish out of water in a strange place, where even her Palmetto Senior High classmates who joined her at Harvard were spread out across other dorms and classes, making their own new friends. "I was in a strange place far from home . . . no one knew it was my 18th birthday and certainly no one cared." *Why do I feel like I'm drowning / When there is plenty of air / Why do I feel like frowning / I think the feeling is fear . . . In a different place / In a different time / Different people around me / I would like to know of their different world / And how different they find me.*

Ketanji was still questioning whether she really belonged there. Could she fit in? Had she made the right choice to come? It was one of the few times she doubted herself. She wasn't sure if she could make it in that environment. But way down, she is also a fighter and not a quitter. She dug deep inside, back to the feeling she had when she was excluded from her high school play because of her race. And she decided she wasn't going to let Harvard exclude her, especially if that feeling was coming more from her than from others. She picked up her books and trudged up the thirty stairs to the entrance, and disappeared inside, swallowed up by the cavernous institution.

It was close to midnight when she headed back to her freshman dorm. Being a thoughtful, courteous roommate, she didn't turn on the light, since her roommate was already in bed asleep. On her bed was a package and letter, which she brought out into the hallway to open. In the package was a cassette tape, and there was a card from her mom and dad. Written inside in her mom's handwriting were happy birthday wishes. She wrote that they missed her, that Ketanji was growing into a lovely young lady, and that she prayed Ketanji would reach her full God-given potential.

The letter was from her Aunt Carolynn, who'd picked out her African name meaning "lovely one." She too remarked on how time was flying, and Ketanji was growing into an adult. She reminded her to remain aware and on guard, and trust that God would protect her, and that people at home were praying for her.

Back in the room, Ketanji pulled out her Walkman, put on her earphones, and played the cassette tape. On it, her mother sang "Happy Birthday" to her. Her mom had never serenaded her before. And it helped, in that moment, to break Ketanji's blues. She might have been feeling alone, but she was being thought about with love and joy all the same. Ketanji said that knowing her parents "remembered me, believed in me, were praying for me, and wanted me to be successful," left her feeling encouraged, and she was thankful to God that she'd been given the opportunity to go to this school, that she had support even from afar, and that she had already come a long way toward achieving her goals. Her parents, her aunt, and that woman from the Yard were like angels watching over her, lifting her up, lifting her spirits. It was everything she needed to put her sadness behind her and restart her college experience from a place of strength, hope, and resilience.

With a renewed spirit, Ketanji dove into her coursework. One of her Moral Reasoning classes was called "Justice," which she found to be one of the most important and influential toward her future career. It dealt with "moral dilemmas"— situations where a choice must be made, but all the choices are equally troubling. Her instructor, Professor Michael J. Sandel, had students in a theater-like setting debate various issues like affirmative action (what today might be called "diversity, equity, and inclusion," or DEI), income inequality, free speech, hate speech, and same-sex marriage. Ketanji was in her element. He asked questions like: Is it justifiable "to torture a suspect to get the information"? or "to steal a drug that your child needs to survive"? Ketanji said, "The kinds of questions that he was asking overlapped with philosophy and law," and she described it as "just really, really formative, and I think it set a path for me."

She also dove headfirst into writing in her Expository Writing class and received the only A her teacher, Professor Richard C. Marius, gave out for the entire course! That means she did better than the other kids who'd come from prep schools, or whose parents had money, or who walked through the campus seeming so confident to Ketanji. That kind of validation was exactly what Ketanji needed as she found her voice again and pushed that self-doubt out of her head. She wasn't in over her head and out of her depth; she was right where she belonged.

From here on out, Ketanji knew she could make it there, and that she was a force. She could persevere through the homesickness and find her purpose and joy again. Not necessarily any that came from teachers, or peers, or even strangers on the sidewalk. The kind you can only find within.

*Much of the research for this chapter came from Harvard's own report studying its past: *Harvard & the Legacy of Slavery*.

*The university had not renamed itself or any of its schools since 1638, when New College became Harvard College, until 2014, when Harvard's School of Public Health was renamed after T. H. Chan, the father of billionaire alum Gerald L. Chan, whose Morningside Foundation donated $350 million. It did it again in 2015, when Harvard's School of Engineering and Applied Sciences was renamed for hedge fund billionaire John A. Paulson upon receiving his $400 million "gift." And it did it once more in 2023, after alum Kenneth C. Griffin, who has given the school more than half a billion dollars, paid $300 million for his name to go on the Graduate School of Arts and Sciences. Still no W. E. B. Du Bois building yet.

VI

IN ON THE ACT

IN THE LATE SUMMER OF 1989, as notes of cedar and centuries-old history formed the distinctive, lingering scent of Harvard Yard, Ketanji hurried from one end of campus to another, harboring a juicy secret. Perhaps not so much a secret, but rather some big news she was dying to get off her chest.

She recognized Stephen in the distance ahead and cut a sharp angle across the lawn to catch up. When in earshot, she called his name and stopped to catch her breath. Stephen swung around, always happy to see his friend, but slightly startled this day by the urgency in her voice. Her brilliant smile put his mind back at ease, and she asked if he'd heard of a new television show that had recently premiered on NBC. Stephen admitted he wasn't familiar with it, and Ketanji gave him his marching orders: "Oh my God. It's the best show. You gotta watch this show." It contained unexpected humor about the most mundane, ordinary things, but it took them to the extreme. It wasn't super popular at the time, like *The Cosby Show, A Different World, Martin,* or *Cheers,* but it spoke to her soul: the minutiae of life, our little pet peeves, friend dynamics, the writing. The journey the jokes took before sticking the landing. It had blown her away and she knew, if given the chance, it'd change his life too.

After he assured her he would give the show a shot, she went on her way, satisfied and relieved to have spread the word about the second coming of comedy. This teenager had had her finger on the pulse of pop culture and had gotten in on the ground floor of a new wave in TV humor, well before the rest of the campus and country had caught on. She'd felt its cross-cultural connection and communal talking points. So on this issue, there could be no debate: People had to start watching *Seinfeld.*

But for a college kid it was no easy feat. There were no videos streaming on the internet—and personal computers had barely begun to pop up on campuses. Word processors had only recently replaced typewriters. There was no such thing as an iPad or smartphone. No YouTube, Instagram, or TikTok. Televisions certainly weren't LCD, plasma, or flat-screen, and they were nonexistent in dorms or common rooms—so one had to find a group that got together each week to watch the show. And if you missed an episode, you'd either have to find someone who'd taped it on their VCR (video cassette recorder) or wait until NBC aired it again in reruns. In order to watch *Seinfeld*, one had to seek out *Seinfeld*.

NBC executives didn't really understand the show and tried to sell it to another channel. It started off small with a cult following, and relied on word of mouth to build its audience. It needed time for people to find it. It broke boundaries and rules and opened up the imaginations of creative artists and writers everywhere. And the show was able to do that while technically adhering to the nation's laws.

Barely ten years earlier, the Supreme Court had heard arguments in a case about a comedy routine, Seven Words You Can Never Say on Television, that a comedian named George Carlin (a friend of Jerry Seinfeld's) had performed on his album. The radio station WBAI aired the routine around two p.m. on October 30, 1973, during host Paul Gorman's "Lunchpail" program. John H. Douglas, a man on the national board of Morality in Media, and his fifteen-year-old son had heard the broadcast, which Douglas thought wasn't appropriate for his child to be listening to at his age.

He wrote a letter, which found its way to the Federal Communications Commission (which keeps tabs on what is played on the radio, satellite TV, television, cable, or over the wire). The FCC decided that the routine, which used "bad" language, should not have been aired during a time children might be awake to hear it. They did not fine Pacifica, which owned the radio station, but they let them know they would be disciplined if they received more complaints in the future.

Pacifica appealed the ruling to the United States District of Columbia Circuit Court on the grounds that the FCC was censoring them (not allowing them the right to speak freely without being punished for it by the government)—a violation of the very first amendment of the United States Constitution! The court agreed and reversed the FCC's ruling. But the FCC filed a petition for *certiorari*, meaning they were asking the Supreme Court, the highest law of the land, to review the DC Circuit Court's ruling and, hopefully, side with the FCC this time.

In a split 5–4 decision, on July 3, 1978, the court reversed the lower court's ruling, deciding that the government does have the right, in limited circumstances, to restrict free speech if it serves the public's interest. This decision remains controversial, but it still stands. So if television shows wanted to discuss topics that brush up against what the FCC might conclude was indecent rather than protected speech, people had to get clever.

Larry David and Jerry Seinfeld, the creators of the television show *Seinfeld*, chose to push the envelope. Despite this Supreme Court decision, they decided not to police what their characters said, only the *way* they said it, presenting controversial topics in a way that wouldn't get them canceled. Writers and comedians found ways around censorship, making the comedy funnier because they never mentioned taboo topics by name. Seinfeld said his team was "very good with language" and he found it "funny to be delicate with something that is explosive." It became a game and they played by the rules, never using any of those seven words one could "never say on television."

The show's audience grew, year upon year, until it hit number one in the Nielsen rankings and ratings. The sitcom had its audience to thank for having lasted that long and embracing it even before the network did, giving it time for others to catch on. People like Ketanji, who spread the word, helped to push comedy—and the culture—forward, by seeing something new and exciting in the show before others did.

Not long after this, Ketanji convinced Stephen to join Harvard's comedy group On Thin Ice. There they'd take comedy, culture, and content to the next level, just for fun. As Stephen remembered, "We would do rehearsals together a lot, and we'd perform in front of student audiences." It might seem strange that people who perform improv comedy actually practice, but it's true. By practicing, performers find ways of thinking quickly and reacting to shifting scenes on the spot. That's a lot of pressure—both the pressure to think fast and the pressure to be funny! Like anything you want to be good at, practice is key. "And that was a really challenging thing. She brought . . . her dramatic skills. But it was, for everybody . . . really tough . . . trying to think really quickly on your feet."

Christiane Pendarvis was a classmate of Ketanji's and had found her to be "always very outgoing, social, but not the social butterfly center of attention, but genuinely interested in people." Ketanji was someone who could balance her studies with her student life—causes, organizations, and social events. "Ketanji wasn't the person who was always in the library. . . . She had diverse interests." She managed her schedule and budgeted her time wisely, so she was able to do all those things well. As she moved through her college career, her performance skills grew more sophisticated and her tastes in different types of entertainment deepened.

Bitten by the acting bug when she was younger, and now considering herself something of an actress, Ketanji participated in Common Casting—that's when all the plays and musicals on campus hold auditions and cast actors. She got the part of Ronette, a member of a trio of singing doo-wop girls—the backbone and narrators of the play *Little Shop of Horrors*, the comedy horror rock musical by Howard Ashman with music by Alan Menken. Staged at the Hasty Pudding Theater in December of 1988, the show got a positive review from the main newspaper, *The Harvard Crimson* ("'weed' recommend it"), though they found the trio's performance to be spotty. You can't win them all, and despite that critique, Ketanji kept on pursuing her love of the theater.

She joined the Political Drama committee, part of the Institute of Politics at the Kennedy School of Government, and was elected chair her junior year. She tried producing and directing and put on a production of the 1984 play *I'm Not Rappaport*, by Herb Gardner, about two elderly Jewish and Black men reminiscing about their difficult lives.

But the highlight of her acting and singing at Harvard might be her tribute to the late famous jazz singer Billie Holiday, during the tail end of her junior year. Her sophomore-year roommate, Nina Simmons, found the show "extremely powerful," yet given all her gifts, Ketanji was "very humble about that. It's that balance that so impresses people."

The *Crimson* was equally impressed, calling it "an unprecedented Harvard production. It is not, strictly speaking, a play, a musical nor a concert. Instead, *Yesterdays* is about the possibilities of jazz." They noted how Ketanji was the only performer who opted to speak with the same accent as Holiday and perform with the same flair and vocal style. Ketanji even wore Holiday's trademark white gardenia flower over her left ear—something Holiday decided to do to cover a section of her scalp where she'd accidentally burned the hair off with a hot comb or flat iron—a tool women used to flatten and straighten their curly or wavy hair. (Historically, it was something that enslaved women and women of color specifically did in order to fit in better with white society.) Ketanji had adapted the music for the play from Holiday's 1956 autobiography, *Lady Sings the Blues*. The opus *Yesterdays*, "a fresh interpretation of Holiday's life that manages both to entertain and to challenge the boundaries of theater at Harvard," was Ketanji flexing her singing and acting muscles, and honoring the part of herself that loved theater, debate, creativity, language, new ideas, and art.

To this day, she goes to a musical in every new city she visits and with every new job she gets.

VII

THE FLAG

KETANJI WANTED TO MAKE CERTAIN she maintained close ties to her roots, the way her parents had helped her do while she was growing up. So she joined the Black Students Association (BSA). One day, she invited Stephen to join her for one of their mixers, and on their way home from the event, he admitted how out of place and awkward he felt, being the only white person there. He had never before experienced that feeling of sticking out like a sore thumb. Ketanji told him that's how she felt every day throughout high school, which stunned him. It had never occurred to him that Ketanji might not have felt completely comfortable at school, since she was so popular and bubbly. "I'm so sorry," he said.

It was a moment of genuine understanding between them. Ketanji felt seen in a way she hadn't before. She had tried so hard as a kid to be perfect, wanting never to come across like one of the stereotypes held against Black people. Somehow, this moment freed her from needing to prove people wrong in their anti-Black beliefs. Instead, she felt free to be exactly who she was. Their stupidity was their burden to carry, not hers.

Ketanji was a junior when, on February 18, 1991, transfer student Bridget (Brigid) L. Kerrigan chose to hang a Confederate flag outside her fourth-floor Kirkland House window. Ketanji and her friend Lisa were walking back to their suite and froze in their tracks, among several other students who were staring at the offensive image. Kerrigan was born near Chicago, a very diverse city, but grew up in Virginia, where the idea of "Southern Pride" could often be found among white residents whose ancestry was rooted in the South, or whose family survived or fought in the Civil War on the side of the slavers (the Confederacy or the "South"). The South believed each state had the right to decide whether slavery should be allowed in that state ("states' rights") and fought against freeing the enslaved and against those who wanted to keep the United States whole (the Union or the "North").

Almost 130 years before Kerrigan did this, Abraham Lincoln, a Republican, issued the Emancipation Proclamation abolishing slavery on January 1, 1863. That was over two years after he was elected president (November 6, 1860) and South Carolina had separated from the United States (December 20, 1860). It was also nearly two years after the South fired its first shot against soldiers from the North at Fort Sumter at 4:30 a.m. on April 15, 1861, in Charleston, South Carolina. This started the Civil War, and Virginia broke away from the Union on April 17, 1861. That same year, the National Flag Committee of the Confederate States of America held a contest on how the design of their flag should look.

After the Confederacy was defeated and General Robert E. Lee surrendered on April 9, 1865, with 642,427 deaths on the Union side and 483,026 on the Confederate one, the country went through a period called Reconstruction (1865–77). The badly bruised nation had to rebuild. It had to deal with the harmful, long-lasting impact slavery had on the individuals who'd been enslaved as well as manage the larger social, political, and economic effects the war and the end of slavery would have on the states that could no longer rely on free, immoral labor.

On April 11, 1865, President Lincoln gave a speech in which he proposed that "very intelligent" Black males and veterans be allowed to vote in elections. John Wilkes Booth was in the crowd and was furious Lincoln wanted to give rights to any Black Americans. He turned to his friend beside him and vowed, "That is the last speech he will ever make." Three days later, Booth assassinated the president.

The renowned author, speaker, and abolitionist Frederick Douglass said in his eulogy that Lincoln was the first president to "show any respect" for Black men's rights. On December 24 of that same year, a group of former Confederate soldiers in Pulaski, Tennessee, started a terrorist organization called the Ku Klux Klan (KKK), founded in order to spread the idea of white supremacy across the nation. It was designed to prevent any Black advancement in America. Its members used intimidation, violence, and murder against Black and white people who believed in the equality of the races or who tried to advance that cause. W. E. B. Du Bois estimated the Klan committed roughly 197 murders and 548 violent assaults in the Carolinas from 1866 to 1867 alone.

The Senate ratified the Fourteenth Amendment of the United States Constitution on July 9, 1868, which granted citizenship to all people born or naturalized in the United States, *including* those who had been enslaved. It also allowed the federal government to reduce the congressional representatives of any state that interfered with citizens' rights to vote. Former Confederate states, which all tended to vote Democrat, had to ratify the Fourteenth Amendment in order to regain representation in the federal government. Congress then passed the Fifteenth Amendment on February 26, 1869, and ratified it a year later on February 3, 1870, granting Black men the right to vote.

The Reconstruction Acts of 1867 made it so those same former Southern states were required to write new state constitutions allowing Black and white men to vote and hold office. During Reconstruction, around 2,000 Black men were elected to public office nationwide, one of their major contributions to society being the establishment of tax-funded public schools. Even Florida sent a Black man, Josiah Wells, to Congress in 1871. And Black men really did gain wealth and vote in elections during that time, temporarily changing the composition of state governments as well as the federal one. The Civil Rights Act of 1875 made it illegal for anyone to deny "the full and equal enjoyment of any of the accommodations, advantages, facilities, and privileges of inns, public conveyances on land or water, theaters and other places of public amusement; subject only to the conditions and limitations established by law, and applicable alike to citizens of every race and color."

But the promise of Reconstruction was short-lived, because the presidential election in 1876 did not have a clear winner. Democrat Samuel J. Tilden led Republican Rutherford B. Hayes by 260,000 popular votes and 184 electoral votes to Hayes's 165 (Tilden needed one more to win the election). Congress created an Electoral Commission in 1877 to settle the dispute, and Hayes promised the former Confederate states that, if they would back his win, he would remove federal troops (armed police) from their states, who were there to protect the rights of Black citizens. With that promise in mind, the presidency ultimately went to Hayes and the troops left, as did any hope for equal treatment of Black citizens for the next ninety years.

The United States Supreme Court struck down the Civil Rights Act in 1883 in an 8–1 ruling (Justice John Marshall Harlan being the only dissenting voice), with the majority, led by Justice Joseph P. Bradley, agreeing that the Fourteenth Amendment did not give Congress the authority to prevent discrimination by private individuals, only by the states.

Meanwhile, the terrorist campaign against Black citizens by the Ku Klux Klan, whose membership even included police officers and politicians, went virtually unchecked. They scared Black people away from the voting booths, ran them out of town, intimidated Black community leaders who were teaching people how to register to vote, or murdered them. There were also white men, some of whom were called "Redeemers," who took on the mantra that the "South shall rise again," because they wanted government power back.

In general, whites who owned small farms were resentful of Blacks, whose votes kept conservatives in power. White men, including the "Readjuster Party" in Virginia, overthrew some state governments and then passed restrictive voting laws, such as poll taxes (meaning you had to pay to vote) and literacy tests (since the enslaved had been forbidden from learning to read), where the white person administering the test could give a Black applicant an impossibly hard question on purpose. That person might ask the Black person to recite the entire Declaration of Independence or United States Constitution from memory or tell him he had failed even if he'd passed.

On May 18, 1896, in the case of *Plessy v. Ferguson,* the Supreme Court ruled that separate-but-equal facilities were constitutional. Segregation became the law of the land in the South in public spaces and public transportation, like trains, buses, hotels, diners, restaurants, theaters, and schools. Then in 1915, D. W. Griffith's silent film *The Birth of a Nation* was released in movie theaters. Based on a novel by Baptist preacher Thomas Dixon, the movie depicted the Ku Klux Klan (in hoods and robes) and former Confederates as heroes needing to restore the South to its "former glory," waving the Confederate battle flag, while formerly enslaved Black people, abolitionists, and Northerners were the evil villains. It was a giant hit, and though it was an advancement in motion picture technology, it was pro-Confederate propaganda. It used white people in blackface and other racist imagery and ideas to fan the flames of racism, division, fear, and discrimination in the country. Ultimately, along with the Plessy ruling, *The Birth of a Nation* helped birth the Jim Crow era in America.

Ketanji has described Jim Crow as follows:

". . . in many places, Black people were required to pay special poll taxes or take literacy tests before they were permitted to exercise their right to vote. Black Americans did not have full and equal access to public transportation—they were relegated to certain cars on trains and certain seats on buses—and could only take advantage of public accommodations such [as] restaurants and theaters on the specific terms that white shop owners dictated, usually that they had to sit at separate tables away from white patrons. There was segregation in housing, and, of course, Black children were not allowed to attend public schools alongside white children, as a practical matter, even after the *Brown v. the Board* decision. In the South, there was also the ever-present threat of physical harm and even death to Black people (men especially) who stepped out of line as far as white society was concerned."

Even after women won the right to vote through the Nineteenth Amendment, which Congress passed on June

4, 1919, and ratified on August 18, 1920, Black women, like Black men, still had to fight discrimination and intimidation at the polls and in their daily lives, even beyond that fateful *Brown v. Board of Education* Supreme Court case. And it was all due to the color of their skin.

President Harry S. Truman, a Democrat from the South, wanted to run on a civil rights platform, but a group of his colleagues called "Dixiecrats" walked out of the party's 1948 convention in disgust. In 1964, Democratic president Lyndon B. Johnson signed the Civil Rights Act into law, which his Republican opponent Barry Goldwater had opposed publicly. That night, as Johnson sat in his bedroom feeling depressed, he confessed to his special assistant Bill Moyers that "I think we just delivered the South to the Republican party for a long time to come."

President Johnson signed the Voting Rights Act in 1965. Black voters, who used to vote Republican because the 1866 Civil Rights Act promised them equality, switched to the Democratic Party, and white Southern voters, who resented the gains of Blacks, fled to the Republican Party. By the 1980s, the parties had completely switched platforms and voters, and in the 1960s and '70s, towns, mainly in the South, created hundreds of inexpensive private schools for white students to attend, so they wouldn't have to mix with Black students. Many of those "segregation academies" still exist. Combined with "white flight," the country and its schools remain as segregated today if not more than they were in the 1960s. Truly separate and still unequal.

Right around the turn of the twentieth century, heralding in the Jim Crow South, white Southerners, still not over the gains made by Blacks during and immediately after the Civil War, began erecting statues to Confederate generals and continued to display the Confederate battle flag on their lawns, in their homes, on their vehicles, etc., supposedly as a source of pride. But for Black people, it remained strictly another threat and means of intimidation, where Black people needed to be put back in their place—threatened, intimidated, and under the foot of whites.

Bridget Kerrigan had transferred from the University of Virginia to Harvard-Radcliffe in 1989. When she tried hanging her Confederate flag out the window of her apartment in Peabody Terrace that year, the superintendent there made her take it down because it was against regulations. Her roommate at the time, Katherine Florey, said Bridget "knew what she was getting herself into" when she'd hung up the flag.

The next year in Kirkland House, Bridget refused to budge and seemed to bask in the negative attention that hanging her flag had brought her. She suggested she just wanted to get respect, as a Southerner, from the Harvard community. Speaking with a Southern drawl, which her high school classmates did not remember her ever having before, she said that the flag reminded her "of home. That's all," and that she's "just the average blond girl from Virginia." She claimed that holding a different viewpoint from the majority of students at Harvard, who were more open-minded and liberal in their beliefs, meant that she represented "diversity." "If they talk about diversity, they're gonna get it. . . . If they talk about tolerance, they better be ready to have it."

She wasn't the only one to hang that flag. Jon P. Jiles had hung a Confederate flag at the end of 1990. The Leverett "House master" John E. Dowling told him what he'd done could offend others, and Jon eventually took his flag down to display inside his own suite instead. Years later, Jon said, "Just because you can stick a flag up on the wall, doesn't mean you should do it."

Only days after Kerrigan had hung her flag, in sympathy for her, a white student, Timothy McCormack of New Sweden, Maine, hung his own up outside a window in Cabot House (named for Thomas Dudley Cabot and Virginia Wellington Cabot), alongside a sign that read: "Racism No."

Other students quickly got upset. Some strung rubber chickens in their windows. One, whose window was above Tim's, had a message for him and his display. This student's sign, which had an arrow pointing down at Tim's, read: "What a Fool!" Ketanji lived in Cabot House too.

The BSA and Black students overall, who made up about

10 percent of the student population, saw these acts as clear attempts to offend, humiliate, and dehumanize Black students, because the Confederate flag has always been about intimidating, overseeing, and controlling the lives of Black people. And it needs to be stated that back then the "Quad" (North House, Cabot House, and Currier House, originally Radcliffe student housing) was home to a large proportion of Black students, making this display especially harmful.

The BSA, led by its president, Mecca J. Nelsen, got together to strategize how to protest these offensive acts. They started marching through campus, such as on March 8, from Kirkland to Cabot House; organizing rallies; circulating petitions; shouting their disapproval; and being vocal and visible on campus at all hours in order to get the school administration to act or help them. They made a poster with the Confederate flag and the words "This is a signifier of white supremacy" and "The official flag of a defeated nation born of treason and financed by inhumanity" on it. Campus "House masters" (now called "faculty deans," since the other name could be too easily associated with slavery) met and there were "eat-ins" staged in Kirkland and Cabot House cafeterias to protest the disgusting displays.

A Black student, Jacinda Townsend from Kentucky, hung a sheet with a swastika and "Racism No?" spray-painted on it from her window in Cabot House as a response to

McCormack's flag. Townsend wanted to emphasize that both the swastika and the Confederate flag were symbols of hate and genocide and should never be allowed to be displayed publicly, as both are used to terrorize and target people because of their race (and/or religion). Isn't it true that two wrongs shouldn't make a right?

Harvard's campus police came within a day and asked her to remove her flag. But why her, and not Kerrigan? Townsend recorded an outgoing message on her answering machine that said, "If you're calling me to tell me to take my flag down, I hope you'll call Dean Fred Jewett and ask him to make me take my flag down."

Though they were on her side regarding the Confederate flag's awful history and need for removal, Harvard's Jewish student organization, Hillel, asked her to take the swastika sheet down because of how offensive it was, especially to Jews.

The BSA, of which Jacinda was not a member, also stepped in and asked her to remove the swastika flag, so as not to create anger between Black and Jewish students. "That wasn't the intent," she agreed. Understanding the pain of her fellow students, she took down her sheet.

In a letter released on March 12, the school agreed with Jacinda that hanging the Confederate flag was "insensitive and unwise." But President Derek Bok decided not to intervene. He and the undergraduate student council (which voted against asking the students to remove the flags) and the student-run newspapers believed the students were exercising their right to "free speech."

The Harvard Crimson recommended "censure, not censor," meaning to state you disapprove of something rather than silence the voice of the person you disagree with. Free speech is a guaranteed right laid out in the First Amendment of the United States Constitution and was reinforced by a 5–4 Supreme Court decision in the 1989 case of *Texas v. Johnson*. Gregory Lee Johnson had burned an American flag outside the 1984 Republican National Convention in protest of President Ronald Reagan's policies. He was arrested and convicted of desecrating (destroying in a disrespectful way) a venerated (sacred) object. But the Supreme Court decided burning the flag was "symbolic speech," and even if society found it offensive, the government could not silence or jail him for it.

University president Bok didn't want to focus on debating what is and isn't free speech at the expense of getting Harvard business done. He suggested students instead "take more account of the feelings and sensibilities of others" and had assembled a faculty committee to create "Free Speech Guidelines." The introduction read: "As a community, we take certain risks by assigning such a high priority to free speech. We assume that the long term benefits to our community will outweigh the short term unpleasant effects of sometimes noxious views. . . . Because we are a community united by a commitment to rational processes, we do not permit censorship of noxious ideas."

Ketanji realized that if the Black students, who were protesting night and day instead of going to classes, started doing poorly in school, and were focused only on getting Bridget and/or the school to remove the flag rather than concentrating on their coursework, that was exactly what someone like Bridget would want. They would have succeeded in distracting and hurting Black people, thrilled to watch them fail and prove their twisted point that Black students didn't belong.

Ketanji expressed her concerns to the BSA students: *Wait a minute, as we're doing this, we're missing out on classes. As we're fighting against this injustice, we're actually doing them a service because we're going to be failing.* She said, "While we [are] busy doing all of those very noble things, we [are] not in the library studying." She thought it was incredibly unfair to the Black students that the school was "unacceptably lax" in its response to their pain, and on top of that, that the Black students were missing classes. It could be exactly what people like that wanted: "for us to be so distracted that we failed our classes and thereby reinforced the stereotype that we couldn't cut it at a place like Harvard." She quoted the Nobel and Pulitzer

Prize–winning author Toni Morrison, who said that "the very serious function of racism . . . is distraction." If it wasn't the flag, racists would find something else to try to discredit you. So instead of missing classes, the students made sure to attend class, do their homework, protest in shifts, and excel at the school so that they could make their point to the administration while resisting the racists.

Bridget Kerrigan, who went on to share the copyright on the novel *Legally Blonde*, later adapted into a Reese Witherspoon movie in 2001, left her Confederate flag up the remainder of the academic year. Even though the student protesters were unable to get the flag removed, Ketanji's wise approach had left its mark on the school and other Black students, including Antoinette Sequeira, someone who'd become one of her lifelong best friends.

Harvard initially took the position of erring on the side of free speech again in 2023 when the Islamic Resistance Movement (Hamas) launched a vicious attack against primarily Jewish people in Israel on October 7. Thirty-three Harvard student organizations, along with the Harvard Undergraduate Palestine Solidarity Committee, cosigned a statement blaming Israel alone and its treatment of Palestinians in Gaza, who are mostly Muslim, for Hamas's kidnappings or slaughter of approximately 1,450 people. The university did not acknowledge the statement at first. But after backlash from political figures, as well as students, many of whom felt targeted because they were Jewish, it issued statements from the university leadership on October 9, stating the school was committed to fostering an environment of dialogue and empathy. It issued another statement the next day, and on the twelfth, Claudine Gay, the thirtieth (and first Black) president of the school, spoke out directly against the attack.

But that wasn't good enough for some politicians and wealthy donors, although universities were supposed to be spaces where free speech was encouraged. President Bok had refused to make Kerrigan remove her flag in the 1990s. This time, a former university president, Lawrence Summers, who had been forced to resign in 2005 for suggesting women are not as successful in science and math partly because they are born that way, criticized the school for not immediately condemning the attack. Gay and two other female university presidents (one from the Massachusetts Institute of Technology and another from the University of Pennsylvania) were made to testify before Congress in the House Education and Workforce Committee about what they were doing to discourage and fight any rise of anti-Semitism on their campuses. After the hearing, Claudine Gay had the full support of the board of Harvard Corporation and the Alumni Association executive committee to remain in her position. The Black Harvard-Radcliffe

Alumnae and Harvard Black Alumni Society also shared a letter of support with thousands of signatures on it.

However, billionaire Bill Ackman, a Harvard alum who had claimed Gay had only been hired due to her race (DEI), as well as a few others in the conservative party went on a mission to get her removed. This included accusing her of plagiarism (copying someone else's ideas or writing and not giving that person credit) in some of her old school papers. It seemed to be an exaggerated accusation, since the Harvard Corporation found only a few instances where credit needed to be given, and did not find evidence of misconduct. Still, Gay resigned, tired of being used by people in politics to advance their political, anti-Black racist agendas. Not long afterward, Ackman's own wife was accused of plagiarism, but in that case, he defended her. (The publication that made the allegations stood by its story and she later apologized for failing to properly cite some of her work.)

Thirty years after Kerrigan's flag incident at Harvard, when Minneapolis police murdered a Black man named George Floyd in plain sight on May 25, 2020, it sparked #BlackLivesMatter protests against police brutality across the globe. Statues of and memorials to Confederate soldiers throughout the South were vandalized or brought down. State and local governments soon took action to remove them from public places as well, cutting some into pieces and burning them to ashes. The statue of Confederate general Stonewall Jackson in Richmond, Virginia, was removed on July 1, 2020.

Ketanji learned a lesson from the whole flag experience. "So what does it take to rise through the ranks despite those who don't think you have it in you and will remind you of their feelings at every turn? It demands that you tune out those voices, block out their little flags and ignore the haters, rather than indulging them." She said it helped her get a tougher skin. This way she wouldn't get as upset in the future when someone tried to cause her emotional pain. She quoted the Pulitzer Prize nominee, renowned poet, and author Maya Angelou: "You may write me down in history, with your bitter, twisted lies, you may trod me in the very dirt, but still, like dust, I'll rise."

VIII

A REAL EDUCATION

KETANJI EXCELLED IN HER SOPHOMORE year. She was a government major, like two of her roommates, Antoinette Sequeira and Lisa White. Antoinette found Ketanji to be both funny and an amazing storyteller. And Ketanji impressed Antoinette because she was getting As in her classes, while Antoinette was getting Bs. Antoinette asked her how she did it. Ketanji told her, "My mother told me, 'If anybody is going to get an A in this class, it should be [me], and it can be [me] because [I] can do it.'" That changed Antoinette's outlook immediately. Antoinette could and should be a star student too, if she followed Ketanji's lead. And she did.

Ketanji's grandmother Euzera had passed away from cancer that June, and as Ketanji went through the stages of grief back at school, Antoinette had become her rock. She introduced Ketanji to St. Paul African Methodist Episcopal

Church one Sunday, where Ketanji could almost feel the spirit of her grandmother in the hymns and spirituals they sang. Ketanji would continue to attend services there.

Nina Simmons was another of Ketanji's roommates. She came from Philadelphia, Pennsylvania, and south New Jersey and attended a majority-white junior high. After that she went to a predominantly Black high school where she finally felt comfortable. But when she got to Harvard, she too felt out of place—just like Ketanji had—as though she were moving backward in terms of fitting in. One of the first times she saw Ketanji was at a welcome event for freshman students the first week of school. Ketanji came "bopping" into the room. Nina was stunned—she was so tiny. She thought, "Who is this person?" Then Ketanji started talking. Nina was drawn to her and doubled down: "Wow, who is this person?"

Nina recalled that Ketanji was unique. When she introduced herself to Nina, "she spelled out her name and she made me pronounce it twice, so I got it because that was important to her. And she told us the history of her name from day one. And so immediately you know she's proud of where she came from."

Ketanji helped Nina open up her world and let in people from all backgrounds. "Through her eyes, I could see that there are people out there who don't look like you, who do share your values and can be supportive," she said. Nina was used to studying by herself, but Ketanji explained how helpful it could be to study in a group.

Ketanji invited Nina to join a study group she'd organized to both discuss their books and assignments from their African American women's literature course and help encourage the wonderful type of debate she'd enjoyed in high school. In the group, made up mostly of other Black women, several students would gather to go over their notes, ideas, and talk through their points of view on the course material. Through Ketanji, Nina ended up learning "that the best learners are those who hear different perspectives."

Similarly, Lisa White felt out of place too. "I was feeling a little lost and like I didn't belong." She'd even considered leaving the school her first semester and transferring to the University of California, Los Angeles (UCLA). Lisa was raised in Compton, California, and had gone to schools with mostly Black students. Every night she slept under a poster of the great civil rights leader Malcolm X. She was a track star and straight-A student in high school, but her confidence wavered when she got to Harvard. Once Lisa returned from the winter break holidays, Ketanji invited her to join her study group. "It was the first time that I was around a community of learners that were like me, but also just incredibly thoughtful, and interesting and giving.

It was in Ketanji's room." In fact, it was there that she met Antoinette. "It was the first time that I was like, 'I can make it here,'" Lisa said.

Ketanji, surrounded by Lisa, Nina, and Antoinette, was the heart of their study group, and planned outings and parties as its social chair, while making sure everyone kept on top of their academics. They became like the sisters she never had growing up. Ketanji's room turned into a kind of safe haven for Black women on campus. Yet even when offering sanctuary to her friends of color, she made sure people of other backgrounds were invited too. Lisa said Ketanji would welcome "her very diverse group of friends" into their conversations because she always believed "'You have to talk to different people.'" And when Ketanji had something to say, people stopped to listen. "She's extremely intelligent, probably one of the smartest people I know," Nina said.

But Ketanji didn't just read her books or whatever was required on her syllabus, she took the time to also critique and debate what those books and texts said. She would sometimes attend events and lectures on the subject matter in order to understand it on a deeper level. What she would not do was blindly accept that what was written was the end of the story or even the truth—instead, she made sure to use her own reasoning skills, life experiences, and exposure to other points of view to come to her conclusions.

This way of approaching knowledge allowed her to understand the subject backward and forward, be able to repeat it, dissect it, confirm it, deny it, expose it, use it, or build on it, and become something of a reliable source on it, rather than just pass a test on it and forget it.

Early on, recognizing her friends were exhausted and feeling out of place, uncomfortable, and feeling the stress of their new environment and responsibilities, Ketanji invited them to come home with her to Miami and spend time with her parents. "Her parents really took us in and made us feel at home and kind of loved us up," Nina said. "We got some of the strong support that she had her whole life."

Nina, Antoinette, Ketanji, and Lisa, who chose to be roommates their sophomore year, called themselves "the ladies" and would go out dancing together, arriving early and heading straight for the dance floor. Her three roommates all came from single-parent homes, so seeing Ketanji's parents, John and Ellery, on campus—and they came a lot—was inspiring to them. Her parents were a support not just to their daughter but also to her friends, who could look to them as a shining example of a strong and powerful Black couple. They had confidence and sass and held their heads high, even in mostly white spaces.

Ketanji was busy and thrived in her academics as well as in her after-school activities, which her parents often attended too. Their belief in their daughter reinforced her belief in herself and her talents. From the beginning through to the end, Ketanji's parents let her know she could do anything she set her mind to. Lucky for Ketanji—and the rest of us—she inherited their self-confidence too.

Not long into their sophomore year, Antoinette told Ketanji, "You are going to be the first Black woman justice on the Supreme Court, if there's ever going to be one." She just saw in Ketanji the markings of greatness—the skill, smarts, compassion, intellect, logic, and passion. "I could see it. She has it, she has everything that you would need to do that and represent us the absolute best."

Through her classes, activities, and performances, Ketanji earned the respect of the Harvard community and made friends from all walks of life. Roger Fairfax, a student who was two years behind her, noticed her "piercing intellect." And she made a particularly close connection with Patrick Jackson, a white student who was in the same Historical Studies class as her: "The Changing Concept of Race in America."

He was sitting behind her and started talking to her, tapped her on the shoulder, and did other "silly things." They often stayed behind to discuss the subject matter, like Reconstruction, Japanese internment camps during World War II, and other important issues. He started walking her to her next class every other day as they discussed what they were learning, and they became friends. But on the other two days of the week, when she was in her government class, he acted standoffish or rolled his eyes when she smiled and waved. Her roommates told her to forget him if he was going to act that unstable and nuts! When Ketanji asked him about it on one of the days he was being friendly, he told her he wasn't in a government class. Ketanji had been confusing his identical twin brother, William, for him!

While Ketanji and her roommates were all pre-law, Patrick was a sociology major, though he also took math and the pre-med courses he would need to do well on the Medical College Admission Test (MCAT) and get into a top medical school. Ketanji would describe Patrick's background as being that of a "quintessential Boston Brahmin," meaning he came from wealthy, educated, elite members of nineteenth-century Boston. A "Boston Brahmin" was someone who usually had Puritans as his ancestors, who went to Harvard, whose relatives made their fortunes as merchants, who typically lived in the ritzy Beacon Hill area of Boston, and who, in the past, did not tend to believe in all people being equal or deserving of equal rights.

The author, doctor, and educator Oliver Wendell Holmes, Sr. (one of Patrick's distant relatives, whose son, Oliver, Jr., was a Supreme Court justice), coined the term "Boston Brahmin" in his 1861 novel, *Elsie Venner.* He referred to Boston's elite families as "the Brahmin Caste of New England." The term *caste* comes from a social system in India that assigns people of the Hindu faith into four different groups, with Brahmins at the top of the social ladder. (Conditions got much worse for those in the lower castes once the British colonized the nation.)

Patrick and his brother William are seventh-generation Harvard men, with Cabots, Gardners, and Saltonstalls on their family tree. Their family roots date back to King Edward I of England; four *Mayflower* passengers; former Massachusetts governor Thomas Dudley; Nathaniel Gorham, a judge who ran the Continental Congress and signed the US Constitution; and his great-great-great-great-grandfather Peter Chardon Brooks. Brooks is the same man who insured ships, including slave ones, became one of the richest men in New England, and donated a small fortune to Harvard. Patrick's male ancestors of his maternal grandfather "owned" 189 enslaved people in total; and at least one of his ancestors was also a Confederate soldier.

On the flip side, Patrick is also a descendant of the Lowells, including John Lowell, a lawyer, politician, and judge who contributed to the elimination of slavery in Massachusetts; and Patrick Tracy, a wealthy merchant who defied his family and freed an enslaved man named Apropos and his wife. President John Quincy Adams is a distant relative.

Meanwhile, Ketanji's ancestors consist of the enslaved, with her being only the second generation of her family to graduate from any college at all. Ketanji's great-great-great-grandfather Armstead Rutherford, who was born around 1820 and married a woman named Lucy (born near 1825), lived forty miles south of Macon, Georgia, on John H. Rutherford's 700-acre cotton plantation near what is today's Hayneville. A 1867 sharecropping agreement between the two shows that after emancipation, Armstead wasn't paid any money. His only "earnings" were his ability to keep some of what he harvested—in what amounts to living just one step up from slavery.

Ketanji and Patrick spent hours talking about wealth differences in America, and how people had gained wealth based on race or by taking advantage of the less educated laborer. He came across as very self-aware too. One afternoon, as the two were studying together, sharing notes, and quizzing each other with flash cards, Ketanji challenged him: "Why are you doing this?" she asked. She wanted to know why he was working so hard to learn these things, since he came from such a privileged background and could use his wealth or family connections to "important" people to get almost any job he wanted.

Patrick told her he'd wanted to be a doctor since he was a kindergartner. But he chose to focus on sociology. He wanted to learn why the diverse kids he tutored his freshman year in a local public school through a program called the Committee on Help for the Advancement of Needy Children Through Education (CHANCE) might not have the opportunity to go to college, even if they had all the potential in the world. He thought it was unfair that someone like him happened to be born with "all the advantages" and he wanted to "help level the playing field." Ketanji saw in his eyes, as they watered, that he meant what he said. And it was then that she realized she had developed a huge crush on him. But it didn't matter. How could it? He had a girlfriend.

The two maintained their friendship and continued to hang out at parties or study one on one. He'd sometimes have dinner with her and her roommates in the Quad, and even helped build the stage and sets for a fashion show she put on as president of the African American Cultural Center. He participated in campus protests, including the one against the Confederate flag being hung on campus. And in the middle of all this, his girlfriend broke up with him. But that didn't change his and Ketanji's friendship, so her feelings—a crush—continued to go unreturned. Ketanji's roommates wondered why Patrick spent so much time with them—and her, especially—and questioned if he might have feelings for her. But Ketanji, who had never had a boyfriend before, was convinced: No, he just liked being her friend. She didn't tell them about her feelings for him, though.

At the end of her sophomore year, his junior year, Patrick invited Ketanji to spend an afternoon with him on his family's private island off Cape Cod, Massachusetts, which they've owned for almost a hundred years. Patrick and Ketanji took a walk on the beach and talked deeply and honestly about almost everything. . . .

Then he brought her to meet his parents at their home in Dedham, Massachusetts. They enjoyed a lovely meal together and talked about what Patrick, William, and their older brother were like growing up. Afterward, Patrick and Ketanji sat in the den to watch a movie he'd rented, called *Sea of Love*. Patrick then pulled a smooth move—he yawned, raised his arms in the air, and then brought one down across Ketanji's shoulders. She was flustered, knocked his arm off her, leapt to her feet, and told him to stop! Now he was the one who was surprised. He asked her what was wrong. Ketanji searched for the right words to convey what she was really feeling and told him she didn't want to get hurt.

That's when Patrick confessed that he would never hurt her. "I love you," he said. Ketanji was in shock and he in turn was shocked she didn't know that already! Since he had never confessed his feelings or even tried to hold her hand, she had no idea. He told her he always tried to be a gentleman and make sure she felt safe around him, not trapped, especially when they did things alone together like go for a walk on the beach. The reality of what was happening was slowly dawning on Ketanji, and she asked when he first realized how he felt about her. That's when Patrick confessed it was the first day she "walked into history class."

Sophomore year, Ketanji announced Patrick would be stopping by the dorm. "He's coming over," she told her roommates. She first introduced him as just a friend. But the truth was that she was pretty serious about him, and her roommates made it clear they wanted to keep their eye on him. She hadn't been serious about anyone before then, and now a white guy was going to pick her up for a date? "What do they have in common?" Nina thought, not wanting her friend's heart to get broken.

They gave him the "side-eye" and "once-over," and let him know they would be making sure he treated her well. They grilled him—politely—on his family, goals, and values. He needed to understand what it might mean in America to get involved with a Black woman or have children with her. But he didn't back down. He wanted Ketanji in his life, and he did his best to fit in with her friends and in her life. He had a sense of humor that drew people in and he used humor to show his utter devotion to Ketanji and prove his heart.

Antoinette noticed how seriously he took getting educated in Black history. He took classes on social justice. And he walked the walk when injustices arose around him. He was what people would consider a true "ally." "I did not realize that he was from a family with long roots in the area because he came off as so down to earth, so friendly, so unassuming," said Lisa. "If we had an image of a quintessential prep school boy"—Patrick had attended Groton School in New England—"he was not it. . . . That was not his personality at all."

Patrick graduated a year before Ketanji, in 1991, and they kept dating while he started his courses in medical school in New York. She spent that first summer in an internship at the Neighborhood Defender Service of Harlem, where she sat in on meetings and interviewed twenty-five judges and lawyers, all in her pursuit of becoming a lawyer and, later, a judge. And she brought Patrick home to meet her parents. Although her mom had met Patrick and already knew they were dating, Ketajh and her father didn't know he was white! Her parents spoke to her privately about how it might be difficult to be in a mixed-race relationship or marriage. They had lived through segregation and the Civil Rights Movement. Too many people hadn't lost their racist beliefs just because laws had changed and might treat them poorly, or worse.

Ketanji assured them she hadn't lost any of her Blackness just because her boyfriend was white, and that it was a little too soon to be thinking that far ahead. Her parents accepted her position, but they tested Patrick, wanting to know his intentions. The undertone of their interactions, according to Nina, was about Ketanji's parents making sure Patrick understood "this is not a color-blind society and you're going to have Brown children." But the bottom line was, "Patrick really demonstrated that he saw things through her eyes and was sincere, and amazing, and so sweet to her."

The problem was, Ketanji had other thoughts swirling inside her head. Patrick's parents had been warm and welcoming. But how would his other relatives react? Her questions had more to do with her own insecurities—she had spent so long being invisible to boys, then men, and society at large, even rejected by white children who weren't allowed to play with her. Was Patrick truly into her? It took Ketanji realizing that she had grown up believing white society's standards of beauty were right for her to be able to start putting her doubts aside. Who is to say who or what is attractive? She didn't believe she was pretty because TV shows, movies, and magazines up until that point didn't present people with her color and features that way. So she didn't believe someone else could find her attractive either.

That would be a big turning point for her—when she realized she didn't have to measure herself against white society's standards in beauty or anything else. Because she was in a class all by herself.

Just as Ketanji felt compelled to act when the university was discounting and disrespecting its Black students when a handful of white students insisted on displaying their Dixie flags, she similarly got fired up to make her opinion and presence known in 1990. At that time, the university had an appalling lack of full-time faculty in the Afro-American (now known as "Black" or "African American") Studies Department.

When she started at the school in 1988, only 1.8 percent of the permanent faculty was Black, and the school could not even see fit to lessen that gap by making changes in its own Black history department. Anthony McLean, a junior majoring in Afro-American studies, organized one of the protests demanding the school hire more Af-Am Studies faculty. "We are out here because of this university's atrocious neglect of Afro-Am Studies. We have begged them, sent them letters, and have requested meetings, but they still haven't made any solid commitment to the program. We're sick of it."

The students asked for six new professors, with three of

them assigned to teach in the department full-time. They submitted to Dean Archie Epps their list of five "expectations" that they wanted the university to meet in order to address their demands. They also wanted to be granted weekly meetings to discuss staffing with university officials.

On November 15, 1990, eight students slept outside Dean Epps's office in University Hall. Another group spent the night on the lawn outside the building. A junior in Afro-American studies, Reed Colfax, one of the eight, said Epps asked them to leave that next morning and took their student ID cards from them, warning they could be punished, maybe even expelled from school! But Colfax was determined. There were more than 200 students involved in the protest, who got together on the front steps of the building the morning after the sleep-in.

Ketanji understood, through her parents' stories, how powerful activism could be. "Young Black professionals like my parents were finally on the verge of getting to enjoy the full freedom and equality that is promised to citizens of the United States. Change does happen, and . . . even the most dire circumstances can be overcome." Her friend Nina said, "She was always the person trying to find the middle ground." She wanted to use measured moves, dialogue, moderation, and persuasive debates to confront the college officials about its race and equality issues. She'd say, "They're not going to listen to us if we're screaming at them." And Lisa saw how Ketanji could move the chess pieces to win the game: "Ketanji moves the crowd, and it's a very diverse crowd."

Ketanji was set on making the most of her studies— nothing and no one, not even a school, was going to deter her from her goals. She drew a line between standing up for herself and ignoring the noise around her. And she believed sometimes there could be power in silence. Ketanji thought there might be an even more effective way to make their point. She suggested less confrontational tactics, which some of her classmates found too mild, even questioning if she was "Black enough." But Ketanji had grown used to people thinking she was too middle-of-the-road.

Nina was clear: "If they knew her or her family, they'd never ask that question. She taught me never to shrink myself, never to be afraid to take up space. I was raised to keep your head down, don't make noise. You don't want them to think this or that because you're a Black person. But Ketanji would say small things. In a restaurant, she'd say, 'My order is not correct,' whereas I had this fear and I'd take it as it came."

Antoinette agreed: "She knows who she is, and she remembers where she comes from. . . . Her parents are graduates of historically Black colleges, they're accomplished people in their own right that instilled in her their values of hard work and discipline and giving back. And she brought all of that with her to school."

By Saturday the seventeenth, following Ketanji's lead, the students had come up with another plan to make a bigger, "louder" statement to get the university's attention. Instead of wearing Harvard's school colors of crimson and white, she got the protesting students to wear black to the annual, high-profile Harvard–Yale football game. They carried signs and marched silently around campus. "We can embarrass the university in front of the alumni," she said. It was a bold statement and act that won her fans among her Harvard class and community.

When Ketanji was a freshman, her uncle on her father's side, Thomas Brown, Jr., who looked a lot like her dad, was sentenced to life in prison on a drug charge that had no violence involved. He was a victim of the misguided, if not intentionally racist, mandatory life sentence rules for drug offenses in the 1980s and 1990s (meaning judges were not allowed to hand down a lesser punishment if prosecutors brought up the rule in the case).

These laws affected people of color disproportionately, which means they were applied more frequently to people of color than white people, even when the crimes were the same. The Anti-Drug Abuse Act of 1986 was coauthored by then senator Joe Biden, whose son Hunter would go on to have his own struggles with substance abuse. (Eventually,

Hunter would go on to receive a full pardon from President Biden in 2024 and therefore not serve any time on gun charges or tax crimes.) The law also made it so people who were caught with a small amount of an illegal drug that was more often found in Black neighborhoods were given the same sentence as people who had a hundred times more of the root drug the other was derived from. The parent drug was one that white people were more likely to have. It is no surprise, then, that 75 percent of people sentenced under the law were Black.

Ketanji's uncle was a victim of a newer three-strikes law (three strikes, you're out). He had been involved in two low-level crimes in the 1970s and '80s already. In one of them, he pleaded guilty in 1982 to possessing marijuana and was fined $1,500.

What ultimately sealed his fate was that on April 18, 1989, five federal agents caught him in a sting operation, and he was found guilty of possessing and intending to sell an illegal drug. It was his third strike, so he was given a life sentence.

Ketanji didn't have any communication with her uncle during this time, but by her senior year, she was exploring ideas about America's prison and sentencing system. Before graduating in 1992, she wrote a senior thesis called "'The Hand of Oppression': Plea Bargaining Processes and the Coercion of Criminal Defendants," arguing that people can be tempted into accepting plea bargains when (1) the punishment doesn't fit the crime, (2) they could likely be found not guilty, or even (3) they're innocent. She wrote that if most accused criminals were pushed to take plea bargains (confessing to a crime in order to receive a lesser sentence), neither the accused nor the victims get to know or say exactly what really happened.

Prosecutors and judges want to make cases go away fast because it costs a lot of money to go to trial. So they routinely push defendants toward accepting deals. She wrote, "There is a chance that the very institution which is designed to dispense justice and to protect individual rights could be the most guilty of creating injustices."

Ketanji accepted that there were benefits to plea bargains, in that the accused criminal would get a lighter punishment and the whole nightmare would be over quicker. But she decided it was still wrong to nudge people into accepting guilt for things they swore they did not do.

Her thesis was ahead of its time.

On the coffee table in Ketanji's childhood home was a copy of *Faces at the Bottom of the Well: The Permanence of Racism*, by Derrick Bell, a book about how racism was both built into and would remain a permanent part of American society. Change would only be possible once everyone accepted this as fact. The author himself explained why he chose that title: "Black people are the magical faces at the bottom of society's well. Even the poorest whites, those who must live their lives only a few levels above, gain their self-esteem by gazing down on us." Ketanji couldn't comprehend why the cover showed a happy, smiling person while the title of the book seemed so sad. She'd stare at it endlessly, trying to make sense of that.

She and her father would speak about how to make that smile real for her—how to earn it—and rise to the top of the well or overcome any other obstacle or achieve any career she wanted. She learned, "As a dark-skinned Black girl who was often the only person of color in my class, club, or social environment, my parents knew that it was essential that I develop a sense of my own self-worth that was in no way dependent on what others thought about my abilities."

Ketanji would go on to graduate *magna cum laude* from Harvard—the second-highest honor the school bestows.

IX
THE LAW

AFTER GRADUATION, KETANJI MOVED TO New York City, where Patrick attended medical school at the Columbia University College of Physicians and Surgeons. She had gotten into Harvard Law School but took a detour to work for more than a year as a news reporter and researcher at *Time* magazine. Her father wasn't fond of the idea, until HLS allowed Ketanji to defer her enrollment and start school the next year.

She reported on stories on "The Job Freeze," in which the writer John Greenwald suggested that after an economic recession (when across the country a lot of people start losing their jobs and people spend less money on anything other than things they need, like food and clothing), most large corporations are too nervous to rehire people full-time again. She also covered rising prescription drug prices in Greenwald's piece "Ouch!" For Janice Castro's 1993 piece, "Hollywood Rocks Madison Avenue," Ketanji reported on how regular people thought Coca-Cola's television advertisements were boring and "flat," so the company hired a Hollywood agency for its new ad campaign in order to make a big buzz (since Hollywood is where they make exciting movies).

And she reported on trouble within the human rights organization the American Civil Liberties Union (in Richard N. Ostling's piece "A.C.L.U.—Not That Civil"). The president of the ACLU called for the four white police officers who were found "not guilty" in state court of unnecessarily beating a Black man, Rodney King, to be tried in federal court. Federal court is "higher" than state court and deals with crimes that violate the Constitution or other federal laws, as opposed to just state laws. The beating had been caught on video camera and when the officers were acquitted in 1992, Black people especially were disgusted. Many of them went outside to protest, and things got out of hand. Some people started breaking things, burning down buildings (a large number of which belonged to Korean people), stealing property, even shooting others (this event is known as the Los Angeles Riots). Some members of the ACLU believed that trying the policemen in federal court after they had been acquitted in state court went against the ACLU's own position that prosecuting an acquitted person again for the same crime (double jeopardy) was unconstitutional.

Just before Ketanji returned to Harvard University, where her three roommates from undergrad had also been accepted, there was a big change on the Supreme Court. Ruth Bader Ginsburg, who'd attended Harvard Law School for two years, was confirmed as an associate justice of the Supreme Court on August 3, 1993. She was the first Jewish woman and only the second woman ever to sit on that bench. And this made a huge impression on Ketanji.

That summer, Ketanji and Patrick took a trip to Europe, visiting Paris, Venice, Florence, and Rome. They got to spend time together, just the two of them, without the pressures of school or work looming over their heads. And despite any hiccups, they got along well, enjoying each other's company and laughter. It was yet another important step in their growing relationship.

At Harvard Law School, Ketanji was a remarkable student who stood out—not because there were only fifty-six other Black students, but because, according to her friend Kimberly Jenkins, of all the students there, Ketanji was "a woman of character and integrity." Ketanji dug in her heels, and once again applied her "I'll show them" mantra to her studies at HLS. She was open, brilliant, humble, and honest.

Her childhood friend Stephen Rosenthal, who also went

to Harvard Law School, spoke of her "remarkable combination of gifts: charisma, [and] penetrating intelligence." In their first year of the three-year program, she and Stephen worked together in mock trials, arguing their cases in a fake court—kind of like acting in a play.

In law school, Ketanji was studious, well-rounded, and always kind. Before their final first-year exam in civil procedure, which was going to last for hours, she reminded her friend Njeri Mathis to bring extra pencils and a cushion to sit on. It was that concern for others that also set Ketanji apart. One of her teachers in her first year, Professor Carol Steiker, had been a public defender. She thought it would be hard for people who had not been defense attorneys to really understand how much pain and fear criminal defendants experienced. She wanted them to understand how going to prison affects them, their families, and even society. It was an interesting perspective to have—one that Ketanji would come to appreciate more as she moved along in her career.

Sometimes other students or professors would think the Black students were too quiet or reluctant in class. And people would unfairly assume it was because they couldn't keep up with the students of other races. Rarely did they imagine it might be because the Black students felt isolated, the way Ketanji had felt when she first got to Harvard as an undergrad. But again, Ketanji defied that label. Njeri never saw her back away from a challenge, calling her "tiny but mighty," and "always saying thoughtful, knowledgeable things." According to Njeri, "We were all focused on school. We were all intelligent, hard-working people. But she was on a totally different level." She said that "[Ketanji] was a very strong law student. Very, very smart and very hard-working. Like, next level hard-working but she was also very, very kind."

Stephen watched her be "brave, poised, and outspoken in classroom discussions on legal issues." Even when people might have strong opinions, such as in their large class called "Race Relations and the Law," Ketanji made "insightful remarks that would steer the classroom conversation in a valuable new direction."

Toward the end of her first year of law school, right after final exams, Ketanji competed in a six-day writing competition to win a spot on the distinguished *Harvard Law Review*. *Law Review* is "essentially an honor society" within the school. It consists of a group of students who publish a journal of the same name. It features articles, book reviews, and essays by lawyers, judges, authors, as well as student editors, who'd sometimes write "Notes" on recent cases and laws. Unfortunately, the number of people of color on the review was limited, so Ketanji stood out.

Kimberly Jenkins attended HLS at the same time as

Ketanji, and during their first year, they decided to room together. She found Ketanji to be "a considerate roommate and a supportive friend." Kimberly was an articles editor on the *Harvard Law Review* during their second and third years of school and she and Ketanji joked they spent more time together there than at home. *Harvard Law Review*, much like the school itself, was competitive, with some people wanting to show off their smarts to the others. That was not Ketanji's way.

Even as the group of editors argued over which articles should be accepted for publication, Kimberly noticed that Ketanji didn't force people to listen to her nor did she feel like she needed that validation. "But when she spoke, we listened, because her comments were consistently insightful and valuable." Ketanji possessed leadership qualities and a "brilliant legal mind that could critique any legal argument." That, along with her "humility and tenacity," is why her colleagues elected her supervising editor (volume 109), where her job was to check the articles submitted and make sure their style matched that of the journal.

For Kimberly, Ketanji's elevation to that role was "proof that she had a brilliant legal mind," and was someone "humble and easy to work with." Njeri said: "There are lots of smart people at Harvard, but what I really admired and adored about her was that she was so kind and down to earth."

The editors on *Law Review* literally review what's being written about in the law. Authors submit articles, and the editors help them rewrite their material so it reads better. They also double-check that the authors have cited their sources correctly (given their sources proper credit). Ketanji found it to be an "especially significant" time in her career, because it helped her better analyze what she read, and being on *Law Review* "opened doors to other opportunities." She thought the *Law Review* was "a wonderful experience for a law nerd like me!"

Working on the *Review* added at least forty more hours of grunt work a week to Ketanji's and Kimberly's plates, on top of their already difficult studies. They often worked late into the night and on weekends. But Kimberly never heard Ketanji complain. "She always kept a sense of humor and positive disposition, even when we worked long into the night." Yet by the spring of their second year, Kimberly wasn't sure if all that extra time and energy was worth it. It was Ketanji "who encouraged me to stay the course while herself being a role model of quiet perseverance."

In 1994 and 1995, Ted Ruger worked on *Law Review* with Ketanji and thought "she stood out for her brilliance." He found that she had a deep respect for the rule of law, and later, for the people her rulings affected.

Maeghan Maloney was a year behind Ketanji and served with her on the *Review* as well. Ketanji was a kind, patient mentor to her, especially when she had to deal with tougher issues, such as during her work with the Prison Legal Assistant Project, where students took on Massachusetts inmates' cases. She was struck by Ketanji's brilliance, but also her kindness. "She was a great person, a great mentor, someone who was never too busy to answer a question."

Ketanji wrote an article for the *Harvard Law Record*, published on April 22, 1994. In it, she highlighted the experience of legal scholar Professor Lani Guinier, who was speaking at the eleventh annual Black Law Students' Association spring conference. It was taking place on the fortieth anniversary of the landmark *Brown v. Board of Education* Supreme Court decision. Guinier's nomination to Assistant Attorney General for Civil Rights had been withdrawn by then president Bill Clinton the year before.

Guinier had written several articles that suggested the systems of voting in America were flawed, and she supported the restructuring of voting rights. She believed the system discouraged "participation by minority groups and turns government into a self-interested and unaccountable monopoly." She believed that fairness in a multiracial democracy "cannot be achieved in a system in which 51 percent of the people always enjoy 100 percent of the power." Her belief was that "we are facing the problems of a democracy in which people of color have a vote but no voice."

After her nomination, several senate Republicans and

conservative journalists attacked her character. They accused her of advocating for racial "quotas," which they claimed would benefit Black people at the expense of whites. George Will, a political journalist and commentator, claimed she believed "only Blacks can properly represent Blacks." And Clint Bolick, now a justice of the Arizona Supreme Court, dubbed her a "quota queen." The word *quota* is used here as a racial dog whistle (a term meant for white people and not others to understand) to rile up white people who feared affirmative action. They wrongly believe quotas are about hiring a set number of unqualified minority candidates over more qualified white people. And the word *queen* is used here as a dog whistle to rile up people afraid of the mythical "welfare queen." "Welfare queen" was a term made up in 1976 by future president Ronald Reagan. The aim was to suggest that certain Black people who live in poverty and depend on welfare were abusing the system by spending the money given to them by the government on luxury items and fancy trips instead of basic necessities like food and clothing. Yet the majority of welfare recipients are white. And even (predominantly and disproportionately white) American farmers get social assistance—another word for welfare—every year in what is called the farm bill.

Guinier is quoted in the article as saying she was expressly warned "not to speak" before her confirmation hearing as a courtesy to the Senate. "While I remained silent, the media and those who opposed my nomination took control over my image. Like the welfare queen, the 'quota queen' was a racial stereotype and an easy headline looking for a person."

The smear campaign worked. Even Democratic senators got cold feet after meetings with Guinier—who tried to set the record straight and clear her name—and urged Clinton to backtrack on the nomination. After he did, William Thaddeus Coleman, Jr., one of the Harvard Law grads who'd laid the groundwork for *Brown v. Board of Education*, wrote, "The loss of Lani Guinier as Assistant Attorney General for civil rights is a grave one, both for President Clinton and the country. . . ." Coleman, who served as the secretary of transportation under former president Gerald Ford, continued, "[It] was not only unfair but some would say political cowardice. . . . [Guinier] suggests that some localities may prefer a race-neutral plan to a race-conscious plan. This idea is hardly radical. During the [George H. W.] Bush Administration, the Justice Department approved alternative voting systems in at least 35 different jurisdictions." He concluded, "I would ask the country to read again what was said about Thurgood Marshall when he fought against white primaries and segregated schools and lunch counters. These battles . . . are now thought by most Americans to be among our finest hours. Thurgood Marshall's successors, such as Lani Guinier, should not be condemned for working through the system to reverse the lingering effects of two hundred years of slavery and another one hundred years of segregation." And Representative Kweisi Mfume, a Democrat and chairman of the Congressional Black Caucus, called Clinton's withdrawal "a giant step backward. . . . Fairness and due process were abandoned for political expediency."

That Ketanji covered Lani Guinier's speech in this article, which mentioned her treatment during her nomination process, is notable. Many years later, Ketanji would find her record similarly twisted to suit a political agenda, and her character and writings skewed and questioned. She would need to take a different approach so she wouldn't find herself in the same boat as Guinier, a Black Jamaican and Jewish woman, who'd dared to have a voice.

Back in the *Law Review* offices, Ketanji thought the publication needed to feature different viewpoints and represent many voices. Richard Schragger found her to be "a principled person" who didn't have a particular agenda to push. She didn't shove a certain way of thinking on anyone, which he respected. He believed she "stood out for her consideration of others . . . and her kind words to lots of people." And because she was so thoughtful and personable, according to Stephen, "she was always well-liked and respected by those who held differing views."

Ketanji wasn't shy about tackling difficult, sensitive subjects either, and wrote a "Note" for the *Review* that explored how the monitoring of or certain punishments for child abusers might be considered constitutional or unconstitutional.

Meanwhile, Ketanji and Patrick were still seeing each other. "We were an unlikely pair in many respects, but somehow we found each other," she has stated. He would visit her at her dorm and once, while upstairs, Njeri overheard him say from below, "I love you, Ketanji," which she found "so sweet" that she always remembered it. In fact, as he applied to surgery programs mainly around Boston, he also got an interview at the University of Miami Jackson Memorial Hospital. He stayed with Ketanji's parents the night before, and after dinner, asked if he could speak with them in the den. It was then that he requested permission to ask for Ketanji's hand in marriage.

Johnny confessed that there would have been a time that he would not have allowed it. But society and laws had changed a lot in his lifetime. And he had witnessed how well Patrick treated Ketanji, so he agreed. Ellery was a different matter. She had remained silent through their exchange, but finally piped up. She asked, "Do you love my daughter?" to which Patrick replied he did. And she asked, "Do you believe in God?" Patrick confirmed he did, and Ellery gave him her support too. Patrick told them his parents were aware of his intentions already—he'd expressed them to his dad after his and Ketanji's European vacation. Both his parents had given him their blessings and made sure he was aware of what discrimination his family might face. Patrick also knew that if he and Ketanji had children, they would be Black and raised with that awareness. That brought Ketanji's parents even more relief, to know that he was going into this with both eyes open.

Toward the end of Ketanji's time at law school and in the front pages of one of the last *Law Review* journals she'd work on, an ad appeared for a new book just published in May 1996, called *Critical Race Theory: The Key Writings That Formed the Movement*. The book and the ideas behind it would, in the next decades, go on to be taught in law schools across the country. It concerns ideas and research that began with Derrick Bell, an academic and scholar, suggesting that America's history of white supremacy cannot be forgotten or left in the past, given that our laws and systems are based on it.

The book summed up a movement that was growing, which studied the racial inequality the United States planted in its laws and documents since its founding. Ketanji would later discuss how Bell was someone she admired—the first Black Harvard Law School professor to receive a permanent position (tenure). He left his job in 1992 out of principle over the school's lack of women of color on the faculty.

Although the book's publication happened right before she graduated *cum laude* (with honors) from law school, the book and its teachings would resurface nearly three decades later as a reason some would use to try to keep her from achieving her lifelong dreams and hopes for her career....

X

THE REAL WORLD

AFTER SHE COMPLETED HARVARD LAW School, there was a lot of change in store for Ketanji. She passed the Massachusetts bar exam in 1996, and until 1997, she clerked for US judge Patti B. Saris for the District of Massachusetts.

Of Judge Saris, Ketanji said, "She has become a lifelong friend and mentor of mine in the real world." When it came to balancing work and life, Ketanji saw her as a role model: "Hearing cases, ruling on things, and then coming back into chambers and taking a call from her kid who was a kindergartner, talking to the teacher," etc. Patrick was now a surgical resident at Massachusetts General Hospital.

In August 1996, she attended her childhood friend Denise Lewin's wedding to Bernard Lloyd in Chicago. There, she spied a young Black couple who were Harvard Law grads (and two of only a few other lawyers at the event). She recognized one of them as having become, in 1990, the first Black person to be elected president of the *Harvard Law Review*. He'd also graduated magna cum laude from Harvard Law School in 1991. His historical first meant a lot to her, and she enjoyed spending time talking with Barack and Michelle Obama, both friends of Bernard's. It turns out, the community organizer was also known for his diplomacy at HLS—someone who tried to find common ground rather than picking sides during heated arguments. For instance, he lent his voice to the 1991 student protests demanding more Black faculty at HLS while also leading from behind the scenes. They got their picture taken together—one of only two pictures the photographer took of the Obamas at that event.

Ketanji and Patrick got married on October 12, 1996, in Coconut Grove, one of Miami's oldest neighborhoods. It was built by Black immigrants from the Bahamas, and is now one of the most affluents enclaves in south Florida. The wedding participants walked down the aisle of the Plymouth Congregational Church to "Love Changes Everything," sung by Ketanji's aunt Carmela, from Andrew Lloyd Webber's 1989 musical *Aspects of Love*. It was her soon-to-be father-in-law's favorite song, which was why Ketanji had picked it. She took Patrick's last name as hers once they wed.

Patrick recognized the significance of the Supreme Court *Loving v. Virginia* case, which made it possible for him to marry his beautiful bride. In a unanimous decision, the court had concluded on June 12, 1967, that the miscegenation laws (laws that made it illegal for Black and white people to marry) that many states, including Virginia, had on their books, were unconstitutional. They violated the equal protection and due process clauses of the Fourteenth Amendment. Years later, he wrote, "Happy Loving Day! I am especially thankful to be walking through life with a brilliant and compassionate partner who still takes my breath away, made possible by sacrifices like Richard and Mildred Loving."

With her own wedding behind her, and only a few months into her clerkship with Judge Saris, Ketanji Brown Jackson was getting her feet wet in the real world. She was a full-on adult, with full adult responsibilities, like finding and keeping a job, maintaining a household, and being a newlywed.

Patrick would sometimes visit Judge Saris's courtroom after working all night as a doctor "on call," having not slept and looking scruffy and unkempt. He found the world his wife was now operating in fascinating. And one night, as Patrick sat in the back of her courtroom, Judge Saris's courtroom marshal (deputy) approached her and whispered, "Judge, would you like me to remove the homeless man in the back row?" The marshal didn't realize who Patrick was or that he was allowed to be in there.

On March 31, 1997, the *Boston Herald* newspaper published a piece by columnist Don Feder, who by then was in his fifties, titled "Despite Liberals Race Does Matter." He argued that America was becoming too race conscious, and that it was Black people's fault for calling out racism ("liberals intent on sowing division and race-hustlers"), not the fault of those who are racist.

Twenty-six-year-old Ketanji, just over half his age, wrote a letter to the *Herald* in response, which the paper published on April 10, 1997:

> Feder's as racist as those he condemns. For someone who claims not to consider certain groups morally or intellectually inferior to his own, Don Feder spends much of his column, "Despite liberals race does matter" (March 31), spewing out disagreeable facts about the high-crime rate in the black community and denouncing black voters for selecting incompetent, incorrigible or inebriated leaders.
>
> By his own definition, Feder is a racist.
>
> To my mind, he's also like the liberal's purported view of American history—irredeemably evil.
>
> Ketanji Brown Jackson, Boston

Ketanji was calling out the irony—she concluded that in his attempt to accuse liberals and Black people of being racist, he proved himself to be racist. In writing this response, Ketanji demonstrated her morals and expressed her opinion openly to someone who had more power and influence than her, who held views that were problematic, if not just plain evil.

Over the next two decades, Ketanji Brown Jackson had several different jobs, each offering her experiences and lessons that she would take with her as she moved closer to achieving her dream of being on the Supreme Court.

In 1997, she accepted a clerkship for Bruce M. Selya on the United States Court of Appeals for the First Circuit in Providence, Rhode Island. "I learned writing skills in a different way with him," she said, "the attention to detail, the way in which he would work with the law clerks in crafting opinions was really something that I had not seen up until that point." Patrick was still in Boston, so there were many times when she felt lonely. She decided she would try her hand at writing a novel in the evenings, after work. But she kept starting and stopping, never quite getting to the finish line on any of her drafts. Eventually she came to terms with the idea that it wasn't going to happen—at least not then—nor was she going to get to act in a play, despite that lingering love she had for the theater. So she set those dreams aside for the time being, and got back down to business.

Next, in 1998, Ketanji became an associate at the Miller, Cassidy, Larroca & Lewin LLP law firm in Washington, DC, since Patrick was there, doing a research fellowship at

A young Ketanji and her mother, Ellery Brown

Hall of Fame

Ketanji Brown and Stephen Rosenthal posing for the "Hall of Fame" section of the Miami Palmetto Senior High School yearbook

Hall of Fame member KETANJI BROWN enjoys traveling and meeting debate squads from all over the country. She has had plenty of opportunities to do so at numerous local, state and national tournaments where she has placed high competing in different debate events.

In addition to her many debate trophies, she is most proud of being the recipient of the Harvard Book Award. As an officer for both NFL and NHS and a member of three other honor societies, she rarely has spare time. Regarding her future, Ketanji said, "I want to go into law and eventually have a judicial appointment."

Hall of Fame member STEPHEN ROSENTHAL enjoys tennis and basketball in addition to playing and umpiring baseball for Howard Palmetto League. Also, his involvement in extemporaneous speaking has him competing and placing in local, state and national tournaments. Besides serving as junior and senior class vice-president, he belongs to several honor societies and clubs. Other achievements include winning school English and Debate awards.

"I'd like to attend an Ivy League college and perhaps get involved in politics," Stephen said. Although he is unsure of a major, he knows that happiness is his major goal.

Ketanji Brown, Vice-mayor

Ketanji when she was voted vice-mayor of Palmetto Junior High

Ketanji (right) and members of the On Thin Ice improvisation group at Harvard during the 1989–1990 school year

Ketanji (right) in 1997 with her Harvard classmates, from left: Antoinette Coakley, Nina Simmons, and Lisa Fairfax

Ketanji (left) and Lisa Fairfax

Ketanji Brown Jackson at her wedding with Nina Simmons (left), Antoinette Coakley (right), and Lisa Fairfax

ASS OF 1996

Robert L. Brainin
Emory University
Rockville, Maryland
LaShanda D. Branch
Howard University
Jackson, Mississippi
Yellow L. Breen
Harvard University
St. Albans, Maine
David F. Bresenham
Wofford College
Rock Hill, S.C.

Matthew A. Brill
Dartmouth College
White Plains, N.Y.
David C. Brooks
Temple University
Philadelphia, PA
Elizabeth A. Brown
Harvard University
Malden, MA
Ketanji O. Brown
Harvard University
Miami, Florida

Ketanji's
Harvard Law School
yearbook photo

Leila, one of Ketanji's daughters, smiles at her during her confirmation hearing with the Senate Judiciary Committee.

Newly confirmed Supreme Court Justice Jackson acknowledges the cheers of the crowd on the White House lawn while President Joseph R. Biden and Vice President Kamala Harris applaud her historic achievement as the first Black woman to serve on the US Supreme Court. April 8, 2022

Ketanji Brown Jackson sits with President Barack Obama as they celebrate her confirmation to the Supreme Court.

Chief Justice John G. Roberts, Jr., looks on as Justice Ketanji Brown Jackson signs the Oaths of Office in the Justices' Conference Room, Supreme Court Building.

Chief Justice John G. Roberts, Jr., and Justice Ketanji Brown Jackson

Justice Stephen G. Breyer (retired) and Justice Ketanji Brown Jackson in the Justices' Conference Room, Supreme Court Building

Chief Justice John G. Roberts, Jr., administers the Constitutional Oath to Justice Ketanji Brown Jackson in the West Conference Room, Supreme Court Building. Her husband, Dr. Patrick Jackson, holds the Bible.

From left to right: Justices Amy Coney Barrett, Sonia Sotomayor, Ketanji Brown Jackson, and Elena Kagan in the Justices' Conference Room prior to the investiture ceremony

President Joseph R. Biden, Jr., Justice Ketanji Brown Jackson, and Vice President Kamala Harris at a courtesy visit in the Justices' Conference Room prior to the investiture ceremony.

Members of the Supreme Court with President Joseph R. Biden and Vice President Kamala Harris. From left to right: Associate Justices Amy Coney Barrett, Neil M. Gorsuch, Sonia Sotomayor, and Clarence Thomas, Chief Justice John G. Roberts, Jr., President Joseph R. Biden, Vice President Kamala Harris, and Associate Justices Ketanji Brown Jackson, Samuel A. Alito, Jr., Elena Kagan, and Brett M. Kavanaugh

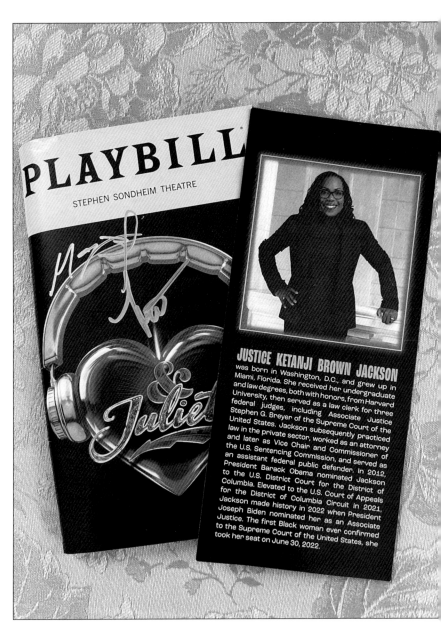

JUSTICE KETANJI BROWN JACKSON was born in Washington, D.C., and grew up in Miami, Florida. She received her undergraduate and law degrees, both with honors, from Harvard University, then served as a law clerk for three federal judges, including Associate Justice Stephen G. Breyer of the Supreme Court of the United States. Jackson subsequently practiced law in the private sector, worked as an attorney and later as Vice Chair and Commissioner of the U.S. Sentencing Commission, and served as an assistant federal public defender. In 2012, President Barack Obama nominated Jackson to the U.S. District Court for the District of Columbia. Elevated to the U.S. Court of Appeals for the District of Columbia Circuit in 2021, Jackson made history in 2022 when President Joseph Biden nominated her as an Associate Justice. The first Black woman ever confirmed to the Supreme Court of the United States, she took her seat on June 30, 2022.

Justice Ketanji Brown Jackson featured in her one-night-only Broadway debut in the musical *& Juliet* on December 14, 2024, fulfilling a lifelong dream.

George Washington University Hospital. Richard Schragger, from law school, also worked at the firm, and witnessed how easily Ketanji worked with people from most every political background. She was admitted to the Washington, DC, bar in 1998.

"Tell me, Ms. Jackson, have you ever thought about becoming a law clerk at the Supreme Court?"

In 1999, a former law professor put a bug in Ketanji's ear—would she like to clerk for a Supreme Court justice? She was in the right place (DC) at the right time, and he put her name forward for a position with "eternal optimist" Associate Justice Stephen G. Breyer. After a whirlwind of calls and interviews over just a few days, she got her first exposure to the behind-the-scenes workings of the United States Supreme Court when she was offered the position!

Ketanji praised the experience, saying, "It's hard to even describe the degree of influence" he had on her career, "in terms of just his character. He is the ultimate consensus builder, the one who was always trying to . . . build bridges, talk to the justices who disagreed with him about issues. My memories of him are of him constantly coming out of his internal office saying, 'I've got to go talk to Sandra [Day O'Connor], I've got to go talk to Tony [Kennedy]'—because he was always trying to come up with something that we could all agree on."

She made a lasting impression on other clerks during

her 1999–2000 stint as well, as they worked together some-times on high-profile cases, including those dealing with prayer in school, women's rights to govern their own bod-ies, as well as the rights of criminal suspects (who are inno-cent until proven guilty, which is laid out in the Fifth and Fourteenth Amendments).

Amanda Tyler clerked for Justice Ruth Bader Ginsburg at that time, and said that Ketanji "was someone who was very careful and thoughtful about considering the argu-ments on both sides and working through them in a very methodical way. But also someone who had a bigger vision—a grander vision about the Constitution and what she thought it required." Not only that, Amanda observed Ketanji to be "very calm under fire" and careful in her approach to interpreting the law.

A clerk for Justice John Paul Stevens, Sonja West thought Ketanji was a "natural leader" when they first met, and they've remained friendly since. She believed Ketanji approached "the world with openness, honesty, and a presumption of good will in others." She found that Ketanji and Justice Breyer shared similar, positive personality traits: "She will always listen carefully to the views of others, but she will also never hesitate to say and do what she believes to be right." Ketanji would find that to be high praise since she also thought Jus-tice Breyer was "just extraordinary in his thought processes about the way the law works. So just having the chance to sit and hear him discuss it, or to look at drafts that he had written of opinions and the way in which he analyzed things—it's the kind of experience that can't really be replicated."

Deborah Pearlstein, also a clerk for Judge Stevens, thought Jackson was insightful and funny. "I don't know anybody there at the time who didn't get along with Ketanji," who she said was "incredibly good at her job."

At the end of her clerkship, Ketanji, Patrick, his brothers, and their wives, went on safari to sub-Saharan Africa. When they landed in Nairobi, Kenya, they had to go through customs, where officials make sure travelers have all the right documents, don't bring anything forbidden into their country, and don't overstay their welcomes. The officer Ketanji and Patrick dealt with spoke very abruptly and matter-of-factly as he asked them questions, until he read Ketanji's name on her passport: "Ketanji Onyika." Her African name moved something in him and his manner softened. Ketanji explained that her aunt, who'd spent a long time in Africa, had given her the name. "Welcome home," he told her kindly.

The words overwhelmed Ketanji. She was too close to tears to speak or thank him for that small gesture. He'd given her a bit of healing, for all she and her ancestors had had stolen from them. He'd given her a bit of recognition, making sure she knew that she was welcomed and loved—that this place was friendly to her and she was regarded as family. In Mother Africa.

They had a magical experience, witnessing all sorts of wildlife and encountering many wonderful people. The Samburu, whose men guarded their camps, invited them inside their own settlements. As semi-nomads, the Samburu will take apart their homes and huts and move their goats to another area where the goats can graze happily. They rebuild their huts in the new location and remain for as long as the goats have food. They were welcoming and created a joyous gathering for the Jacksons one night, dancing, eating, and singing the songs of their culture. The tour guide told Ketanji and her family that it was rare that the Samburu would invite people inside their world this way. And Patrick wanted to thank them and give back in the best way he knew how—using his medical knowledge. He offered to counsel them on any ailments they might be experiencing, and see if the Royal African Safari company would get them medical supplies too. The guides spread the word among the Samburu about the "white healer" who would help them.

On the final day of their trip, Patrick, Ketanji, and her parents-in-law waited at the only schoolhouse for miles as countless Samburu people arrived and sat with Patrick, who answered all their medical questions. Ketanji's trip was healing in so many ways. She felt at home, like a "goat who was stolen" from African tribes, but had now returned. She'd been treated like a long-lost kidnapped sister finally reunited with her people. And what the trip did for her was allow her to feel at home anywhere, because she had found that peace within, in a place where she finally belonged.

Ketanji went to work as an associate at law firm Goodwin Procter LLP in Boston, from 2000–2002, and was six months pregnant the day she joined the firm. For one case, she wrote an amicus brief. (*Amicus* is Latin for "friend.") As a "friend of the court," Ketanji's firm was not officially involved in the case, but they offered relevant information in support of Massachusetts women's rights groups that wanted six feet of space between guests approaching their buildings and protesters who wanted to block their entrance. A three-judge panel of the First Circuit Court of Appeals, including Judge Selya, unanimously agreed with her position, believing the state legislature was "making every effort to restrict as little speech as possible while combating the deleterious secondary effects" of the protests. From there, she became "something of a professional vagabond," moving from place to place as her family needs and circumstances changed.

After she returned from her four-month maternity leave,

she had her work cut out for her as a new mom to her first-born, Talia, and as someone who always had to prove herself in any new job situation. Women and people of color have not historically been given the same grace and presumption that they're up to the task in many professional fields, but especially not in old, established law firms. And the lack of mentorship they receive is a large part of the reason why they tend to leave. Needing to be able to spend time more with her toddler as her husband's demanding job and commitment to childcare kept him busy day and night, Ketanji set out to find a better work-life balance for herself and her family.

XI

VAGABOND YEARS

WITH THE DEMANDS OF RAISING a child added to her responsibilities, Ketanji decided to shift her career focus toward a job that was more stable—one with a paycheck that was more predictable and not tied to the number of hours she worked, but rather to the quality of the work she did during normal hours.

Ketanji moved to another private practice, a smaller firm called the Feinberg Group, in 2002. She then joined the United States Sentencing Commission in 2003 (an agency made up of both Republicans and Democrats to determine the sentencing guidelines for various federal crimes, and which analyzes whether criminal sentences are handed down fairly and without bias). There she was an assistant special counsel and stayed until 2005, after having her second daughter, Leila, in 2004.

One of her colleagues, Rachel Barkow, who also had been on *Law Review* with Ketanji, observed her to be "a very careful reader of text" and an originalist who "cares about the original meaning and history of the Constitution." In fact, the one time they ever had a difference of opinion was when Ketanji agreed with the government's position, not the defendant's, even if she didn't personally agree with the law. She didn't let her personal beliefs sway her opinion. That was an example of how she could remain impartial (unbiased and fair) in applying the law.

It was in 2005 that the course of her career shifted and her eyes were really opened to problems facing defendants in criminal cases in America. She noticed that sentences passed down by judges were not consistent among the convicted, but she knew she didn't understand criminal law and procedures well enough to understand why—or how to fix it. For that reason, she applied to be an appellate public defender in Washington, DC—a lawyer who represents people accused of a crime who cannot afford their own attorney. She found it to be like doing an "autopsy on a case"—reviewing and dissecting something that was already over and done.

She represented people held by the United States government in Guantánamo Bay, Cuba ("Gitmo"), some of whom were suspected of being terrorists (or "enemy combatants" suspected of having ties to the 9/11/2001 terrorist attacks on the United States, committed by nineteen plane hijackers, fifteen from Saudi Arabia, two from United Arab Emirates, one from Egypt, and one from Lebanon), but had not been officially charged with a crime and/or had no trial date set. Gitmo did not have to follow United States laws that require defendants be given due process, nor did it fall under international law. It had no laws, so human rights abuses took place there, including the torturing of prisoners.

Ketanji was assigned to one such person, Khi Ali Gul, who was eventually released and transferred back to Afghanistan during President Barack Obama's administration, as the administration worked to close the controversial detention center. Among her many cases, she represented an attorney charged with tax fraud (in *United States v. Ponds*) and a person charged with gun possession, several times successfully winning cases against the government, getting people's sentences reduced or erased entirely. She credits her time as a public defender with informing her later work and perspective as a judge. "There is a direct line from my defender service to what I do on the bench, and I think it's beneficial." Her former teacher Professor Carol Steiker had planted that seed.

She also made sure not to allow any negative personal feelings about defendants or their actions cloud her ability to represent them well, saying that every lawyer has "a duty to represent her clients zealously," which included not "contradicting her client's legal arguments and/or undermining her client's interests by publicly declaring the lawyer's own personal disagreement with the legal position or alleged behavior of her client. Because these standards apply even after termination of the representation, it would be inappropriate for me to list the cases in which I previously represented a client whose views I disagreed with or whose alleged crimes I found offensive."

A. J. Kramer was Ketanji's supervisor, and he allowed her and the other assistants to work almost entirely independently on their cases! They were trusted with their responsibilities, which let them feel pride in their work as well as grow from the experience. It made the office atmosphere feel both positive and collaborative. Even fun, sometimes.

Ketanji was a fan of reality TV shows. Of *American Idol* (during its original run on Fox), A. J. said she would come into the office the day after the show aired each week with wise critiques of the contestants' performances that she'd share around the watercooler. She was an even bigger fan of *Survivor* from its second season forward. For Ketanji, "... it's like a social experiment. It's human nature, what do people do when they're starving and how do they react to one another? It's like this Hobbesian state of nature: How are we going to deal with this situation? I love it." In fact, she took lessons from the show and applied them toward being a good lawyer.

She told American University's law school graduates that the show teaches you to: set priorities, make the most of the resources that you have when it seems the deck is stacked against you, do your best to shut out distractions, use your time wisely, know your strengths, and play the long game. "Season after season, the players who tend to do really well are those who appear to come in with the understanding that this game is about existing both in community and conflict." By this, she meant that you will always be operating both on the same side as others on your team, and oftentimes against them. She noticed, however, that the ones who tended to go farthest in the game would "choose optimism, lifting the spirits of the other tribe members, no matter what happens" and not get too excited by their wins or upset by their losses.

In 2005, Ketanji volunteered to lead an online discussion for the "Justice" course she took at Harvard, led by her former teacher, Professor Sandel. This was the course that had helped steer her on her career path. Although he hadn't known her from among the hundreds of other kids who'd attended his lectures, now Professor Sandel could watch her in action. He found her "enormously impressive, very much in touch with the philosophical texts and arguments we had explored in the course, now ably convening them to her peers with a gentle but compelling charisma."

Beginning in 2007, Ketanji went back to private practice in DC, to work "Of Counsel" (she wasn't an associate or partner but still had a relationship with the firm, doing specialized work, and could control her own hours) at Morrison & Foerster LLP. Her duties focused on appellate cases (where one party didn't like the outcome of a lower court proceeding and wanted a higher court to weigh in and overrule the lower court) and she also did pro bono work (free services done for the public good). Both her prior work on appeals and as a public defender served her well here.

She submitted many amicus briefs to the Supreme Court, including in *Arizona v. Gant*, where a defendant's vehicle was searched without a warrant. (The court ruled for her client, the defendant.) She also cowrote amicus briefs for other Guantánamo Bay detainees, such as Qatari national Ali Saleh Kahlah al-Marri on behalf of the libertarian Cato Institute, the Christian civil liberties nonprofit Rutherford Institute, and the Constitution Project. (From 2003 through 2009, he hadn't received a fair trial.) She also wrote one for a patent case (*Quanta Computer, Inc. v. LG Electronics, Inc.*), where the court reversed the Federal Circuit court's ruling and unanimously sided with her client.

Ketanji was also taking a big leap with her decision to make a huge change with her hair. After so many years in the workforce, coupled with all the demands at home with two children—one who was in need of extra attention for reasons Ketanji did not yet understand—as well as a marriage to nurture, she wanted to find a style that was easy to care for. She wanted to be able to stay on top of the upkeep, and wanted a style that still looked beautiful.

One day she saw a Black woman passing through a courtyard into a new smoothie shop. The woman was the shop owner and looked regal, her hair professional and refined. Ketanji followed her inside and as she ordered a smoothie, she told her how impressed she was with her hairstyle. The woman told her about a relatively new 'do called Sisterlocks, created by Dr. JoAnne Cornwell, who founded the company of the same name in 1993.

Sisterlocks are done by professionals using a curved, interlocking tool to build locs from the ends to the roots in a specific grid. They differ from and are more expensive than microlocs, a smaller version of traditional locs (crafted through matting or palm rolling with a balm or loc wax), which can be made in any grid pattern or technique, including braiding, twisting, coiling, etc. The style is low-maintenance, with salon appointments required once every two months. The woman gave Ketanji her practitioner's (stylist's) information, and Ketanji got in touch immediately, moving on from the straightened styles that white society prizes and imposes on Black women, to embracing her natural hair texture with this new signature look.

From the outset, Black women's hair has been a source of conversation and, oftentimes, controversy in the United States. Black hair was yet another means for slavers to justify the inhumane practice of slavery. Slavers considered every part of the Black body and mind to be inferior to white people's. That belief was force-fed from the white community into the Black one, to the point where many Black people came to agree with it and internalized the racism, turning it on themselves and each other in "self-hate."

During slavery, Black people who had lighter skin complexions and straighter hair were most likely the children of a white "master" or "overseer" who'd taken advantage of (or raped) an enslaved woman. Those Black people were usually treated better, considered prettier or handsomer, and given easier work inside the slavers' homes, away from the fields.

Black people themselves began to adopt the idea that natural Black hair was bad, or that darker skin was unattractive. This is called colorism and can be compared to the concept of caste in India. In 1786, Governor Don Estevan Miró of New Orleans, Louisiana, pushed this gross lie and enacted the Tignon Law, forcing women of African descent (including Creole women) to cover their hair with scarves or handkerchiefs, shaming them for their crowning glory. They had to hide their beauty and show they were members of the "slave class," whether or not they were in fact enslaved!

The women defied the law by wearing gorgeous scarves made of fantastic fabrics or covered in jewels, remaining fashionable and claiming their attractiveness despite the law wanting them to hide it. Still, European beauty standards penetrated the Black community, even after slavery was abolished. Black people have come to reject that self-hatred and recognize the versatility, loveliness, and uniqueness of their skin colors and various hair textures and lengths, however they wear or protect it. Society at large, however, is still catching up.

In May of 2010, in Mobile, Alabama, Catastrophe Management Solutions took back a job offer they'd made to a woman named Chastity Jones, because Chastity refused to cut her dreadlocks. She filed a complaint with the Equal Employment Opportunity Commission (EEOC), claiming this was racial discrimination. But in 2014, the company succeeded in getting her case dismissed.

Senior US district judge Charles Butler, Jr., agreed with CMS that people cannot change their race, but they can change their hair, so hairstyles are not protected under

Title VII of the Civil Rights Act of 1964. That means you *can* discriminate against people based on their hairstyle. The EEOC appealed this ruling to the Eleventh Circuit of Appeals, which, in 2016, agreed with the lower court. Because of the way dreadlocks are made, the only way Chastity would be able to change her hair would be to cut it all off. She filed a petition on her own for *writ of certiorari*, to go before the United States Supreme Court. But on May 16, 2018, SCOTUS declined to hear her case.

On August 20, 2018, eleven-year-old Faith Fennidy, who'd been wearing her hair in braids for two years, was sent home from her private Roman Catholic school in Terrytown, Louisiana, for using extensions in her braided hair. The school had added a policy over the summer: "Boys and girls: Only the student's natural hair is permitted. Extensions, wigs, hair pieces of any kind are not allowed." They told her not to come back.

The policing of Black hairstyles continued in 2023, when the mother of Darryl George, a junior at Barbers Hill High School in Mont Belvieu, Texas, received a letter from Principal Lance Murphy stating that her child would be suspended for more than a month for wearing his natural hairstyle. The letter listed a bunch of unrelated reasons for the suspension, but Darryl thought the real reason was because he'd already filed a lawsuit against his school district for targeting his hairstyle with a discriminatory dress and grooming policy. For Darryl, his hair was an "expression of cultural pride." He changed schools.

Several states across the country have passed laws banning discrimination against natural hairstyles, called the CROWN Act (Creating a Respectful and Open World for Natural Hair). Though Representative Bonnie Watson Coleman from New Jersey got a national CROWN Act passed by a vote of 235 to 189 on March 18, 2022, in the US House of Representatives, it failed to pass in the Senate. Given that Black women are 80 percent more likely to feel pressure to change their hairstyles to fit in at work, Black people, especially women, who take a stand to wear their hair in natural or protective hairstyles are, in effect, peaceful resisters and fighters. Fighters against discrimination, fighters for change, fighters for a better future.

Though Ketanji's decision to go natural was a personal one, it is significant on a national scale, as it helps with representation, visibility, and acceptance of women of color and their natural hair, beauty, and power. It makes it clear that they don't need to trade or sacrifice one of those in order to achieve the other. And that matters.

In 2009, President Barack Obama nominated Ketanji to the US Sentencing Commission, where she'd already worked in 2003, and in 2010 Republicans and Democrats confirmed her appointment as vice chair. The nomination and confirmation process was so stressful that she taught herself to knit in the meantime, to "channel my nervous energy. . . . If anybody wants a scarf, I'm your source," she said with her trademark wit.

Among other actions, she and the other commissioners unanimously agreed to attempt to correct the outsized difference between sentencing for drug possession established in the Anti-Drug Abuse Act of 1986. The difference in sentencing for that illegal drug found mainly in Black communities versus the other found mainly in white communities "cast a long and persistent shadow," according to Ketanji. "It has spawned clouds of controversy and an aura of unfairness that has shrouded nearly every federal [illegal drug] sentence." Ketanji stated, "I believe that the commission has no choice but to make this right."

After public outcry about the unfairness of the "war on drugs" punishments, and after many studies showed the laws were racially biased and did nothing to prevent crime or drug use, Congress passed a new law, called the Fair Sentencing Act. Thanks in no small part to Ketanji, the new sentencing guidelines didn't just apply going forward. Roughly 12,000 federal prisoners, 85 percent of whom were Black, could get their sentences reduced, though the racial unevenness in drug sentencing remains far from fixed.

"The decision we make today, which comes more than 16 years after the commission's first report to Congress . . . reminds me in many respects of an oft-quoted statement from the late Dr. Martin Luther King, Jr.," Ketanji said at a hearing in 2011. "He said: 'the arc of the moral universe is long. But it bends toward justice.' Today the commission completes the arc that began with its first recognition of the inherent unfairness of the 100:1 crack:powder disparity all those years ago. I say justice demands this result."

President Obama then nominated Ketanji in 2012 to be a federal judge for the US District Court for the District of Columbia (Washington, DC), but her hearing was stalled because Obama needed to win reelection before Congress would entertain the nomination. (If Republican Mitt Romney had won the presidency, the Republicans hoped he would nominate someone else whose judicial philosophy lined up more with their politics.) The wait was confusing and stressful for Ketanji, who said, "And when you add to that the fact that I am related by marriage to . . . Paul Ryan, who was at that point running for vice president against President Obama, you can get the sense of what that period was like for me."

Obama won reelection and on January 4, 2013, he nominated Ketanji again for a seat left open by Henry Harold Kennedy, Jr. She sat before the United States Senate to answer questions before they would vote to confirm her for the seat, and was asked if, in public education, "fifteen years from now, the use of racial preferences will no longer be necessary." She replied that the Supreme Court had already determined that "race-conscious admissions policies must be limited in time." But that she had no way of knowing how long those policies would be needed or when that time would be up: "I have no particular insight into the future need for, or ramifications of, the continued use of race in admissions." Both diplomatic and constitutional.

While all this was going on, Ketanji's friend Nina found out she had been diagnosed with breast cancer. Despite the pressure and stress that Ketanji was under, she made sure to be there for her friend. "One day I woke up and Ketanji and Lisa are at my door," Nina recounted. "She just appeared on my doorstep in the middle of everything she was going through." Her friends are her family, and her family's needs are her own. "That was a time where I wasn't telling people. I wasn't really sharing it, and she showed up, didn't ask any questions, she just showed up." Nina emphasized her point: "Ketanji can organize something, bring people together, and she recognizes the strength of everyone and makes sure that you recognize your strengths as well."

Judge Ketanji Brown Jackson was confirmed (with support from both parties) on March 21, 2013. US District Court judge Saris, chair of the US Sentencing Commission, said at her investiture (promotion) ceremony, "Judge

Jackson will be the kind of judge who blends common sense and pragmatism with this overarching sense of justice." Ketanji affectionately refers to Judge Saris as "my judge," because she considers her to be both a mentor and a friend.

She was only the second Black woman to be appointed to that court in thirty-two years. The first was one of her personal heroines, Constance Baker Motley.

Ketanji was "robed" on May 9, 2013—meaning she was given the black robes worn by judges at an official swearing-in ceremony. She was only forty-three years old, but through years of work and dedication to her job as a lawyer, she was ready for this next big step.

The dream, hope, and plan that she had written in her high school yearbook in 1988 had finally come true: Ketanji was now a judge. (Though, in order to get her bearings, she would need to attend "baby judge school," an orientation run by the Federal Judicial Center.)

Her aunt Carolynn had been unable to attend. She had lung cancer and was in New Orleans at the time, though her heart was no doubt in DC. She passed away that June— another person, like Grandma Euzera, who'd helped raise Ketanji and who'd lifted her up so she could one day soar, whose spirit lives on in her.

In her new role as judge, in order to remain impartial in her rulings, Judge Jackson would employ a three-step methodology: remain neutral (don't pick sides) at the start; then evaluate the facts and materials presented; and finally interpret and apply the laws that fit those facts. "I'm methodically and intentionally setting aside personal views, [and] any other inappropriate considerations" in determining the outcome of a case, she noted.

"Part of the frustration that I feel, as a Black woman," noted her friend Antoinette, "is the idea that because she is a Black woman that perhaps she is not going to be able to be fair and impartial, that somehow it's going to be a detriment to her in presiding over cases."

In Judge Jackson's office, she displayed a handwritten petition to the Supreme Court from a white Florida prisoner, Clarence Earl Gideon. He, who had not advanced past the eighth grade, had been charged with breaking and entering. He was not provided counsel to defend himself in court and was forced to represent himself. He lost, and received a sentence of five years in prison. In his 1961 case, *Gideon v. Wainwright*, after he wrote to the court himself, the Supreme Court decided having counsel in a criminal trial was a fundamental right, and if one could not afford an attorney, the state had to provide one.

Her photo with the Obamas from 1996 also hung inside her chambers, which her friend Denise had forwarded to her years later in 2008. In it she was standing beside the future president, who'd be the one to nominate her to the Sentencing Commission and then to the federal bench! She said, "I now use this photo to teach my daughters that the world is much too small to disregard the people that you meet along the way."

Her work as a judge seemed to suit her interests and talents well. Being a "judge is a very active process, primarily because a trial-level case is like a living organism—it is constantly moving and changing and responding to new stimuli."

In addition to her performing at her day job, she was elected to the thirty-one-member Harvard Board of "Overseers" in 2016, the university's second-highest governing body, which advises the university on how it should operate, and assesses the quality of its various schools, goals, departments, activities, and programs. Ever since she attended Harvard-Radcliffe (now called Harvard, after the two schools merged in 1999) as an undergrad, she had been passionate about improving the institution and its value to the students. Joining the board was another way for her to give back to the school where she'd learned so much, not just about academics, but also about herself.

At one point, her friend Stephen Rosenthal's law firm tried and lost a case before Judge Jackson. They appealed the decision, with Stephen presenting their argument. "Because she did such a good job in her opinion, it was like a nightmare to try to handle as the appellant." He was resigned to the outcome: "I lost the appeal, as I knew I would." Judge

Jackson would soon become famous for how thorough and well-reasoned her decisions were.

President Obama interviewed her for the spot on the Supreme Court of the United States left empty when Associate Justice Antonin Scalia passed away in 2016. The president ended up nominating Merrick Garland instead, but the Republican-led Senate refused to hold confirmation hearings for Obama's pick, they claimed, because it was an election year. But really it was because they believed having another Democrat-appointed judge on the court could allow the court to make more progressive rulings, as opposed to the conservative ones they wanted.

Mitch McConnell, the Republican Senate majority leader from Kentucky who set the agenda for the Senate at the time, said: "One of my proudest moments was when I looked Barack Obama in the eye and I said, 'Mr. President, you will not fill the Supreme Court vacancy'" and boasted it was "the single most consequential thing I've done in my time as majority leader of the Senate." (He was still in that leadership position in 2021 and hinted he wouldn't allow a Supreme Court vote for any nominee of that president, a Democrat, either.)

Judge Jackson participated in a mock trial in 2017, alongside future Supreme Court associate justice Brett Kavanaugh, where they debated whether to annul (undo, so legally it never happened) the marriage of characters Olivia and

Sebastian from William Shakespeare's comedic play *Twelfth Night*. She joked, "I hear the tax benefits are going to be enormous for two wealthy people getting married in 2018."

Richard Rosenthal was chairman of the high school reunion committee, but he said Judge Jackson was actively involved in planning the reunions even after she became a federal judge. "She'd help plan, and she'd come back to Miami for the event and it always went well," he said.

"She was on the organizing committee for all the reunions. We'd have them every five years, and she'd help arrange the location and the food and the DJ," David Kujawa said. "They were always a lot of fun."

Judge Jackson often mentions her high school in speeches—usually adding an enthusiastic "Go, Panthers!" when she does. She returns home when she can. "I'm a Florida girl," she'll say.

She also applied to be the chief marshal of alumni for commencement at her twenty-fifth Harvard reunion. She confirmed how much the school had meant to her and how many doors it had opened for her. "It is impossible to over-state the impact that Harvard has had on my life since graduation. I got married to my college boyfriend (Harvard '91) the year I graduated from Harvard Law School, and have spent the better part of the last quarter century doing what I can to give back to the institution that has given me so much." She was an interviewer for high schoolers applying to the school and would always make "sure to emphasize how difficult my transition from Miami public school kid to Harvard freshman would have been had it not been for the warm and welcoming environment of the Yard and the Union, and the emotional support that I received from various advisors and faculty that first semester." She also highlighted:

> . . . the enduring friendships that experiencing college life in Cambridge creates—there is nothing like braving the collective crucible of academic anxiety and endless winters to bring people together! . . . some of the people I met while at Harvard have become my closest friends, while others remain my biggest professional allies. . . . I would not be a federal judge today . . . without the extraordinary network of Harvard graduates . . . who routinely open doors and pave paths for one another. I have also cherished the complexity, depth, and range of the many people I have gotten to know through my connections to Harvard; in this regard, to interested interviewees, I say this: the University's commitment to diversity and inclusion is real, and it yields intangible benefits for all those who have the privilege of getting to know people from other walks of life.

Unfortunately, when Donald Trump was elected president again in 2024, after having been defeated by Joe Biden in

2020, Harvard, as well as many universities and corporations nationwide, would cave, abandoning their commitment to "diversity and inclusion," after he issued an executive order called "Ending Illegal Discrimination and Restoring Merit-Based Opportunity." Trump's mission seems to have been to reverse any gains won by people of color (and to an extent, women) since the end of the Civil War, as well as dismantle any of their protections, in order to restore a hierarchy of white supremacy throughout all of American life. A very large faction of Americans have chosen to go along with his policies without challenging them. But there are fighters out there whose names people will one day come to know . . . and remember.

In 2018, Ketanji presided over a different half-day mock trial, this one to determine whether Vice President Aaron Burr, who shot Alexander Hamilton in a duel in 1804, was guilty of murder. The story of these men is what Lin-Manuel Miranda's 2016 Tony Award–winning blockbuster play *Hamilton*, one of Judge Jackson's favorites, is based on. (She quoted *Hamilton* in one of her written opinions while on the DC Circuit Court.) One of the songs that really hit home for her for obvious reasons, given the microscope her life had been under, was "History Has Its Eyes on You." In this production, the roles of the white men who "founded" America are all played by Black or Latino actors. It shook up the Broadway and theater world with its boldness, embracing rap and spoken-word as elevated art forms. And it makes one wonder how Ketanji's old theater teacher might think about casting plays now.

Judge Jackson, who loves art, plays, and musical theater, identified three musicals from which people, and recent law graduates in particular, could learn valuable lessons. First, from *Little Shop of Horrors*, the play she was in at college, she suggested people remember "to always start by asking *why* when you confront a new situation," which the main character from that show did *not* do when he stumbled across a bloodsucking, flesh-eating, Venus flytrap–looking plant.

Second, regarding *Hamilton*, she told the graduates "if [Aaron Burr] really wants to have a say, then he needs to do whatever it takes to get himself a seat at the table, and help to make a change." There's not much one can accomplish from the outside looking in. "Find something you care about, and get yourself into the room where it happens."

And third, in Charles Randolph-Wright's show *American Prophet*, about Frederick Douglass, Douglass's own words are used and repeated often in different ways. It helped the audience get to know the man and really land his points. Of that, she said, "It's not just what you say that leaves an impact . . . it's also how you say it."

Over the years, Judge Jackson received many honors and

awards, including being named the University of Chicago Law School's Edward H. Levi Distinguished Visiting Jurist (2014–2015) and being an elected member of the American Law Institute (ALI), serving on its council since 2016. She was keynote speaker at *Harvard Law Review*'s 130th Spring Banquet (2017) and in 2019, she was named the David T. Lewis Distinguished Jurist-in-Residence for the University of Utah's S. J. Quinney College of Law; received the Stars of the Bar Award from the Women's Bar Association of the District of Columbia; and was profiled in the NBC News program "She Thrives: Black Women Making History." She was given the Distinguished Visiting Jurist, Third Annual Judge James B. Parsons Legacy Award from the Black Law Students Association, University of Chicago Law School (2020); and the Constance Baker Motley Award, Empowering Women of Color, from Columbia Law School (2021).

At the Columbia event, she spoke again about one of her main inspirations and heroes, Constance Baker Motley, and had this to say:

The lawyers of color in the generation prior galvanized a movement that would change their lives, and that of their decedents, forever, and they did so during a period of time in which they themselves did not have the many benefits that we now enjoy. . . . The mantle that Judge Motley and others took up in their time has been passed to us—as judges, and lawyers, and soon-to-be law graduates—we are now charged with the responsibility of making the most of our legal education and considerable good fortune, and of doing the work that is necessary to protect the rule of law and to promote equality and justice for all.

XII

DECISIONS

"KAY! HOW ARE YOU? THIS is your uncle Thomas. . . . I'm calling because I've been trying to get someone to take another look at my case."

With those words, a man Ketanji hadn't seen or heard from in more than fifteen years, since she was a little girl, was suddenly back in her life. "Your dad tells me you're a public defender."

The voice Ketanji heard over the phone that day in her law office in Washington, DC, was familiar, yet at the same time, distant. Her uncle, Thomas Brown, Jr., was calling her from a federal prison in her home state of Florida.

Emotions and thoughts swirled in her head as she listened to him explain his situation and ask her for help. She felt great sympathy for him. She might not have known him well over the decades, but she knew his story. By the time he called her, she and most other people involved with the country's justice system knew that severely punitive drug laws pushed by politicians for many years were not only racially biased, but they also didn't work. Instead, they disrupted and even ruined the lives of so many people like her uncle, who was told he had to spend the rest of his life behind bars for a nonviolent crime.

That moment in her office merged two of Ketanji's guiding principles of the law: It should mean justice, but also fairness.

The two ideas are similar, but not the same. Justice means making sure people follow the laws, and holding them accountable if they don't. Fairness means treating people the same, without showing favoritism, no matter how rich or poor they are, or whether they're Black, Brown, white, or any other color.

Our laws must be rooted in fairness, equality, and justice for all Americans, Ketanji has said about her philosophy of law.

Her entire career had been channeled toward those bedrock beliefs. But her education, her research, and her own life experience had shown her that those essentially American beliefs were too often cast aside, especially for people who are marginalized because of their race or economic status.

Ketanji often reminded people when she was invited to

make speeches that Americans should take note of what the architects of the US Supreme Court building in Washington, DC, etched into the marble above the main entrance.

"You may have seen it in person, or in pictures. And of all the things that could have been engraved above the front door of our highest legal authority, what is there standing alone are four words: Equal Justice Under Law," Ketanji told a group of law school students in a speech. "That is a stark reminder that equality is a critical component of our justice system."

She was encouraging the students, no matter what type of law they went on to practice, to sometimes represent people who can't afford to hire a private attorney, to make sure they also got equal justice. All lawyers are expected to take some clients pro bono. And people without means make up a large portion of the cases before judges.

"Practicing lawyers are also obligated to ensure that every member of society has access to justice," Ketanji said. "There will come a time when you're asked to take on clients who may not be able to pay for your services, and you might even be called upon to represent indigent individuals who are unpopular or who have been accused of committing crimes. When that opportunity arises, please take it. The rule of law to which we are all committed cannot flourish unless the legal system is fair and open to all."

Ketanji knew that asking students who may have been

looking to get very rich in their law careers to give away their work for free was asking a lot. Lawyers in high-profile cases who have rich or famous clients have charged as much as $2,000 an hour for their work. Most lawyers charge far less, and public defenders in many states, who represent indigent clients every day, make around $30 an hour.

No matter how high their salary or how "important" their clients were, Ketanji said, "Our justice system can only function properly if talented lawyers like you step up and do the work of representing people who do not have financial means with just as much zeal as the work that is done for paying clients."

Ketanji had spent much of her early career working to review and change practices in the legal system that were unfair to poor people, people of color, and others. The harsh penalties for minor drug crimes was one of them.

Black people were swept up in raids and punished more severely than white people who had committed similar crimes. Black Americans were nearly six times more likely to be jailed for a drug crime than white people, despite the fact that the level of drug use was equal. The drug laws, like so many in America, favored white people over people of other races and ethnicities.

Ketanji's uncle Thomas, her father's older brother, was just one of many thousands of people convicted under the harsh laws and sentenced to serve the rest of their lives in prison for a crime that today would mean, at most, five years in jail. When he called her in 2005 from prison, he had already been incarcerated for fifteen years. But he thought he might have one last chance if his niece agreed to help him.

She did. She processed the situation the way she did most things in her life: not from a personal or emotional stand-point, but with a sense of duty, a sense of fairness, and a certainty in doing what was right.

Although Ketanji couldn't help her uncle directly—her job at the time was as a federal public defender in Washington and it did not include representing people in other states— she agreed to try to find someone else to represent him.

Her uncle sent her a big package full of documents on his case. She forwarded it to a powerful private law firm in Washington, where she knew lawyers who could help. They represented Thomas Brown, Jr., pro bono, in his quest for clemency.

Ketanji didn't ask for special favors for her uncle, but she did, coincidentally, help change the justice system to try to undo some of the damage the punitive drug laws had done to people like him, and to make America's justice system more fair.

For Ketanji, sentencing—the punishment a judge gives

to someone found guilty of a crime—was among the most important things a lawyer should know about. She called sentencing fairness "my passion in the law."

It is the "ultimate exercise of the power of the government to subjugate the free will of individuals, which has enormous implications in a society in which the government derives its power from the will of the people," she said.

It took twelve years from the time of his phone call to his niece, but in 2017, Thomas Brown, Jr., walked out of a Florida prison a free man. President Barack Obama had issued him a pardon for his crime. The then president commuted the sentences of more than 1,700 people after the unfair "war on drug" laws were changed. Thomas had spent twenty-eight years behind bars. By the time he was freed, he was seventy-eight years old, and in frail health.

He moved to Georgia, where his family—Ketanji's grandparents and ancestors going back more than 150 years—was from. He lived only a year after his release. But he died a free man, not in a prison cell.

"I chose to become an Assistant Federal Public Defender because public service is a core value in my family," Ketanji said. "And after becoming a lawyer, I determined that being a public defender was the highest and best use of my time and talents."

Once she became a judge, first as a District Court judge in 2013, then on the US Court of Appeals in Washington, Judge Jackson issued more than 578 judicial decisions.

Her decisions were rarely overturned, meaning higher courts—in this case, the only one higher being the US Supreme Court—agreed that she got her rulings right.

Judge Jackson already had a reputation for being one of the smartest and hardest-working legal minds of her generation, and her reputation grew once she became a judge.

It didn't matter what kind of case came before her; she gave each one her careful attention. Her decisions, crafted with the help of her team of law clerks, were often more than 100 pages long—the longest being 186 pages.

Some of the more important decisions she made during those years include:

- ruling in favor of a man who was deaf and needed an interpreter to understand what police and jailers were telling him after he was arrested. Judge Jackson said the prison officials violated his rights by not making sure he could understand them.
- ruling in favor of a biology teacher who lost his job of twenty years when his school district began hiring younger teachers. Judge Jackson said he had a case for age discrimination.

- temporarily blocking a plan by President Donald Trump in 2019 to expand a program that "fast-tracked" deportations of people who were in the United States illegally.
- also in 2019, writing one of her most famous decisions, ruling against the Trump administration again. In this case, Trump wanted to prevent a White House lawyer from testifying to Congress about election interference. Judge Jackson said that, just like other Americans, Trump couldn't defy an order from Congress to have his aide testify.

"Stated simply, the primary takeaway from the past 250 years of recorded American history is that presidents are not kings," the judge wrote in her decision. "This means they do not have subjects, bound by loyalty or blood, whose destiny they are entitled to control."

That decision endeared her to millions of Americans who worried that the country might slip into tyranny if people believed that anyone, including the president, was above the law.

"In this land of liberty, it is indisputable that current and former employees of the White House work for the People of the United States," she said. In other words, the president and his staff have to follow the law too, just like every other American.

Judge Jackson's sharp intellect, tireless work ethic, and reputation for trying to reach consensus, or agreement among her colleagues, made her more respected than ever. More important, she believed in fairness for everyone, not just for some.

XIII

MOTHERHOOD

"DEAR MR. PRESIDENT," BEGAN THE letter from an eleven-year-old girl to President Barack Obama. "While you are considering judges to fill Justice Scalia's seat on the Supreme Court, I would like to add my mother, Ketanji Brown Jackson of the District Court, to the list."

With that, young Leila Jackson embarked on a campaign to see her mom win a seat on the highest court in the land.

The letter was neatly written in pencil on a sheet of three-hole-punched, wide-ruled lined notebook paper, ready to be put into a school binder or sent to the White House. Leila did the latter—getting an envelope and stamp and sending it off to 1600 Pennsylvania Avenue.

"I, her daughter Leila Jackson of eleven years old, strongly believe she would be an excellent fit for the position," Leila wrote about her mom.

*She is determined, honest, and never breaks a
promise to anyone, even if there are other things
she'd rather do. She can demonstrate commitment,
and is loyal and never brags. I think she would
made a great Supreme Court justice, even if the
workload will be larger on the court, or you have other
nominees. Please consider her aspects for the job.*

She closed her letter with: "Thank you for listening!"
and signed it "Leila Jackson."

Judge Jackson thought that her daughters were, at that
point in their young lives, "oblivious to Supreme Court
politics and the process of nominating justices."

But Leila and her older sister, Talia, knew what their
mom was all about, even if she didn't realize they had been
paying attention to her work the whole time.

Leila told her parents that some of her middle school
friends had been talking, and they said to her, "'You know,
your mom's a judge—she should really apply for that position.' Now Leila thought that was a pretty good idea, and
so she had come to tell me that I should submit an application for the open Supreme Court seat," Judge Jackson
recalled.

She and Patrick explained to her "that getting to be on
the Supreme Court really isn't the kind of job that you apply
for—you just have to be lucky enough to have the president

find you among the thousands of people who might want to do that job."

Leila, undeterred by that news, said, "Well, if the president has to find you, I'm gonna write him a letter to tell him who you are!"

Leila's heartfelt recommendation to the president didn't work, at least not then, but it did mark the official beginning of Judge Jackson's roller-coaster journey toward the highest court in the land.

The support of her daughters, along with her husband, Patrick, and the rest of her family, was central to who she was, and who she aspired to be. "My parents actively and intentionally built me up from a very early age to believe that I could do anything I wanted to do, and I have actually been reflecting on this extraordinary gift over the past few years as I now raise my own daughters," she said. But it has not always been an easy journey, especially not motherhood.

The letter Leila wrote brought her "a brief, shining moment" that her role as a mom—one of the most important in her life—was valued. And that the choice she had made to juggle her personal and professional life, with Patrick's help and support, had been the right one.

"It is difficult to put into words how it felt to get such a ringing endorsement from my own daughter. It was an actual testimony that was, by far, more meaningful than any make believe account of how my daughters feel," Judge Jackson said, at long last not having to guess what her daughters were thinking on the topic. "I realized not only that I'm raising an assertive young women who isn't afraid to speak her mind, even to the president of the United States, but also that my daughters are not oblivious to my work, and are proud of me, as I am of them and our entire family."

But she cautioned that parenting and having a successful career was a difficult balance. "It has been a lot of hard work—trying to balance work and motherhood, and like so many other people, I often feel as if I'm failing."

Judge Jackson was not accustomed to that feeling, so parenthood left her in unfamiliar territory. "I was, in fact, terrified at the prospect of becoming a mom and of having to juggle work and family," she said, expressing emotions that so many women in the workplace also share.

Former first lady Michelle Obama described it as "feelings of not-enoughedness."

She and her husband had raised their two daughters, Malia and Sasha, in the White House over the span of eight years.

"The images of maternal perfection we encounter in advertisements and across social media are often no less fake than what we see on the enhanced and Photoshopped female bodies," Mrs. Obama wrote in her book *The Light*

We Carry. "But still, we are conditioned to buy into it, questing after not just the perfect body, but also perfect children, perfect work-life balances, perfect family experiences, and perfect levels of patience. It's hard not to look around as a mother and think *Is everyone doing this perfectly but me?*"

Mrs. Obama had won many awards for her work, including International Mother of the Year. But she still understood the pressure working moms face.

"Self-scrutiny is something women are programmed to excel at, having been . . . fed fully unrealistic images of female 'perfection' from the time we were kids ourselves," she wrote. "None of us—truly none—ever live up."

Judge Jackson wanted to live up to those parental expectations, though. She was working fourteen- to sixteen-hour days in 2000 as a clerk for US Supreme Court justice Stephen Breyer when she got pregnant with Talia. Then she and her husband decided to move back to Boston, where Patrick would finish his residency in general surgery.

"And so began the delicate balancing that many young lawyers face in their professional lives: how *does* one manage the demands of your career and also the needs of your family?" she asked. She went to work for the prestigious private law firm Goodwin Procter in Boston. Talia was born a few months later, and the conflict between parenting and career hit her hard.

"Like many young women who enter Big Law, I soon

found it extremely challenging to combine law firm work with my life as a wife and new mother." Women often find they need to leave the workforce and their careers behind when they have children, or they end up falling behind, career-wise, if they take time off for child-rearing. "In my case, it was the inflexibility of the work schedules and assignments that became the deal-breaker."

Although the bosses and partners in the firm were supportive, and she knew of women who somehow managed the pressure of simultaneously holding down two full-time jobs—of mother and lawyer—she discovered early on, she was not one of them.

"That period of my life taught me . . . as much as I had enjoyed developing trial-practice skills in law school—and, in my mind, I had many Perry Mason moments—if I was going to make life as a lawyer work for me and my family, I needed . . . a more predictable, more controllable working environment," she said. "Armed with that realization, I then began what I can only characterize as a professional odyssey of epic proportions."

Before they decided to have their second child, the Jackson family moved back to Washington, DC, with Ketanji going a year ahead to work at the Feinberg Group as Patrick stayed back at Mass General to work as "super chief." She brought the nanny Joanne along to help with Talia. Once Leila was born in 2004, she went back to working in the public sector, which had always been her true interest when it came to the law.

Those jobs weren't easy, but at least the hours in public service jobs were more predictable. It also brought her back to the reason she loves the law: ". . . to help people in need, and to promote core constitutional values . . . that every person who is accused of criminal conduct by the government, regardless of wealth and despite the nature of the accusations, is entitled to the assistance of counsel."

Her more stable and predictable life allowed her to become involved in her children's day-to-day lives. There were times when the Jacksons had a nanny to help out with the girls, but Judge Jackson also devoted much of her free time to the girls' school activities. The family adopted a rescue dog; they went to annual family reunions with both sides of the family.

She became a classroom mom and joined the boards of Talia's and Leila's schools. She valued Georgetown Day School's "rigorous progressive education that is dedicated to fostering critical thinking, independence, and social justice" (something she'd get quizzed on later, with a senator asking if that meant she thought babies could be racist!).

She studied how to be a mom by reading books and also by learning from others.

Her friend Judge Patti Saris "mothered me in my first

job out of law school; she taught me how to think and write like a litigator; she showed me how to balance work and family."

When Patrick's and her early careers seemed to make parenting almost impossible, Ketanji would step back and think, "What would Patti Saris do?" It wasn't going to be an easy path, no matter how prepared she was, and her mentor let her know that.

Judge Jackson found some parts of parenting could be compared to sentencing guidelines for people convicted of breaking the law.

"One thing I learned is that 'to discipline' actually means 'to teach,' and that . . . parents should strive to establish rules that incentivize children to make good choices themselves rather than rely on structures designed solely to penalize children harshly after they have misbehaved."

She even co-taught a class for a parenting group on how parents can discipline kids, called "Push Me, Pull You: Understanding and Diffusing Power Struggles at Home."

Judge Jackson once joked that she was "a judge in the federal trial system who moonlights as a mother of two daughters" and talked about the difference between her work life and her home life.

"One moment, you have this beautiful, sweet baby, and then suddenly, as if out of nowhere, you look around and she is taller than you are and absolutely certain that she knows much more than you do. About everything." She explained she was experiencing "near daily whiplash from the jarring juxtaposition of my two most significant roles: United States District Judge, on the one hand, and mother of teenage daughters on the other."

Ketanji faced another parenting challenge that took her years to understand and accept: her first daughter was neurodiverse. That means her brain works differently in some ways. She would later be diagnosed at age eleven with mild autism spectrum disorder. Talia was remarkably smart and interested in specific subjects, especially cooking. But in preschool and through much of elementary school, teachers told Ketanji and Patrick that Talia had trouble stopping one activity and moving on to another. She sometimes had difficulty interpreting other people's reactions.

At home, Talia was chatty and engaged with her parents and younger sister much of the time—both she and Leila took piano lessons and sang around the house. Talia also played the violin and "had an exquisite singing voice," as her proud mother commented. Talia could also be bossy with her little sister. But Leila was devoted and protective of her sister.

School was a struggle for Talia, though. And her parents—both self-admitted overachievers whose early lives were based around education—worried about her future. Ketanji had been preoccupied for years about finding the best classroom for her daughter, who didn't always act like other kids and was sometimes teased because of that. Ketanji said the autism diagnosis was devastating, but also a relief, because she and Patrick finally knew, for sure, the best way to help Talia realize her own dreams.

Her neurodiversity meant that Talia "would have to fight harder for what she needed as an autistic person," her mom said, but it was a fight her parents did their best to prepare her for. They found schools and teachers that would encourage and support her, smaller classes with students who would respect and not tease her, and ways to help channel her interests and passions at home.

"Talia was autistic, and she was also our bright, witty, doe-eyed adolescent whose neurodiversity fueled her very specific interests—her passion for cookbooks and love of baking, for example, and her enjoyment of animation, especially anime," her mother said.

Ketanji figured out how to navigate her work and her home lives as separate but also connected, even as both parts of her life continued to grow and thrive. She had a happy, if sometimes challenging, family and a demanding, high-profile job. Home life kept her centered, though—especially her daughters, who had ways of bringing her back to earth, no matter how important their mom was to the public.

While at work, people would treat her with respect, ask her opinion, and listen to what she had to say and do what they were told.

"But . . . when I leave the courthouse and go home . . . all of my wisdom and knowledge and authority essentially evaporates, and my daughters make it very clear that, as far as they are concerned, I know nothing and should not tell them anything; much less give them any orders—that is, if they talk to me at all."

But most of what the judge learned about being a parent came from how her own mom, Ellery Ross Brown, raised her. She gave a speech at the American Law Institute Dinner Council in 2017 titled "Four Lessons My Mother Taught Me." The main takeaways were:

1. Be Proud of Who You Are and Where You're From
2. To Whom Much Is Given, Much Is Expected
3. Learn Something
4. *Always* Show Respect for Others

She worked to pass those lessons on to her own daughters.

She explained that she and her husband share "the indomitable spirit of hard work" and are "those long-suffering, 'early-to-bed, early-to-rise' no-rest-for-the-weary kind of people, who have high standards and sincerely believe in the prioriti-zation of work over play in most circumstances."

Her daughters were not always on board with that. But she and Patrick would tell them to "do what you need to do before what you want to do." Because that was how she was raised. "My mother," she added, "would be very proud."

XIV

NOMINATION

JOE BIDEN MADE A PROMISE to the American people when he asked them to vote for him for president in 2020.

"I'm looking forward to making sure there's a Black woman on the Supreme Court, to make sure we, in fact, get every representation," Biden said. No matter whom he chose, Biden knew she would face an uphill battle to get through a politically divided US Senate. But he was determined to try, because he saw the importance of bringing more diverse voices to the seats of power in the country.

When President Joe Biden nominated Judge Jackson to be on the US Supreme Court, her friends and family and most people in the legal world were thrilled but not surprised.

The president said he wanted somebody truly special for the important job.

"Someone extremely qualified, with a brilliant legal mind, with the utmost character and integrity, which are equally as important," Biden said. "Someone with extraordinary character, who will bring to the Supreme Court an independent mind, uncompromising integrity, and with a strong moral compass and the courage to stand up for what she thinks is right."

It was a tall order, but he found that extraordinary person in Judge Jackson. The president said he also wanted a Black woman for the job, because none had ever been on the US Supreme Court.

"For too long, our government, our courts, haven't looked like America," Biden said.

The US Supreme Court is a branch of the federal government that is supposed to have power equal to that of the Congress and the Executive Office (the president). As Biden put it, "the court is equally as important as the presidency or the Congress. It's co-equal."

And because of its importance to every American, Biden said the court should look like America. For 177 years, only white men served as justices on the Supreme Court. In 1967, Thurgood Marshall became the first Black person to be named to the court. Prior to that, Associate Justice Marshall had been a famous attorney and a leader in the Civil Rights Movement.

Despite strong opposition, President Lyndon Johnson,

who had signed monumental civil rights laws, said Thurgood Marshall was "best qualified by training and by very valuable service to the country. . . . I believe it is the right thing to do, the right time to do it, the right man and the right place."

There were senators, mainly from Southern states (Florida, the Carolinas, Mississippi, Louisiana, and West Virginia), who objected to his being on the bench. They questioned his impartiality (in essence, whether he would favor Black people over white people in his opinions, though where was the opposite concern when white men were nominated or confirmed?). He had led the fight against school segregation as an attorney for the NAACP. He was successful in convincing the Supreme Court in 1954 to issue one of its most famous decisions: *Brown v. Board of Education*. Despite those senators' "Nay" votes, Justice Marshall prevailed and was confirmed by a vote of 69–11. He served on the court for twenty-four years, until his retirement at age eighty-two.

The first woman on the court wasn't chosen until 1981, when President Ronald Reagan nominated Sandra Day O'Connor, who was confirmed by a vote of 99–0. She served for twenty-five years until she retired in 2006 to care for her ailing husband. President George W. Bush then nominated her replacement, Justice Samuel Alito.

Like President Biden, Reagan had made a promise while

he was campaigning to be president that he would name a woman to the Supreme Court if there happened to be an opening. Since then, more women have joined the bench, though they are still outnumbered by men:

Ruth Bader Ginsburg was named to the court by President Bill Clinton in 1993.

President Barack Obama nominated two women to the court—Elena Kagan in 2010 and Sonia Sotomayor in 2009. Associate Justice Sotomayor is the first Latina to serve on the high court.

Then Donald Trump appointed Amy Coney Barrett to the court in 2020.

Justices Sotomayor, Kagan (who is Jewish), and Barrett were still on the bench in 2022, so the court had become more diverse. Three of the nine members were women, and of the six men, one was Black—Clarence Thomas, who was appointed by President George H. W. Bush in 1991.

When Supreme Court justice Stephen Breyer announced his retirement in January 2022 after twenty-eight years on the bench, the White House staff set about finding a candidate to fit President Biden's conditions. It wasn't a simple task. The US Constitution doesn't have explicit requirements for Supreme Court justices—they don't even have to be lawyers. The only rule is that the person practice "good behavior" while they're on the bench.

It's the job of the president to nominate a justice, with the "advice and consent" of the Senate, which must confirm the nominee by a simple majority—meaning the nominee must get at least fifty-one out of one hundred votes.

While the Constitution doesn't require it, for the past sixty years, the Senate Judiciary Committee has played a major role in the selection process by investigating the nominee's background and qualifications. As America's first president, George Washington was the first to appoint the country's original Supreme Court justices. The qualifications Washington wanted in a prospective justice included "love of country," prior judicial experience, and also "distinguished service in the American Revolution." Most important to Washington, the nominee had to show "support and advocacy of the U.S. Constitution."

But another rule that was left unsaid at the time because it was so obvious to Washington and the other founders of the United States of America was this: the nominee would be a white man.

Black Americans weren't even considered full citizens when the country began. But even after the Civil War and the passage of the Fourteenth and Fifteenth Amendments guaranteed Black people the Constitutional right of full citizenship and Black men the right to vote, Jim Crow laws and anti-Black customs violently suppressed the rights and ability of Black people. They affected everything from voting to going to college and also made it difficult for them to gain entrance into the American government's highest ranks, in particular the US Supreme Court.

It wasn't until 1937 that a Black person became a federal judge. William Henry Hastie, Jr., was appointed to the federal bench in the Virgin Islands by President Franklin Delano Roosevelt.

Hastie, a Harvard Law School graduate, was Roosevelt's race relations advisor, a post the Democratic president created to try to deal with the scourge of Jim Crow laws, although Roosevelt tolerated many of them.

During World War II, Hastie was also assigned to focus on race relations in the armed forces. He found that racism was rampant in the army, air force, and other branches of the military. Black and white soldiers were separated into different units, trained separately, and it was much more difficult for a Black soldier to climb the military ranks. (In 1946, out of 776 generals in the army, only one was Black.)

The segregation was so corrosive and deeply entrenched in the military that even the blood used for transfusions to save soldiers on the battlefield was segregated—it was against army rules to give a white soldier blood donated by a Black person. Hastie fought those absurd rules and laws and, as previously noted, helped lay the groundwork for the *Brown v. Board of Education* decision. He was one of the brightest legal minds of his era.

Several Americans active in the Civil Rights Movement said that Hastie would be an excellent Supreme Court justice. President John F. Kennedy considered nominating him in 1962, but decided against it and instead, like every president before him, chose a white man. Kennedy's successor, President Lyndon Johnson, became the first to appoint a Black person to the Supreme Court when he nominated Thurgood Marshall in 1967.

In 2005, President George W. Bush was reportedly considering nominating the first Black woman to the Supreme Court. Janice Rogers Brown was a US Court of Appeals judge who then senator Joe Biden voted against. He and other Democrats believed Brown was too conservative. Progressive groups said she had a "strong, persistent, and disturbing hostility toward affirmative action and civil rights." Conservative groups lauded her accomplishments and interpretation of the law.

When he became president, Biden was determined to keep the promise he'd made to voters and nominate a Black woman, and it would be a woman whose outlook would fall more in line with Democrats and their policy goals. But because America's judiciary has been marred by racism for so long, the "pipeline" to the Supreme Court—beginning with education, success in law school, connections to important judges and politicians—had been and continues to be challenging for anyone other than white men to navigate.

Yet, thanks to people like President Barack Obama, a two-term president and the most powerful person in the world for eight years, there was a whole new field of diverse connections and networks for lawyers to help them advance in public service.

Even so, Black women face more impediments to finding success in the legal profession than most other people. They encounter bias, stereotyping, and more inequality in job opportunities than white women do. They find it more difficult to advance in their jobs, get support for their work, or be paid equally. A study conducted by the American Bar Association in 2020 showed that only 4 percent of partners in private law firms were women of color—a pattern President Biden wanted to change and believed he could by naming a Black woman to the most important legal job in the country.

The White House staff found three women for the president to interview—Leondra Kruger, an associate justice on the California Supreme Court; J. Michelle Childs, a US District Court judge in South Carolina; and Ketanji Brown Jackson, an appellate judge.

Each of them was supremely qualified and accomplished, but Judge Ketanji Brown Jackson stood out and was considered the front-runner from the very beginning. Biden had already nominated her to another important legal job on the US Court of Appeals in Washington, DC, considered the most important court in the country behind the Supreme Court. She'd been there for about a year, distinguishing herself with well-informed decisions and clear rulings. Of that nomination, she'd said, "It is the beauty and the majesty of this country, that someone who comes from a background like mine could find herself in this position. . . . I'm just enormously grateful to have this opportunity to be a part of the law in this way, and I'm truly thankful for the president giving me the honor of this nomination."

Judge Jackson had clerked for Supreme Court associate justice Stephen Breyer over two decades prior, so she was familiar with the ins and out of the Supreme Court. Clerks assist judges by researching the laws and legal precedent, helping them make their rulings. Clerking for a US Supreme Court justice is one of the most highly sought-after jobs for ambitious attorneys in public life.

Justice Breyer was a big fan of Judge Jackson's, saying she would "interpret the law wisely and fairly, helping that law to work better for the American people, whom it serves."

President Biden gave glowing praise to Judge Jackson when he talked to the American public about why he was nominating her. "Her opinions are always carefully reasoned, tethered to precedent, and demonstrate respect for how the law impacts everyday people." He went on: "It doesn't mean she puts her thumb on the scale of justice one way or the other, but she understands the broader impact of her decisions." Just as important, he said, is that: "She listens. She looks people in the eye—lawyers, defendants, victims, and families. And she strives to ensure that everyone understands why she made a decision, what the law is, and what it means to them. She strives to be fair, to get it right, to do justice."

Were Judge Jackson to be confirmed, she would also be the first justice with experience as a public defender. Most justices have been prosecutors, acting for the government to bring cases against people and companies for alleged crimes. But Judge Jackson had spent two years on the other side of the courtroom, representing defendants, many of whom were poor, and many who were confused about how they wound up in a federal courtroom and what was going to happen to them next.

Courtrooms can be intimidating places. The rules inside are strict and enforced by bailiffs, which can be intimidating or elicit fear in people, especially those who are accused of crimes.

Judge Jackson understood this. She made it a point as a

public defender to explain each step of what was happening to her clients, and what it meant for their cases. She carried that philosophy with her later on when she became a judge.

"I . . . believe in transparency, that people should know precisely what I think and the basis for my decision," she said. "And all of my professional experiences, including my work as a public defender and as a trial judge, have instilled in me the importance of having each litigant know that the judge in their case has heard them, whether or not their arguments prevail in court."

Two presidents and seven years after she penned her letter to President Obama, Leila's wish came true. President Joe Biden—who had been President Obama's vice president and knew about Leila's letter—nominated Judge Jackson to the Supreme Court. He remarked on the judge and her family when he nominated her, telling the country that Judge Jackson was not only an accomplished lawyer and judge, but also a mom who had handled the demands of parenthood and a career. A tough juggling act, which even the president of the United States recognized.

"Like so many women in this country, Judge Jackson is a working mom. She had her eldest child, Talia, when she was a private lawyer in practice. She had her second child, Leila, when she served on the US Sentencing Commission," Biden said, adding that she was "a distinguished American who will help write the next chapter in the history of the journey of America—a journey that Judge Jackson will take with her family."

And with that nomination, despite all the obstacles she'd faced thus far, Judge Jackson was about to encounter the steepest hill she'd had to climb yet: Capitol Hill.

XV

CONFIRMATION

THE EYES OF THE COUNTRY were glued on Judge Jackson as she sat by herself in the big, windowless room in the US Senate building. President Biden was watching. So was Vice President Kamala Harris, as well as Ketanji's parents, brother, husband, and daughters.

Friends from college, friends from high school, former teachers and professors—everybody she knew was watching. Some were there in person, some watching on TV or viewing on their laptops and cell phones. It was day one of a four-day confirmation process that would determine if Judge Jackson would become Justice Jackson, one of the most powerful people in the nation—a justice on the US Supreme Court. The hearings were being broadcast around the world.

How would she handle this intensely pressure-filled moment, face-to-face with US senators, many of whom were hostile to her seemingly because of what she represented? She was a Black woman who wanted to work for a fair and just America. She represented progress, upsetting those conservative politicians who distrusted even the word *progress*.

The final vote would come from the fifty Republicans and fifty Democrats who made up the Senate. She would need fifty-one votes to win. Everybody knew it was going to be close.

But first, the twenty-two members of the Senate Judiciary Committee would have a chance to question her closely—to interrogate her—about every aspect of her life and career and her views on the law. And there were those who'd made up their minds beforehand that she should not get the job.

On that first day of the confirmation hearings, March 21, 2022, and for the next three days, Judge Jackson's immediate family and several longtime friends sat behind her in the Hart Senate Office Building, room 216. It was packed.

Outside the Capitol, huge crowds chanted and cheered for her, some holding signs that read "Confirm Jackson!" and "We Deserve a Justice for All!" People pasted signs on lampposts around the Senate office building with a picture of a smiling Judge Jackson raising her right hand, and a simple message in bold print: "Confirm KBJ."

More than a hundred Black law school students from seventeen schools across the country also gathered at the Capitol to show their support, hoping to see history made. The event was monumentally important to them, and like millions of other Americans, they had pinned their hopes on the possibility that a Black woman would finally make it to the US Supreme Court. They took time off from school and traveled thousands of miles from states across the country to be in Washington, DC.

Others organized watch parties in their hometowns.

Inside, congressional staffers, reporters, and Judge Jackson's friends and family crammed into the dozens of seats in the back. People spoke with excitement and buzzed around the judge as she worked her way through the room and shook hands with senators and well-wishers.

Judge Jackson stood out in the crowd, dressed in a quilted purple amethyst–colored jacket, a string of lustrous black Tahitian pearls around her neck, her signature hairstyle looking sharp and professional. She was wearing her trademark eyeglasses and her brilliant smile beamed. She was a bright spot—a beacon—in a sea of senators, most of them men dressed in conservative navy blue or gray suits.

Throughout the week, Judge Jackson stood out, dressed

each day in a vivid, jewel-toned jacket: bright ruby red on day two, sapphire blue on day three. Her outfits were formal and appropriate for the occasion, yet neither dull nor dowdy.

Even though the hearings were about her capabilities, experience, and thought processes—important intellectual aspects of her life—it was still essential that she project confidence to those in the room.

All her years of theater as both a performer and audience member had taught her that if she was going to be on center stage in the spotlight, her "costume" had better be right.

"No matter what happens, always act the part!" She understood the assignment for those next notable days.

Viewers across the country took note, and fashion commentators praised her clothing choices. In her job as a federal judge, she had to wear a long black robe over her clothes—the same as any other judge. But as a nominee, she had a chance to let her wardrobe tell a story about her and complement her personality, and it did.

Now the hearings were about to begin. When Judiciary Committee Chairman Senator Dick Durbin of Illinois, a Democrat, took his seat at the head of the room, everyone else sat too.

The confirmation hearings were designed to give the

senators on the judiciary a chance to evaluate Judge Jackson's temperament: whether she was quick to anger or if she remained calm. They wanted to know how she would react when she was challenged: Was she defensive or did she remain reasonable? They wanted to test her knowledge of the law and its impact on American life and history. And they wanted to find out if she was biased—that is, if she had already formed opinions about questions that might come up before her as a justice.

In the twenty-five days since President Biden had nominated her, she had spent dozens of hours filling out the answers to complex questions the senators were planning to ask her. Perhaps having learned from Lani Guinier's experience, she let her friends, associates, and colleagues past and present speak on the record about her as a person, scholar, judge, and friend. She had gathered every known record of speeches she'd made, papers she'd written, and actions she'd taken that had anything at all to do with her history and legal training. She even included an essay from one of her high school debate competitions—which she had won, of course—along with book reviews she'd written in college, and newspapers articles she'd been quoted in. In the end, she'd submitted more than 2,000 pages of documents about her life and her experience in the law.

In addition, the senators had access to the more than

500 decisions she had made as a lower court judge, including those that were over 100 pages long. All of it showed that her work and beliefs in the law consistently followed her guiding principles:

That the Constitution must work for all Americans, not just the wealthy and powerful; that judges must show no favoritism; and that the judiciary must live up to those words emblazoned above the entrance to the Supreme Court: Equal Justice Under Law.

If the senators wanted to know who Ketanji Brown Jackson was, both as a lawyer and a person, it was all there, on paper.

Most of the senators had already met her. She had visited ninety-five of the one hundred US senators in the past four weeks. The president had asked former senator Doug Jones of Alabama, a Democrat who was well-liked by most people at the Capitol, to introduce her to his former colleagues. Judge Jackson called him "my trusted sherpa"—her guide—and the two quickly became good friends.

Senator Jones said the judge's winning personality and friendliness encouraged friendliness in return, even from Republican senators who were not inclined to vote for a Democratic appointee. "The reception I got from colleagues on both sides of the aisle was very warm and receptive and that made her feel good," Jones said. "You walk in there and—they were going to give her a lot of respect. . . . The chemistry in those meetings worked out really good. All those meetings went really, really well."

Jones gave Judge Jackson a quick half hug just before she sat down, and before the difficult days of questioning unfolded. He took a seat behind her.

Senators were in the front of the room at tables covered in black tablecloths. Judge Jackson sat by herself at a long desk in the middle of the space, the center of attention. The only things on top of the desk were her notes, a bottle of hand sanitizer, a reusable water bottle, and her nameplate: Hon. Ketanji Brown Jackson.

Before her, more than a dozen newspaper and magazine photographers kneeled or sat on the floor, their still camera telephoto lenses trained on her face in close-ups. The whirs and clicks of the shutters filled the air as photographers captured each historic moment. Judge Jackson didn't seem to notice them.

The room grew instantly quiet after Senator Durbin gave his gavel a sharp rap on the table. The magnitude of the occasion seemed to strike the audience all at once, as a nervous silence blanketed the room.

There was one person, though, who showed no signs of anxiety or apprehension: Judge Jackson was the embodiment of calm within a suddenly tense scene.

This was, after all, the moment she had been working

toward her entire life. She was upbeat and confident, because she knew she was ready. In keeping with the habits that propelled her to the highest level of the legal profession, Judge Jackson had prepared for this and was ready for any question or allegation the senators might throw at her. And for some of them, especially the Republicans who disapproved of President Biden and his nominee, the hearings were also a chance to show their voters at home how tough they could be on her. But she had done her homework and already done the hard work to get there.

She gave her own opening statement, acknowledging her husband of twenty-five years, Dr. Patrick Jackson. "I have no doubt that, without him by my side from the very beginning of this incredible professional journey, none of this would have been possible." She let him know he was "the best husband, father, and friend I could ever imagine. Patrick, I love you." And she spread the love to her beautiful daughters: "Girls, I know it has not been easy as I have tried to navigate the challenges of juggling my career and motherhood. And I fully admit that I did not always get the balance right. But I hope that you have seen that with hard work, determination, and love, it can be done. . . . I love you so much." Her daughter Leila had a yellow sticky piece of paper on her chair with the words "You got this!" and three little balloons drawn on it.

The confirmation process has been going on for as long as there has been a US Supreme Court—273 years. It is often contentious because it's a lifetime appointment. Senators are especially determined to make sure the president makes the "right" choice with his or her pick, which, of course, depends on what the senators' real goals are for the country.

In the country's first one hundred years, the Senate rejected one-third of the nominees put up by presidents. But most were confirmed, and most of the questioning and debate over the nominees was done behind closed doors, out of the public eye. It wasn't until 1939 that the first public hearing for a Supreme Court nominee occurred. Later in that century, all nominees were questioned in public forums.

Even though Supreme Court justices aren't supposed to be either conservative or liberal, they are human, and each of them has opinions. But the most professional of them keep their personal beliefs out of their decisions. People who wanted a more fair and equitable America (including more liberal senators), who wanted to make sure that the Civil Rights Act would help the country make progress in overcoming racism and sexism, would want a justice who would be more likely to support those ideals. People opposed to that (including more conservative senators) wanted conservative justices who they hoped would support keeping most things in the country as they had been for 200 years.

That clash of philosophies made confirmation hearings even more politicized than in the past. By the time Judge

Jackson was nominated, there had only been 115 justices in the history of America. Thus, putting a new person on the court is rare, and a matter of great importance, because they're likely to be there, guiding the country's interpretation of the law, for decades. Many justices choose to stay on the court until well past the age most people retire, affecting how slowly or quickly change happens. If America is making progress toward equality, the Supreme Court is central to keeping that progress going, but because justices are on the court for life, it can take generations to achieve real advancements.

During Judge Jackson's hearings, senators who opposed her tried to get her to admit that she would let her feelings affect her decisions. She pledged to be impartial and not rule with "fear or favor."

"My North Star is the consideration of the proper role of a judge in our constitutional scheme," she told the senators. "And in my view, judges should not be speaking to political issues."

Judges, she said, "can't make law," and she promised to "stay in my lane."

Doug Jones continued to sit behind Judge Jackson every day of her hearings, and he said some of the senators gave her "trap" questions—trying to trick her into saying something that they could claim would disqualify her from the bench. They wanted her to comment on specific cases and issues to show she was biased. But she was unflappable. Neutrality was her mantra.

Senator Durbin told her the second day of the confirmation process is referred to "affectionately by a term of medieval justice, known as the 'trial by ordeal.'" He was warning her it was going to be a difficult and challenging week, and he was right. Before it was over, a handful of Republican senators had accused Judge Jackson of being "soft on crime" and not sentencing criminals, particularly those who took advantage of and harmed children, to long sentences. Many of those statements were proven to be false—in fact, the sentences she had passed down in those types of cases were right in line with the majority issued in the country (in two out of every three cases, federal judges issued sentences below those provided in the guidelines). But that didn't stop the opposing senators, including one from Missouri who'd voted to confirm circuit court appointments of other judges with similar records, from repeating their distortions of the facts on social media.

Judge Jackson kept her cool, even when some senators repeatedly interrupted or talked over her while she tried to answer their questions. Despite the grueling process, Senator Durbin said it was "a proud day for America." He noted that when the Supreme Court met for the first time in 1790, there were nearly 700,000 enslaved people in the newly formed United States of America. They had no right to citizenship, no right to vote. Women couldn't vote either. "There was no equal justice under the law for a majority of people living in America," Durbin said. "In its more than 230 years, the Supreme Court has had 115 Justices; 108 have been white men. . . . Not a single Justice has been a Black woman. You, Judge Jackson, can be the first."

Judge Jackson listened carefully. She was aware of the history of the nomination and the confirmation hearings. Durbin went on. "It's not easy being the first. Often, you have to be the best, and in some ways the bravest. Many are not prepared to face that kind of heat, that kind of scrutiny, that ordeal in the glare of the national spotlight," he said. "But your presence here today, your willingness to brave this process, will give inspiration to millions of Americans who see themselves in you."

Judge Jackson recognized that special honor she had been given. "It's not necessarily easy to be the first, but it's an opportunity to show other people what's possible," she said.

Over those four days, Judge Jackson sat in room 216, answering questions for nearly thirty hours. She pledged time and again to be impartial and to work with the other eight justices on the court if she won the job. At several points during questioning from Republican senators, the mood in the room was tense, tinged with hostility. One senator walked out of the room in frustration. A few senators mentioned critical race theory—a concept taught in law schools that the country's laws were built on white "supremacy"—and demanded to know if she was going to use it in her rulings, implying she would be a justice who would rule unfairly against whites. Senator Durbin banged his gavel over and over each time a line of questioning had instead turned to "badgering" the judge, or the senator in question refused to stop talking. Judge Jackson didn't raise her voice, but she did attempt several times to complete her answers even as an unfriendly senator talked over her.

There were also many easier moments, including some that brought laughter, and some that brought the judge and others to tears. Senator Alex Padilla of California told her about schoolchildren he had met the previous week who were inspired by her nomination. He acknowledged how difficult the confirmation hearings had been at times.

"For the last three days of this hearing your experiences and qualifications have been called into question by some, despite your clear, lengthy record of talent, achievement and accomplishment," he said. Senator Padilla is a Latino American, and he said that, like Judge Jackson, he too had had a high school teacher who discouraged him from applying to an Ivy League college because of his background as the child of migrant laborers. "What would you say, Judge Jackson, to all those young Americans, the most diverse generation in our nation's history, what would you say to some of them who may doubt that they can one day achieve the same great heights that you have?"

Judge Jackson dabbed her eyes, moved by the sincere question from Padilla and his sharing of the obstacles he also faced growing up. "I hope to inspire people to try to follow this path because I love this country. Because I love the law. Because I think it is important that we all invest in our future. And the young people are the future, and so I want them to know that they can do and be anything," she said. She then went on to discuss the time when she was a freshman at college, feeling down in the dumps, and a Black woman read her expression and told her to "persevere." She wanted to share that message with all children. "I would tell them to persevere."

Senator Cory Booker prompted several other such moments. He, a Black Democrat from New Jersey, instead of asking Judge Jackson questions, used his time to offer her support and praise, allowing her those minutes to rest, recover, and regroup after the verbal assaults and attacks she'd endured that day. He told her she had sat, steadfast and strong, through the, at times, "disappoint[ing]" and bitter hearing with "grit and grace." He even noted that a conservative-leaning periodical, the *National Review*, disagreed with those senators who were questioning Judge Jackson's sentencing record on certain child predators, calling their distortion of her record as "meritless to the point of demagoguery" (using people's prejudices against others to win an argument rather than fact-based, rational argument). He countered the claims that Judge Jackson was not "tough on crime" by bringing up the fact that she'd been endorsed by the Fraternal Order of Police, "the largest organization of rank-and-file police officers." She had been endorsed by the largest organization of police chiefs. And he brought up that she had "uncles that are officers. You got a brother, not just an officer, who went to serve [in the armed forces] after 9/11!" Her family was in no way soft on terrorists, he stressed.

Senator Booker mentioned that when Constance Baker Motley, one of Judge Jackson's heroes, was being confirmed to the southern district of New York judgeship, they tried to stop her with outrageous and untrue accusations of being a communist. It was yet another way in which Judge Jackson was following in her footsteps. He told her she had nothing left to prove and quoted the Holy Bible: "Let the work I've done speak for me."

He brought up how much she admired her parents—her father for going into law and her mother for holding down the family in the meantime. How she'd had to make difficult choices in her career in order to balance it with motherhood. He mentioned how the Senate confirmed her to other courts already with bipartisan support (both Republicans and Democrats had voted for her). "Your family speaks to service, service, service," he said. They gave back to their communities and the country, over and over again. Let the work I've done speak for me, indeed.

What Senator Booker was doing was acknowledging the pent-up frustration Judge Jackson might be feeling, and he reminded everyone within earshot and anyone across the globe who was watching and listening that Judge Jackson hadn't gotten as far as she had in life because she skipped steps, or due to quotas, or because people made exceptions for her or went easier on her. She worked as hard as possible; she fought: "You got here how every Black woman in America who's gotten anywhere has done—by being, like Ginger Rogers said, 'I did everything Fred Astaire did, but backwards in heels.'" (Fred Astaire was regarded as one of the best ballroom dancers of all time, and his dance partner, Ginger Rogers, wanted people to know she danced just as well and elegantly, but with harder conditions attached to her exceptional performances.)

He told her how proud and joyous he was on that day, and that nothing anyone else could say, no accusation levied by another senator, was going to dampen that. "Nobody's going to steal [my] joy [today]." He explained why he was getting emotional—that, yes, the judge was more than her race and gender, but that when he looked at her, he saw what her confirmation means to Black people and the hope it inspires in Black women everywhere. His mother. His cousin who insisted on coming to the hearing and sitting behind Judge Jackson and having her back. "I see my ancestors, and yours." He told her, "You have earned this spot. You are worthy. You are a great American."

He pointed out that it was relatively recently that the Supreme Court had made a decision that prohibited states from outlawing marriage between people of two different races: *Loving v. Virginia*. Senator Booker noted how, despite America's historically poor treatment of Black Americans, Black people still loved the country and the promise that it has. People like Constance Baker Motley, Harriet Tubman, Judge Jackson's own parents. "They didn't stop loving this country, even though this country didn't love them back."

He paraphrased the lauded poet Langston Hughes, "O, let America be America again—/ The land that never has been yet—/ But yet must be—the land where *every*one is free . . . O, yes, / I say it plain, / America never was America to me, / But [yet] I swear this oath—/ America will be!"

America has, at various times, treated immigrants badly. The Irish were discriminated against and considered dirty, diseased, poor, prone to criminality, and disliked for being Catholic. Senator Booker recounted how people would put up signs saying "No Irish or dogs need apply," and yet they loved the country and its promise of freedom. "Chinese Americans, first forced into near slave labor, building our railroads, connecting our country, saw the ugliest of America," but they stayed and built their homes here, and they too were going to get the country to love them back and "make this nation live up to its promise and hope." He brought up the struggles of LGBTQ+ people, women, including the Black women Katherine Johnson, Dorothy Vaughan, and Mary Jackson, who worked in astrophysics, computing, and engineering for NASA and whose calculations and flight test analyses were integral in the United States landing on the moon, yet who dealt with discrimination and hostility the whole way.

But he told her, "Don't worry, my sister. . . . God has got you." He discussed how Harriet Tubman, who'd escaped from slavery in Maryland to freedom in Philadelphia, Pennsylvania, returned time and time again to the South to free others, guided by the North Star. "She kept looking up." He told Judge Jackson, "That star—it was a harbinger of hope." And that "Today, you're my star. You are my harbinger of hope," Senator Booker said, his voice breaking with emotion. Judge Jackson wiped tears from her eyes as he spoke passionately about what he believed her nomination meant to the country.

"This country is getting better and better and better," Booker said. "When that final vote happens, and you ascend onto the . . . highest court in the land, I'm gonna rejoice. And I'm gonna tell you right now, the greatest country in the world, the United States of America, will be better because of you."

The fourth and last day of the confirmation hearings was the easiest. There were no questions, just testimonials from supporters, including members of the American Bar Association. That organization had sought the opinions of more than 250 judges, attorneys, and professors who had encountered Judge Jackson and described her using the words "brilliant," "thoughtful," "fair," "thorough," and "eminently qualified."

Frederick L. Thomas, the president of the National Organization of Black Law Enforcement Officers, said his group fully supported Judge Jackson. Thomas pointed out that two of her uncles, along with her brother, Ketajh, had all served as police officers, and that gave her a unique perspective. "It is our opinion that her direct familiarity with the complexities, challenges, and opportunities within law enforcement provides a perspective on criminal justice issues that can be an asset to the Supreme Court," Thomas said. He called her "a stellar nominee."

Richard Rosenthal, now a Miami attorney, also spoke: "From the very first day I met Ketanji, I knew she was special. In my entire life, I have never met anyone like her," he said about the woman he had known for almost forty years. "Ketanji's incandescent brilliance was obvious to all of us from day one. But even more importantly, she has always been one of the kindest, warmest, most humble, and down-to-earth people I've ever met. All this, while still possessing boundless charisma, drive, maturity, and grace. For all of these remarkable characteristics to somehow reside in the same one person—well, I suppose you can understand why everyone who knows Ketanji believed she was destined for greatness."

Next came the waiting—it was ten days before the judiciary committee voted on whether to advance Judge Jackson's nomination to the full Senate. The committee vote was a tie—eleven yes, eleven no, along party lines. With a Democrat, the vice president, leading the Senate, despite the tie vote, her nomination was sent to the full Senate for a final vote on April 4, 2022.

On that bright and cool April morning in Washington, DC, as people across America tuned in again to see if Judge Jackson had won enough votes from the full Senate to become a Supreme Court justice, President Biden, Judge Jackson, and all her supporters still felt confident, but not certain of the outcome.

Schoolchildren from around the country were watching again, with several schools pausing class so they could tune in to at least part of the process. Teachers and principals knew this was a chance to see history in action as the votes were cast.

Judge Jackson and the president watched the vote on

a TV in the White House. They held hands while they waited, smiling but nervous. It had been a tough and grueling battle, and now they would know the result.

Vice President Kamala Harris presided over the Senate the day of the vote. If it turned out to be a 50–50 tie, she, as the leader of the Senate, would cast the tiebreaking vote for Judge Jackson. But Harris, Biden, and Judge Jackson's supporters hoped it wouldn't come to that—they were hoping that at least a few Republicans would support her.

While she was waiting for the votes to come in, VP Harris, seated at the front of the room, wrote a note to her goddaughter. "I told her that I felt such a deep sense of pride and joy about what this moment means for our nation and for her future," Harris said. She told the only two Black senators, Pastor Raphael Warnock from Georgia and Cory Booker, to pen something to a young Black girl in their lives too. Senator Warnock wrote to his daughter: "Dear Chloé, Today, we confirmed Ketanji Brown Jackson to the United States Supreme Court. In our nation's history, she is the first Supreme Court Justice who looks like you—with hair like yours."

When the final vote came in, the president, Judge Jackson, and all her supporters got their wish: it was split 53–47, with three Republicans joining all fifty Democrats in backing her nomination.

Democrats in the chamber broke into loud and sustained

applause; newly confirmed Supreme Court associate justice Ketanji Brown Jackson and the president shared a hug at the White House, and people across the country celebrated the historic moment.

The next day on the lawn of the White House, the president and the new justice spoke about the happy news. President Biden said it was the kind of day where we "turn to our children and grandchildren and say, 'I was there.' . . . This is one of those moments. . . .

"This is not only a sunny day. I mean this from the bottom of my heart: this is going to let so much . . . sun shine on so many young women, so many young Black women, so many minorities," he said. "We're going to look back and see this as a moment of real change in American history."

People across the nation agreed.

"It is exciting to see Judge Ketanji Brown Jackson join the highest court in our land. It is important for my daughters, twenty-nine and nineteen, to see themselves in Judge Brown Jackson as a representation of what they can become, with hard work and dedication," Pamela Swift, a mom in California, told the *Today* show. "I am happy for my girls and I am happy for our country."

"Representation matters in our community. It helps not only with legal maneuverings and fair representation, but for the self-esteem and career trajectories of children of color as well. Seeing people in positions [of power] shifts career ambitions," said Rhonda Mattox of Arkansas. "Being represented on the highest court in the land is not just about the law—it's about who is watching, too. That representation helps to break those proverbial glass ceilings in our minds and our ambitions. It also increases the chances that we will be more fairly represented in the greatest court in the land."

Even Oprah Winfrey took note. "All through the confirmation hearings—especially when I saw young Leila Jackson looking at her mom with such pride—I found myself thinking about parents. Particularly parents of Black children, particularly parents of Black girls—how, for them, Ketanji Brown Jackson is reason to celebrate. A thrilling new example—new living proof—of what is possible. A new chance to turn to their child and say, 'You are possible,'" Oprah wrote. "And congratulations to Johnny and Ellery Brown: Your daughter did good."

With President Biden on one side and Vice President Kamala Harris on the other, Justice Jackson spoke at the lectern and mentioned all the letters and cards she'd received from children, especially girls, which she found to be both touching and powerful. And she mentioned her daughters.

"To my daughters, Talia and Leila, I bet you never thought you'd get to skip school to come to the White House. This is all pretty exciting for me as well, but nothing has brought me greater joy than being your mother. I love you very much."

She thanked her husband, Patrick, "for everything you've done for me over these past twenty-five years of our marriage. You've done everything to support and encourage me. And it is you who've made this moment possible. . . . I don't know that I believed you when you said that I could do this, but now I do."

She thanked her extended family and acknowledged the impact colleagues, law clerks, judges, bosses, Justice Breyer, friends, White House staff, Senator Doug Jones, and many others had on her achievement. And she got a little serious too:

"They also tell me that I'm a role model, which I take both as an opportunity and as a huge responsibility. I am feeling up to the task, primarily because I know that I am not alone. I am standing on the shoulders of my own role models, generations of Americans who never had anything close to this kind of opportunity but who got up every day and went to work believing in the promise of America, showing others through their determination and, yes, their perseverance that good—good things can be done in this great country—from my grandparents on both sides who had only a grade-school education but instilled in my parents the importance of learning, to my parents who went to racially segregated schools growing up and were the first in their families to have the chance to go to college.

"I am also ever buoyed by the leadership of generations past who helped to light the way: Dr. Martin Luther King, Jr., Justice Thurgood Marshall, and my personal heroine, Judge Constance Baker Motley."

The justice also recognized that the hard work that others put in to fight segregation—"The marches, the boycotts, the sit-ins, the arrests"—had made her path much easier than the one her parents had to take. She marveled at the progress that had been made in America in the twenty-five years between her parents' birth and her own.

"Think about that for a moment: in 1963, Dr. Martin Luther King, Jr., could only dream of a day when 'the sons of former slaves and the sons of former slave owners would be able to sit down together at the table of brotherhood,'" Justice Jackson remarked. "And less than a decade later, that was the world that I inhabited. Indeed, so much changed in such a short period of time, that by the time I was born, Black couples in the nation's capital must have felt invincible!"

Ellery and Johnny Brown were the bridge for Justice Jackson between the harsh, segregated past that her grandparents endured, and her path to a seat on the highest court in the land. She acknowledges them every time she's asked to speak about her success.

The justice called her confirmation "an honor of a lifetime" to be selected to serve on the US Supreme Court. "To be sure, I have worked hard to get to this point in my career, and I have now achieved something far beyond anything my grandparents could have possibly ever imagined," she said. "But no one does this on their own. The path was cleared for me so that I might rise to this occasion."

As she choked up, she continued, "And in the poetic words of Dr. Maya Angelou, I do so now, while 'bringing the gifts my ancestors gave . . .'" She was interrupted by rapturous applause, so she paused and then continued, "'I am the dream and the hope of the slave.' . . . We have come a long way to perfecting our union."

XVI
DELTA

THE DELTA SIGMA THETA SORORITY (ΔΣΘ, a Black Greek letter organization) was founded by twenty-two Black women at the HBCU Howard University on January 13, 1913, in Washington, DC. As with most American institutions, secret societies were segregated then, with fraternities only allowing white men to join. Later, when all-female fraternities (subsequently called sororities) began popping up, they too forbade nonwhite individuals from membership.

So Black college students created their own separate secret societies, beginning with the all-male Alpha Phi Alpha Fraternity (AΦA) at Cornell University in New York in 1906 and the all-female Alpha Kappa Alpha Sorority (AKA) in 1908 (also at Howard). By the time the Deltas incorporated, Black societies were growing in popularity and importance, creating safe spaces for people of color to network, socialize, celebrate academic achievements and scholarships, and focus their outside activities on activism, social justice, and the pursuits of human and equal rights. In fact, two months later, their first public service act was to participate in the 1913 Suffrage Parade in Washington, DC, in which women took to the streets to demand the United States government give them the right to vote.

On July 20, 2023, at DST's Fifty-Sixth National Convention held in Indianapolis, Indiana, with over 20,000 members in attendance both in person and by way of video conferencing, Vice President Kamala Harris—the first Black, Asian, and female person to hold that office, and a member of the Alpha Kappa Alpha "Divine Nine" sorority—helped them celebrate the 110th anniversary of their founding, by speaking to a room of 7,000 sorors. She highlighted the sorority's extraordinary accomplishments in the advancement of women's and Black people's rights in America, including the time when Deltas, alongside civil rights icons Roy Wilkins, future congressman John Lewis, and Dr. Martin Luther King, Jr., marched on Washington for jobs and freedom in 1963. The marchers were demanding the government grant people of color fair wages, economic justice, voting rights, equal access to quality educations, civil rights protections, as well as the end to segregation. It was here that Dr. King delivered his enduring, uplifting, and incomparable "I Have a Dream" speech.

VP Harris made mention of how Deltas were also on the front lines in 2020 when, in the middle of the coronavirus pandemic, they organized drives to fight voter suppression (that's when local, state, and/or federal governments or individuals attempt to keep people of color from voting) and got people to the polls for the presidential election— which happened to be the one in which VP Harris, partially through their efforts, was elected to office.

She spoke about how she and President Joe Biden had expanded access to healthcare through Medicaid for expectant mothers, which would save the lives of women of color, since they are three times more likely to die from complications of childbirth than white women. Their administration had also been working with civil rights leaders, law enforcement officials, and leaders of the DST sorority, among others, to advance reforms that would change the way police officers and law enforcement treated Black people. They are 3.23 times more likely to die/be killed during encounters with the police than white people, so it is important for police to find ways to build public trust and ensure their safety.

VP Harris noted that "hard-won freedoms are under attack," such as the right to vote, which women and people of color had fought so hard to win, as well as affirmative action, which had provided equal access to education and jobs to those same groups. On June 25, 2013, in another

5–4 split decision, the Supreme Court took all the teeth out of the 1965 Voting Rights Act in its *Shelby County v. Holder* decision, with the majority opinion essentially declaring racial discrimination a thing of the past, despite all the evidence of discrimination still playing out in every aspect of American life right before the justices' eyes.

Similarly, on June 29, 2023, with an even more lopsided Supreme Court, which leaned toward stripping individuals of freedoms rather than expanding them, in a 6–3 decision (with all three dissenters being women), the case of *Students for Fair Admissions, Inc. v. President and Fellows of Harvard College* (and *Students for Fair Admissions, Inc. v. University of North Carolina*) destroyed affirmative action.

Affirmative action had ensured that qualified students who were female and/or minorities would be able to have those aspects of their identities considered in college admissions. It has benefited white women above all other groups, with Asians, immigrants, and other races next, and Latino and Black Americans, who unsurprisingly bore the brunt of the criticisms and anger against it, coming in last. It benefited people with disabilities and veterans as well. None of the aforementioned groups would have made the gains they have in American society were it not for the sacrifices and battles fought and won by Black people and their allies (especially Jews) during the civil rights era. But that didn't prevent people from using racism against Black people to turn the very people affirmative action and civil rights helped most against the policy, against their own best interests.

In actuality, affirmative action kept people from discriminating against others based on race or sex by ensuring companies and colleges could build staff and/or student bodies made up of diverse peoples, fostering atmospheres of inclusion, understanding, and access. On March 6, 1961, President John F. Kennedy had issued Executive Order 10925, which put the idea of affirmative action into practice—ensuring job and, by extension, college applicants be employed and admitted to schools without their race, creed, color, or national origin being used to exclude them. After Kennedy was assassinated on November 22, 1963, his vice president Lyndon Johnson took office and issued Executive Order 11246 on September 24, 1965, which prohibited employment discrimination based on race, color, religion, or national origin for federal contracts and subcontracts. He amended the order to add sex to the list in 1967.

That meant Justice Jackson, in the 1980s, had every belief that if she worked hard, got good grades, and did interesting things outside school, colleges would want to admit her and her race wouldn't be used against her—it could actually be used toward her benefit. Had this not been the law of the land in the late 1980s, had there been no affirmative action, it could have kept Justice Jackson from being admitted to Harvard, because no one would need to make sure women and minorities had access to equal education (which the country had actively tried to prevent prior to presidents Kennedy's and Johnson's orders). Admission to colleges are not and have never been based solely on one's academic or extracurricular achievements, so her stellar grades would not have necessarily meant she'd have been admitted. Some people are granted admission because their parents donate or have money and influence, or because they are athletes and can bring the school recognition (and by extension, money), or because their parents work for or attended the school (legacies). In essence, people of color and women of all backgrounds would not have been in the "room where it happen[ed]." It could also have deterred the justice from even applying to Harvard, since the people in power would have had no reason to include people who didn't look or think like them. And she, being as smart and practical as she is, would have known this. Then again, maybe she would have shown them regardless.

On top of these things, Vice President Harris explained that there were people in America who didn't want children to read books that told uncomfortable truths about real life, so instead they would get school districts to enact book bans and remove books from their libraries. Similarly, people would try to get "revisionist" history taught in schools. For instance, the day before this convention, in the state of Florida, public schools were mandated to instruct middle schoolers that some enslaved people in America "benefited" from slavery. Facts and the truth were being pushed further to the side in favor of opinions that helped people in power feel less guilty or culpable for prior bad acts. It's important to remember that, just like if you buy a company, when you come to live in the United States, you get to enjoy all its assets and benefits, but you also become responsible for all its debts. And there is a significant ongoing cost that began with slavery that has yet to be repaid.

The vice president made special mention of one particular person in the room full of women clad mostly in crimson red: "For far too long, our justice system has not fully reflected the diversity of our nation. So when we took office, President Joe Biden and I have appointed more Black women to the federal appellate courts than any other administration in history combined . . . including, of course . . ." at which point she and the audience laughed and clapped, "the first Black woman to ever sit on the highest court of our land, and your newest member . . . Justice Ketanji Brown Jackson!" After the enthusiastic applause died down some, VP Harris had one more thing to add about the historic rise of Justice Jackson to the nation's highest court: "It's a good day."

Justice Ketanji Brown Jackson had been offered and accepted honorary membership into this esteemed organization, and this moment was a small slice of her induction ceremony.

The vice president finished up by calling on the women at that convention to fight: "fueled by the love of our children. Let us fight, fueled by the love of our country. And let us fight with the knowledge and faith that when we fight, we win."

Justice Jackson sat among the other honorees, all dressed in creamy white dresses and matching fringe scarves, and took pictures. The new honorees then crossed their arms in front of them and put their hands up against those of the person next to them, making triangle shapes that symbolize the uppercase fourth letter of the Greek alphabet: Delta.

There had been no sorority for women at Harvard-Radcliffe College while Justice Jackson was an undergrad, so she could not have joined one (whether for Black members or otherwise) if she'd wanted to. That is, unless she did so through a nearby chapter at MIT, the Massachusetts Institute of Technology. With concerns of colorism floating around campus in regard to at least one of the Black sororities, as well as having a full academic plate and interests elsewhere, she never ended up pledging. Meanwhile, the fraternities at Harvard, better known as "finals clubs," expressly excluded women from membership—one more example of inequality and unequal access perpetuated by many institutions, not just colleges, nationwide. It was just another means of excluding people and making them feel like they didn't belong, as Justice Jackson had felt early on while there.

As a matter of fact, the first sorority at Harvard was founded a year after Justice Jackson graduated: a division of Kappa Alpha Theta, which had existed and opened chapters at other universities after its founding (for only white members) in 1870. Harvard's chapter rebranded in 2018, due to the university's changing policies against single-gender (all-male or all-female) social organizations, calling itself Theta Zeta Xi and cutting its ties from its mother sorority. In order to keep its doors open, the sorority had chosen to go gender-neutral, meaning any Harvard student of any gender could join. But it had to rebrand once again, this time as Themis Asteri, in order to please the university and disassociate further from the Greek system. With lawsuits and protests from several social clubs spreading across the university, the institution relaxed its policies in 2020 and Zeta Xi was reinstalled on September 11, 2022.

The other honorees at the conventions were also an impressive bunch of Black women: president of television network MSNBC Rashida Jones; United States under secretary of state for arms control and international security Bonnie D. Jenkins; chairman and chief executive officer (CEO) of Warner Bros. (pronounced "Brothers") Television Studios Channing Dungey; WNBA basketball legend and Olympic gold medalist Tamika Catchings; former CEO and chairman of television network BET Debra Lee; and entrepreneur and businesswoman Phyllis Newhouse. Sonia

Issa, president of the Kappa Lambda chapter of the Deltas at Syracuse, said of them, "They are a cohort [a group of people with similar characteristics] of 'firsts' and 'onlys'; trailblazers in their respective fields, and truly represent the organization's mission of providing service to Black people . . . they continue to carry the organization in the direction of breaking barriers and redefining the Black existence in America."

Of the honor, Justice Jackson wrote in a statement to CNN: "Because Delta Sigma Theta only extends Honorary Membership to 'women who have made significant contributions to society while excelling in their chosen fields,' it is a tremendous honor to have been so recognized. I am thrilled and humbled to be among this year's extraordinary group of inductees."

The organization of over 350,000 members, one of the largest sororities in the United States, is extremely proud to call Justice Jackson a member, and let her know that she too belongs. Oo-oop!

XVII

ON THE BENCH

IT WAS HER FIRST DAY on the SCOTUS bench and Justice Jackson was ready for it.

In the six months since she'd made history by becoming the first Black, female associate justice of the Supreme Court of the United States, her life had been a whirlwind.

Oprah Winfrey had sent a $1,200 floral arrangement to congratulate her. She did a photo shoot for *Vogue* magazine wearing elegant designer clothes and posing at the Lincoln Memorial in Washington, DC.

She'd seen her image and her words appear on dozens of products being sold across the world, from T-shirts—"Notorious KBJ" read one; "Persevere" read another—to coffee mugs, socks, pillows, even a special-edition Ketanji Brown Jackson bobblehead.

She'd opened the bins full of letters and cards sent to

her from the American people—including hundreds of children, who had written to let her know she was an inspiration to them.

She moved all her work belongings from her old office at the US Court of Appeals for the District of Columbia Circuit to her new space within the marble-columned Supreme Court Building.

Fellow justice Amy Coney Barrett threw her a welcome-to-the-court party. Barrett knew that Justice Jackson was a huge fan of the musical *Hamilton*, so she hired a performer to sing songs from the Broadway hit during the party.

The justice had learned the lay of the land: where her office was, where her clerks would work, which shelves she would use for her collection of statute books and case law from 232 years of American jurisprudence, books that had traveled with her through her "vagabond years" and beyond.

She'd been in the Supreme Court Building at 1 First Street NE before, during the year she clerked for Stephen Breyer, whom she was replacing. But being a clerk versus being the boss—that was a big difference.

She was given the same assignment all newbie justices at the court are given: She was put in charge of the court's cafeteria committee.

On September 30, 2022, three days before the court began its fall session, Justice Jackson had her formal investiture ceremony, meaning she was officially welcomed to the Supreme Court. She had already been working in her office for several weeks. President Biden and Vice President Kamala Harris attended, and so did her parents, her brother, her husband and their daughters, and dozens of other people who wanted to—yet again—witness Justice Jackson make history.

Her eight new colleagues attended as well, and they all donned their black robes and posed for pictures with her.

That ceremony was different from the ceremony in June when she took the formal oath of office. And it was different from the ceremony on the White House lawn in April, when the country celebrated her confirmation to the Supreme Court.

Justice Jackson even sat in "the historic John Marshall Bench Chair," a mahogany chair that was used by one of the country's earliest justices, Chief Justice John Marshall, from 1819 to 1835. Marshall is often referred to as "The Great Chief Justice," because he was one of the first, and longest-serving, chief justices on the bench. His decisions helped shape how the Constitution was understood in the country at its founding.

He was also a slaveholder and a slave trader. Law schools that had been named for him began rethinking that in recent years. Marshall is regarded as a brilliant jurist, but he also frequently made decisions that perpetuated slavery, and for many, that disqualified him from being honored. That's the kind of tradition Justice Jackson was about to confront.

At a speech afterward, she said she was "humbled by the fanfare" and congratulations from people across the country.

"The people who approach, and especially the young people, they are seeing themselves portrayed in me, in my experience, and they are finally believing that anything is possible in this great country," she said. She said she'd met with people from "all walks of life" who not only congratulated her, but also told her how much hope they now had for the country because of her history-making appointment.

"I can see it in their eyes," she said. "They say this: 'This is what we can accomplish if we put our minds to it.' . . . They're saying to me, in essence, 'You go, girl! We see you, and we are with you.'"

With those thoughts to brace her, Justice Jackson took her seat on the bench on October 3, 2022.

Her chair was the farthest to the left of Chief Justice John Roberts. That's the seat for the most junior of the justices. She'd come prepared—as always—with her notes, and legal analyses, and list of questions close at hand for the two arguments the court would hear that day.

When the justices were seated and the marshal of the

United States Supreme Court called out the traditional "Oyez! Oyez! Oyez!" to call the court to order, Justice Jackson knew: It was showtime.

Her meticulous preparation, her love of the law and of the country, her girlhood dreams, and even her theater training—they all came down to this moment and she rose to it, without missing a beat.

For the next two days, and over the coming weeks, Justice Jackson jumped right into the work, looking and sounding not like a newcomer but like an experienced jurist who was not intimidated by her surroundings or by stuffy, unwritten court rules that in the past had discouraged brand-new justices from speaking up much in their first days. She was fearless, not hesitating to disagree with older justices on the court. It sometimes took other judges years before they would speak their minds independently, but not this justice.

During oral arguments, where both sides in a lawsuit present their case, Justice Jackson spoke far more than the other justices: nearly 1,350 words per argument, according to one count.

"She came to play," said one law professor, who, like many others, was impressed with her debut on the court. Justice Jackson asked so many questions on the first day and posited so many legal theories that the arguments stretched past the allotted time. chief justice John Roberts at one point late in the day scribbled a note to Justice

Jackson, and it was handed down by other justices until it reached her. Nobody except she and the chief justice knows what the note said, but she was slightly less inclined to talk the rest of the afternoon.

That reticence lasted only for one day. By day two, she was back to asking incisive questions, asking for clarifications, and giving context and background to the cases at hand. Her fellow justices often followed up on her questions and used her logic to form their own arguments.

She was already having an impact, without even having voted on her first case on the court.

Evan Milligan had a front-row seat to the action. He was in the courtroom on October 4, 2022, Justice Jackson's second day on the bench, when the justices heard a case that he was deeply and passionately involved in. *Allen v. Milligan* was that lawsuit out of Alabama that was mentioned earlier, which centered on voting rights and whether the conservative Republicans in charge of state politics had come up with an illegal voting map that disfavored Black voters.

Evan was the "Milligan" for whom the case was named. As a longtime advocate for voting rights in his home state, and the executive director of the civic engagement group Alabama Forward, he had sued the leaders of Alabama in an effort to make the voting maps more fair.

He made it a point to be present at the Supreme Court

when his case was heard, although he wasn't optimistic. Then he heard Justice Jackson speak.

She closely questioned the attorney representing the state of Alabama, asking him about the theory put forth by conservative justices and others that the Constitution is "color-blind," and that race shouldn't enter into decisions in subjects like voting rights.

What Milligan heard from Justice Jackson inspired him, he said, and gave him hope that despite the ongoing efforts to make voting more difficult for many people, things might be changing with a powerful woman who not only knew the history of Jim Crow, but whose family had lived it.

She took a legal theory favored by conservatives—that the interpretation of the Constitution should rely on what the men who wrote it said—and used it to prove her point.

She brought up what many scholars call the "second founding" of the United States. That was the time after the Civil War when President Abraham Lincoln succeeded in getting the Thirteenth, Fourteenth, and Fifteenth Amendments passed in Congress. Those amendments to the Constitution abolished slavery, guaranteed all persons due process and equal protection under the law, and allowed Black men who were citizens to vote.

For many, those amendments corrected some of what was left out of the original US Constitution that had been adopted eighty-seven years earlier, or "fourscore and seven years ago," as Lincoln put it in his Gettysburg Address. The original Constitution never mentioned slavery; the amendments passed by Lincoln did, and they outlawed it.

Justice Jackson dug back into history to make her argument.

"I don't think that the historical record establishes that the Founders believed that race neutrality or race blindness was required, right? They drafted the Civil Rights Act of 1866, which specifically stated that citizens would have the same civil rights as enjoyed by white citizens. That's the point of that Act, to make sure that the other citizens, the Black citizens, would have the same as the white citizens. So they recognized that there was unequal treatment, that people, based on their race, were being treated unequally," she said to the Alabama attorney.

"She was confident, and she was idealistic about the law," Milligan said. "She really seemed to believe in the power of her position, and the historical importance of what was being said that day. Even though the numbers weren't on her side, she didn't shrink from that."

Most people watching the case assumed that the conservative supermajority on the court—six conservative justices—would vote against Milligan and allow Alabama to use the maps that diluted the voting power of Black citizens.

But the opposite happened. The court voted for Milligan

in a win that many say saved the historic Voting Rights Act of 1965.

"Just on a personal level, so many of the people I talk to, they all needed that shot of hope," Milligan said about the win that Justice Jackson helped shepherd through.

He said his own young children, including his six-year-old daughter, know Justice Ketanji Brown Jackson's name and the hope people have for her. "She's an inspiration."

The voting rights victory, though, was one of the few decisions on which Justice Jackson was on the winning side in her first two terms.

In another consequential case, the loss came with a surprising bitter response from the other Black justice— Clarence Thomas.

Justice Thomas was confirmed to the bench in 1991. Like Justice Jackson, he grew up in the American South, and he saw firsthand the constraints and violence Black people suffered in order to do ordinary things, like go to school, or vote, or live in safe housing. And like Justice Jackson, Justice Thomas says that race matters, and that America has yet to live up to its principles "that all men are created equal, are equal citizens, and must be treated equally before the law."

But the lessons he draws from his life experience are very different from those Justice Jackson sees.

Thomas is a rock-solid conservative, who says that many of the laws designed to overcome the effects of racism are themselves racist, because they treat Black and white people differently. The Constitution, he says, "is color-blind."

Justice Thomas was from rural Georgia, raised during the height of the Jim Crow era. His background was one of deprivation and hardship. Yet against those odds, he rose to graduate from Yale Law School through the benefits of affirmative action, and later became a Supreme Court justice. But he has become one of the nation's harshest critics of the policy.

The differences between them puzzled her. She had met him years earlier at a judicial luncheon. "I just sat there the whole time thinking: 'I don't understand you. You sound like my parents. You sound like the people I grew up with,'" she said about their meeting. "But the lessons he tended to draw from the experiences of the segregated South seemed to be different from those of everybody I know."

The stark differences between Justices Jackson and Thomas were on full display when the Supreme Court decided two college admissions affirmative action cases in 2023. The first involved Harvard, and Justice Jackson recused, or removed, herself from that case because she served on the university's Board of Overseers.

The second involved the University of North Carolina. The court ruled against the universities in both cases, saying they could no longer use race as a factor in choosing which students to admit. The vote was 6–3, with the conservative supermajority deciding the case over what is called "the liberal wing," which includes Justice Jackson.

The historic decision dismayed those who seek to level the playing field for historically marginalized students to gain entry to higher education.

When the decision was read in court by Chief Justice Roberts, Justice Thomas used the occasion to read his concurrence—or agreement—with the decision. In it, he called out Justice Jackson several times by name, for "articulating her black and white world (literally)" and ignoring other minorities.

Justice Jackson, in turn, wrote a stinging dissent to the ruling, explaining why she disagreed with it.

"Gulf-sized race-based gaps exist with respect to the health, wealth, and well-being of American citizens," she wrote. "They were created in the distant past, but have indisputably been passed down to the present day through generations. Every moment these gaps persist is a moment in which this great country falls short of actualizing one of its foundational principles—the 'self-evident' truth that all of us are created equal."

The rift between the court's only Black justices drew attention because it was unusual for two justices to so publicly and strongly disagree with each other on an issue that is central to how America addresses racism.

From her first moments on the court that October day in

2022, Justice Jackson was ready to use her voice in a more forceful way than she ever had before. She got to work almost immediately—as she always does—and quickly became known for her sharp questions to lawyers who came before the high court, and also for her lively written opinions. Her generally liberal philosophy on the law and racism have been known for a long time, but as a lower court judge and an attorney, she was careful to refrain from appearing to be partisan, no matter what.

But now that she had reached the pinnacle of her profession, she freely and forcefully articulated her thoughts on America's past, and what she hoped to see in its future.

At her speech to commemorate the sixtieth anniversary of the tragedy at the Sixteenth Street Baptist Church in Birmingham, Alabama, she noted that "Oppressors of every stripe, from the slave master to the dictator, have recognized for centuries that knowledge is a powerful tool. They have seen that once acquired, it can be wielded, and once wielded, it is transformative. Knowledge emboldens people. And it frees them."

Many in the audience took that as a reference to a spate of laws passed in conservative states that ban books and make it illegal for teachers to even talk about parts of America's racist past.

"But history is also our best teacher. Yes, our past is filled with too much violence, too much hatred, too much prejudice. But can we really say that we are not confronting those same evils now? We have to own even the darkest parts of our past, understand them, and vow never to repeat them. We must not shield our eyes. We must not shrink away—lest we lose it all," she said.

And she is making her mark, perhaps even changing minds. Even the very conservative George Will, who had condemned Lani Guinier decades ago, wrote an opinion piece siding with Justice Jackson on the issue of whether it was unconstitutional to keep prisoner Michael Johnson in solitary confinement, given that he suffers from severe mental illness, and is sometimes forced to clean his waste from his cell with his bare hands. The prison conditions made his mental illness worse. The conservative justices refused to hear the case; the liberal ones thought it merited discussion. Will wrote, "The court majority's dereliction of duty regarding Johnson illustrates how the labels 'liberal' and 'conservative' can be inapposite [not appropriate] in judicial contexts. The conservatives showed undue deference to government; the liberals correctly construed precedent and the Constitution's original public meaning."

Not long after she took her seat on the Supreme Court, leaders in the Florida community where Justice Jackson grew up asked her to speak at a special ceremony in her hometown. Miami-Dade County Commissioners voted to rename a road where her parents still lived in her honor.

Justice Jackson was just a few months into her new job on the Supreme Court. She had a lot to learn, and her work schedule was full. But she took time to make the trip to her hometown to show her appreciation. In the resolution to rename the road, commissioners highlighted the fact that the Brown family is "deeply rooted in the county."

"Her father, Johnny Brown, worked as an attorney for the Miami-Dade County School Board from 1983 until his retirement as Chief Attorney for the School Board in 2005; her mother, Ellery Brown, served as a teacher for many years and as school principal at the New World School of the Arts located in downtown Miami from 1993 until her retirement in 2007; and her uncle, Calvin Ross, served in law enforcement for over 40 years, including as Chief of the City of Miami Police Department from 1991–1994," the resolution says.

"Justice Jackson has credited her high school experience in this community, and especially her time on the school's speech and debate team, with providing her a strong foundation; and Justice Jackson's exemplary record of accomplishments and ground-breaking ascension to the nation's highest court serve as inspiration to members of this community."

At the ceremony, the county showed a video of workers taking down the old street sign and putting up the new one. Her father was there with the county workers, watching them and taking pictures. The video shows Johnny Brown proudly holding up the new sign before it was planted in the ground for all to see. It's green, with white letters: Justice Ketanji Brown Jackson St.

The video nearly brought Justice Jackson to tears. She took the stage right after it was shown. "It was surprisingly emotional," she said about the video.

She thanked the commissioners for the honor. Eureka Drive, a major road in a county that, just a generation ago, limited by law where Black citizens could live and work and enjoy life, was now named after her.

"I hope that this street naming will also serve as a testament to what is possible in this great country. I hope that people who are driving by might have a moment of reflection about what it means that a person from this neighborhood and someone with my background could take what this place has to offer and be well-equipped enough to then go out into the world and do what it takes to not only become the first Black woman to serve on the Supreme Court of the United States, but also the first former public defender and the first . . . associate justice who is from the great state of Florida," she said.

"It was while I was studying and competing and growing up here in this community that I gained self-confidence in the face of challenges. I learned how . . . despite obstacles, to work hard, to be resilient, to strive for excellence, and to believe in myself and what I could do if given the opportunity. So I really do love this place."

Even amid the regressive policies sweeping several states and the country at large, Justice Jackson said she also has hope for America. Her appointment to the highest court in the land is one of the things that gives her that hope.

"I have faith in our great nation," she said. "The people of this country have seen challenging times before, and still, we rise. We will link arms and step forward together—past the hate and fear, beyond the darkness of division. Knowing what we've been through will only embolden us to lift ever higher the torch of freedom and fairness, justice and equality."

After her first year as a US Supreme Court justice, Associate Justice Ketanji Brown Jackson reflected on the important job she was chosen to do. She said she knew she had been "entrusted with the solemn responsibility of serving our great nation."

It is "a service that I hope will inspire people, and especially young people, to think about what is possible, to understand the law, and to re-commit themselves to the Constitution and its core values: the rule of law, democracy, freedom, justice, and equality."

APPENDIX: JUSTICE KETANJI BROWN JACKSON'S EIGHT KEYS FOR A SUCCESSFUL LIFE

ON THE SURFACE, IT SEEMS that success has followed Justice Ketanji Brown Jackson throughout her life. From childhood to college to law school to her legal career, and now to the pinnacle: a lifetime seat on the Supreme Court of the United States. She's made it look almost easy, almost inevitable!

That obviously isn't the case. But it might look like that because all her achievements share one important factor . . . she's always prepared. And that comes from a personal habit that was instilled in her by her parents and her grandparents, and that she's taught to her own daughters: Focus and work hard.

In speeches, Justice Jackson has also shared other tips for success, but all of them fall under the "work hard" umbrella.

Here is some of what she has said about achievement:

1. KEEP LEARNING, EVEN IF YOU THINK YOU KNOW EVERYTHING ALREADY:

"My mother was (and still is) relentless in this regard, and what that meant for me growing up is that I could never rest on my laurels," she said in a speech entitled *Lessons My Mother Taught Me.* "Yes, I was an accomplished competitive orator; yes, I was president of my high school class, and you would think that would be enough to earn a restful period of unscheduled downtime during the summer. But, no, at my mother's direction, my summers were filled with science camps, and poetry competitions, and writing projects. I grew up a stone's throw from the ocean in Miami, but I couldn't just go hang out at the beach with everyone else. If I was going, I had to have a net and bucket and flash cards with the scientific names of the various species of foliage and marine life that

I was likely to encounter! Every situation presented a 'teachable moment'—and boy did I learn."

2. WORK FIRST, PLAY LATER:

"We have a mantra that emphasizes prioritization of work over play as one of our first principles, as the girls would testify," she said in a speech about raising her daughters. "'Do what you need to do before what you want to do' is a constant refrain in our house."

She reflected on the habits she developed as a child that aren't easy to follow, but are worth it.

". . . self-discipline and sacrifice has carried [me] through at every stage . . . which . . . has also allowed me to have opportunities that my grandparents could not have even dreamed about."

3. HAVE DETERMINATION:

When she became a federal judge, one of her former colleagues, A. J. Kramer, the federal public defender for the District of Columbia, remarked on how Justice Jackson let very few things stand in her way of getting the job done.

"She was unflappable. She is unflappable," he said. "When one of the secretaries begged her not to go over to the courthouse at 11:45 p.m. to file a brief and instead just file it the next morning with a motion, she insisted on trudging over there at 11:45 at night. This was seven or eight years ago, so it wasn't as good an area as it is now, and she walked over and filed her briefs. She was going to do that."

4. **FIND MENTORS:**
She tells her daughters to "look for mentors and role models in each new situation that they encounter, someone who can look out for them and help them . . . navigate the challenges that lie ahead in whatever field they choose to go into."

5. **HAVE A THICK SKIN:**
Justice Jackson told a group of young Black law school students that they were likely to see obstacles put in their way simply because of their race, similar to what she had experienced.

"As a dark-skinned black girl . . . my parents knew that it was essential that I develop a sense of my own self-worth that was in no way dependent on what others thought about my abilities."

That led her to focus on what was important to her, and ignore the insults as much as possible.

"Don't get mired down by the inequities—lift yourself up; rise above them; push them to the back of your mind; and don't let them get in your way!"

6. A LITTLE BIT OF LUCK:

Justice Jackson also believes in good fortune, but the kind of luck that comes if you're ready for it.

"I am the first to say that, in addition to my hard work, the connections that I made and sheer luck played a significant role at numerous points along my professional journey," she explained.

"Nothing I've done—from getting into Harvard, to clerking for the Supreme Court, to getting a presidential appointment—was part of my overall life plan. It just happened. And happenstance favors those who have worked hard and done well in each thing they've done before."

7. NETWORK:

"It is crucial that you make connections and develop relationships. This is, perhaps, the biggest realization that I've had thus far in my career: networking is really how opportunities are created!"

8. HAVE FUN:

For someone as hardworking as Justice Ketanji Brown Jackson, taking time for fun isn't easy. But she says it's important to balance work and play. She recommends hobbies: She knits, crochets, and goes to the theater often. She loves to dance, and she loves to watch reality TV shows.

In a speech to law school graduates in 2023, she was enthusiastic about one show in particular: *Survivor*.

"I have seen every episode since the second season and I watch it with my husband and my daughters, even now, which I will admit, it's not easy to do with the demands of my day job but you have to set priorities, people," she told the audience. "And that's exactly the first lesson that I have for you today. As you leave this wonderful institution and embark on your careers, you will sometimes face difficult choices about how to spend your time as you balance work and family and all of the other things that are important in your life. But no matter how busy you get, you can and should find time for the things you love—and I love that show."

APPENDIX: JUSTICE KETANJI BROWN JACKSON'S TEN SUPERHEROINES

JUSTICE JACKSON FREQUENTLY TALKS ABOUT how she didn't rise to the heights she has achieved on her own. She always mentions her family and her faith. She frequently makes it a point to call out her heroines, the women from the past whom she credits for blazing the trail that she's walked.

Even during one of the most important moments of her life—the opening of her Supreme Court confirmation hearings—the justice gave credit to her heroes:

"I stand on the shoulders of so many who have come

before me, including Judge Constance Baker Motley, who was the first African American woman to be appointed to the federal bench and with whom I share a birthday. And like Judge Motley, I have dedicated my career to ensuring that the words engraved on the front of the Supreme Court building—'Equal Justice Under Law'—are a reality and not just an ideal," she said.

Judge Motley, whom Justice Jackson happily calls her "birthday twin," is her primary superstar. But she has many others. In speeches, she's listed more than three dozen people who have inspired her, and strives to teach others about them.

"For me, many of the women—and men!—I have been privileged to get to know throughout my life have served that function: my mother, my grandmother, my aunt, certain teachers, special coaches, and the judges for who[m] I clerked, as well as those with whom I now work. There are also women I have never met, but who are recorded in the pages of history, and whose lives and struggles inspire me and thousands of other working women to keep putting one foot in front of the other every day," she said in one speech.

Out of the many figures in the past that Ketanji acknowledges with gratitude, here are ten. Some are familiar names in American history, but others are what Ketanji called "the invisible leaders of the Civil Rights Movement"—Black women who guided the movement but are rarely given credit:

1. **Joséphine Baker:** A Black American dancer, singer, and actress who became famous during the early days of moviemaking, and who earned even more fame after she moved to France, where she became a citizen. She was a spy for the Allies during World War II, was awarded the Croix de Guerre and Legion of Honour, and when she returned home to America, she fought for racial justice and was one of the few women allowed to speak at the March on Washington for Jobs and Freedom. One of her famous statements is, "You know, friends, that I do not lie to you when I tell you I have walked into the palaces of kings and queens and into the houses of presidents. And much more. But I could not walk into a hotel in America and get a cup of coffee, and that made me mad."

2. **Daisy Bates:** An Arkansas newspaper editor during the height of Jim Crow who helped plan the 1957 Little Rock Nine school integration. Her success led to threats against her life and she was forced to shut down her newspaper, but she continued to work for civil rights and wrote an influential memoir in 1962 called *The Long Shadow of Little Rock* that won the American Book Award.

3. **Amelia Boynton Robinson:** A voting rights activist in Selma, Alabama, who, alongside John Lewis, helped to organize and lead the March 7, 1965, march from Selma to Montgomery to protest racist voting laws. That day became known as Bloody Sunday, because state police officers met the marchers at the foot of the Edmund Pettus Bridge and began using clubs, cattle prods, guns, and tear gas to stop the marchers. Boynton was tear-gassed and beaten unconscious.

4. **Ruby Bridges:** She was six years old in 1960 when she made history by being the first Black student to integrate an elementary school in New Orleans. Louisiana, like other Southern states, had refused to follow the 1954 US Supreme Court ruling in *Brown v. Board of Education*, but Ruby and others helped to change that. She had to be escorted to class by four federal marshals every day to guard her safety. She grew up to be a travel agent and also continued her civil rights activism.

5. **Fannie Lou Hamer:** An organizer from Mississippi who led protests and voter registration drives, and who helped organize the Freedom Summer in 1964, bringing college students and others from across the country to the South to help with voter registration. Hamer was also a victim of forced sterilization when she was

twenty-three, and later was one of several women who were brutally beaten in a South Carolina jail after being arrested for a sit-in at a bus stop.

6. **Dorothy Height:** She became president of the National Council of Negro Women in 1957, a job she held for forty years. As a prominent civil rights leader, she worked to end lynching, to support voting rights for Black Americans, and she consulted with US presidents as well as other civil rights leaders such as Dr. Martin Luther King, Jr.

7. **Rosa Parks:** A civil rights activist in Alabama who, on December 1, 1955—nine months after fifteen-year-old Claudette Colvin did it—refused to give up her bus seat to a white passenger, was arrested, and saw her case go all the way to the US Supreme Court. The court then ruled that segregation on public buses was unconstitutional.

8. **Gloria Richardson:** An organizer with the Student Nonviolent Coordinating Committee and a leader of sit-ins and protests over segregation who was onstage at the 1963 March on Washington. She didn't shy away from physical danger, and in a famous photo she is seen pushing away a bayonet being pointed at her by a National Guardsman sent to break up a protest.

9. **Eleanor Roosevelt:** The wife of President Franklin Delano Roosevelt, who traveled the country during the 1930s and 1940s and was shocked by the racism she witnessed. She became a strong advocate for civil rights and prompted her husband to push policies that were more fair to Black Americans. She was also instrumental in arranging the famous performance by Black opera singer Marian Anderson at the Lincoln Memorial, after Anderson was prevented by a group of white women called the Daughters of the American Revolution from performing at Constitution Hall in Washington, DC.

10. **Sojourner Truth:** An African American woman born into slavery in 1797 who escaped, gained her freedom, purchased her son from a slaveholder, and then traveled the country in the 1800s, advocating for the abolition of slavery.

AFTERWORD

QUICKLY AND CONSISTENTLY OVER THE next two years, Justice Jackson established herself as one of the court's brightest, most inquisitive minds, with one eye on the history and laws of the country she loves so well, and the other eye on seeing those laws applied with justice and fairness for all Americans. Her buoyant optimism, sense of humor, and sharp intellect were on full display with her questioning during oral arguments for all the world to listen to, and in the thorough and well-reasoned decisions that she wrote privately in her chambers.

She stayed true to her lodestar—that "the entire point of our democratic experiment is, after all, full participation by the people in the systems and structures of government, not exclusion."

Two years into her tenure, she had to confront a sea change in the way powerful people see America and the judiciary.

Donald Trump, whose father had marched in a Ku Klux Klan parade on Memorial Day, 1927, and gotten arrested for participating in the "near-riot" that broke out, was elected president on November 5, 2024. President Joe Biden had listened to calls from people within his party, including Nancy Pelosi and former president Barack Obama, not to seek reelection and instead allow someone else to top the Democratic ticket, after he seemed to struggle collecting his thoughts during a debate against Trump. Vice President Kamala Harris stepped up and ran an exciting, energizing campaign, and beat Trump in their only debate, but had only 107 days between announcing her candidacy and election day to communicate her plans for the presidency and win over voters.

Aware of how his first term had affected the public, most legacy media publications had endorsed Harris over Trump, including the *New York Times*, the *Economist*, the *Atlantic*, and the *Financial Times*. The boards of the *Los Angeles Times* and the *Washington Post* both intended to endorse Harris, but the owners of the publications, including Amazon founder Jeff Bezos, who graduated from Miami Palmetto Senior High School like Justice Jackson, stopped them, causing several journalists to resign in protest.

Despite being aware of all the rollbacks in rights Trump had planned for the American people (outlined in a 900-page policy book called Project 2025), he received 49.9 percent of the popular vote and 312 electoral votes to Harris's

48.4 percent and 226 electoral votes. But 92 percent of Black women still supported Harris, reinforcing their status as the loyal base, backbone, and heart of the Democratic Party.

Trump was inaugurated on January 20, 2025. Michelle Obama didn't attend so she could protect her peace, after having been subjected to disgusting insults and racist attacks by Trump and some of his supporters ever since she entered the world stage. Since then, Trump has ordered companies and colleges to drop all diversity, equity, and inclusion policies, and many have caved.

On September 17, 2025, Trump's FCC chairman, Brendan Carr, appeared to encourage the ABC television network, owned by Disney, to fire comedian Jimmy Kimmel for telling jokes Carr found in poor taste, though that would be a direct violation of the First Amendment and a chilling of free speech by the government. Yet ABC buckled and suspended the comedian's show (though they backtracked nearly a week later after public outcry and an international backlash and boycott of Disney products). In 1722, the founding father Benjamin Franklin, whose brother had been imprisoned by Massachusetts's legislature for criticizing the government, published several letters by British lawyers Thomas Gordan and John Trenchard. In one, they'd written, "Whoever would overthrow the Liberty of the Nation, must begin by subduing the Freedom of Speech;

a Thing terrible to publick Traytors." Free speech is a fundamental right for all Americans—if it is lost, so is democracy.

Trump targeted the Smithsonian Institution museums, including the National Museum of African American History and Culture in particular, for what he called "divisive, race-centered ideology." In the meantime, Trump canceled several education grants, including that of Columbia University and Harvard University, under the excuse that they weren't doing enough to combat anti-Semitism, in an apparent attempt to pit Jewish people against Black people by pretending to favor one group over the other. But in reality, it was to foster an agenda of "diversity of thought" quotas aimed at admitting and hiring politically conservative students and faculty who'd advance a more pro-white agenda. Harvard president Alan Garber had agreed that the school needed to live "up to its steps to reaffirm a culture of free inquiry, viewpoint diversity and academic exploration" months before the grants were canceled. But there is irony in Trump's demand for quotas to be used to elevate and champion potentially unqualified candidates who otherwise would not have been admitted or hired. Harvard filed a lawsuit against Trump on April 21, 2025, contesting the loss in grants.

A lower federal district court ordered the Department of Education to reinstate the grants. But in a 5–4 decision, the Supreme Court ruled in favor of Trump's Justice Department's rush request to pause that ruling. Justice Jackson called the decision by the court to fast-track a hearing on this case "truly bizarre" and said, "I worry that permitting the emergency docket to be hijacked in this way . . . damages our institutional credibility."

On May 22, 2025, the Trump administration blocked Harvard from enrolling any international students in any of its schools and programs, so within twenty-four hours, Harvard filed another lawsuit against them, claiming this was a violation of the First Amendment. US district judge Allison D. Burroughs paused Trump's sanctions against the school until the lawsuit is decided. Harvard learned the hard way—they had given the administration an inch, so the administration took a mile.

Trump claimed white people from South Africa, called Afrikaners, whose ancestors took the land of Africans when they arrived from France and Holland beginning in the seventeenth century, were being discriminated against. These Afrikaners forced African people to live under the oppressive, inhumane, race-based policy of apartheid (based on America's Jim Crow laws) until 1990. Since then, slowly but surely, Africans have been reclaiming their land. Trump proclaimed that the white people were facing a "genocide," despite 75 percent of privately owned land and 60 percent of the top management jobs there being held by white people, though they make up only 7 percent of the population. Trump granted them asylum in the US, while in the meantime he tried to revoke the legal work status of Haitians, Nicaraguans, and Cubans and deport Latinos, Muslims, Jamaicans, and other people of color, including some US citizens, without due process, under the 1798 Aliens Enemies Act.

On April 8, 2025, Justice Jackson said, "The President of the United States has invoked a centuries-old wartime statute to whisk people away to a notoriously brutal, foreign-run prison [Guantánamo]." While a public defender, Justice Jackson had become very familiar with the horrible, torturous conditions there and couldn't stay silent. "For lovers of liberty, this should be quite concerning." She continued, "At least when the Court went off base in the past, it left a record so posterity could see how it went wrong." She was referring to the 1944 Supreme Court case of *Korematsu v. United States*, in which the court allowed for the internment (imprisoning in a camp without a trial) of Japanese Americans in World War II. The court overturned its ruling in 2018, with Chief Justice Roberts calling the original decision "morally repugnant."

"With more and more of our most significant rulings taking place in the shadows of our emergency docket, today's Court leaves less and less of a trace. But make no mistake: We are just as wrong now as we have been in the past, with similarly devastating consequences. It just seems we are now less willing to face it," she concluded.

On May 16, 2025, the Supreme Court stopped the administration from deporting Venezuelans the administration claimed were gang members, sending the case back to a federal appeals court. It directed the lower court to consider the migrants' claim that they could not be legally deported under the Alien Enemies Act, which is the very issue Justice Jackson had raised.

Donald Trump lost the presidential election to Joe Biden in 2020, so on January 6, 2021, unable to accept defeat, he incited a riot of his supporters, whom he referred to as "patriots," who attacked the United States Capitol to try to prevent the Senate from certifying the election results. A bipartisan Senate report found several people died as a result of this terrorist attack, and Biden's Justice Department sought to hold Trump accountable for his actions. Trump was indicted for these crimes, but he claimed he was immune from prosecution for what he did because he was president at the time. The six conservative justices on the court sided with Trump and gave Trump almost blanket immunity from criminal prosecution for "official" acts or crimes he commits while in office, both then and now.

In her dissent, Justice Jackson wrote, "I write separately to explain, as succinctly as I can, the theoretical nuts and bolts of what, exactly, the majority has done today to alter the paradigm of accountability for Presidents of the United States." She noted, "In its purest form, the concept of immunity boils down to a maxim—'[t]he King can do no wrong'"—a notion that was firmly "rejected at the birth of [our] Republic" when the United States went to war and declared its independence from Britain in 1776. She added that "in short, America has traditionally relied on the law to keep its Presidents in line. Starting today, however, Americans must rely on the courts.... Once self-regulating, the Rule of Law now becomes the rule of judges. . . ." And she went on, "To the extent that the majority's new accountability [model] allows Presidents to evade punishment for their criminal acts while in office, the seeds of absolute power for Presidents have been planted. And, without a doubt, absolute power corrupts absolutely."

The justice finished her argument, stating: "The majority of my colleagues seems to have put their trust in our Court's ability to prevent Presidents from becoming Kings through case-by-case application. . . . I fear that they are wrong. But, for all our sakes, I hope that they are right. In the meantime, because the risks (and power) the Court has now assumed are intolerable, unwarranted, and plainly antithetical to bedrock constitutional norms, I dissent."

In addition, in 2024, while out of office, Donald Trump was convicted of thirty-four felonies in New York State Supreme Court for crimes and cover-ups he committed to help himself win the 2016 election. Since he was reelected in 2024, he has not faced punishment for those crimes. And on his first day in office in 2025, he granted clemency and pardons to all the January 6 criminals, fulfilling his campaign promise to do so.

Trump has threatened members of the judiciary with impeachment and imprisonment for trying to uphold laws and constitutional protections that he disagrees with. At a conference for judges held in Puerto Rico on May 1, 2025, Justice Jackson called this out: "Across the nation, judges are facing increased threats of not only physical violence, but also professional retaliation just for doing our jobs." She made it clear that "it can sometimes take raw courage to remain steadfast in doing what the law requires." And in regard to targeting judges in particular, she stated, "The attacks are not random. They seem designed to intimidate those of us who serve in this critical capacity."

Her worries about the threats to democracy kept her up at night, she said. "I urge you to keep going, keep doing what is right for our country, and I do believe that history will vindicate your service." She highlighted how judges who issued progressive decisions during the civil rights era "have faced challenges like the ones we face today, and have prevailed."

It hasn't just been all work for the justice since she ascended to the Supreme Court, though. In fact, she managed to achieve the second half of her lifelong dream of becoming the first Black, female Supreme Court justice to appear on a Broadway stage!

For one night only, on December 14, 2024, the justice made her Broadway debut in a walk-on role in the musical

& Juliet, a send-up of the Shakespearean tragic play *Romeo and Juliet*, with a book by David West Read, featuring the music of Max Martin. In speaking to the William Shakespeare character, who in this musical is writing that play, she said, "I like it too . . . ah, yay! I think what I like about it, is that I am having a very strongly negative reaction to it. Like, I hate it. Which makes me think it must be brilliant." She sang a brief one-line solo, joined in with the chorus, and in what might be the most timely and on-brand line, when Shakespeare's wife, Anne Hathaway, suggests maybe his Juliet character should live at the end of the play, the justice exclaimed in agreement, "Female empowerment. Sick!"

Even when things seem to be progressing backward, or times get rough or even scary, the legacy of Ketanji and her ancestors has proven that the most successful strategy is to march on. Black Americans have seen this before and have made it through, fighting against injustice for themselves and others, while making sure to find the joy in life along the way. Life, laws, and the Constitution are always being written and revised, sometimes moving us in the wrong direction, but hopefully, as Dr. King said, arcing toward justice. So the most important thing to do in tough times boils down to the one word that lady told Ketanji all those years ago: Persevere. And justice will prevail.

ENDNOTES

SOME OF THE SOURCES IN these notes are also included in the United States Senate Committee on the Judiciary, "Questionnaire for Judicial Nominees: Attachments to Question 12(a)," Ketanji Brown Jackson, Nominee to be Associate Justice of the Supreme Court of the United States, which can be found online at www.judiciary.senate.gov/imo/media/doc/Jackson%20SJQ%20Attachments%20Final.pdf. Those citations will be annotated at the end with "see SJQ" followed by a page number.

CHAPTER 1

1   "on the other side . . . the Voting Rights Act": Ketanji Brown Jackson, "Commemorate and Mourn, Celebrate and Warn: Remarks for Associate Justice Ketanji Brown Jackson on the 60th Anniversary of Sixteenth Street Baptist Church Bombing," September 15, 2023, 3, www.supremecourt.gov/publicinfo/speeches/Justice_Jackson_Sixteenth_Street_Baptist_Church_Speech.pdf.

1   "both pride in their heritage and hope for the future": Associated Press, "Read the Full Text of Supreme Court Nominee Ketanji Brown Jackson's Opening Remarks," PBS News, March 21, 2022, www.pbs .org/newshour/politics/read-the-full-text-of-supreme-court-nominee -ketanji-brown-jacksons-opening-remarks.

1   "lovely one": Ibid.

CHAPTER 2

8   "change [was] gonna come": Sam Cooke, "Change Is Gonna Come," *Ain't That Good News* (RCA Victor, 1964).

8   "double duty": Associated Press, "Read the Full Text of Supreme Court Nominee Ketanji Brown Jackson's Opening Remarks."

9   "If she could speak, she can read": "Ketanji Brown-Jackson's Mother Ellery Brown | TVJ Smile Jamaica," Television Jamaica, April 16, 2022, YouTube, www.youtube.com/watch?v=nSEfBQJTW4g.

9   "She had a lot of thoughts and ideas she liked to put down in writing": Johania Charles, "Ketanji Brown Jackson Born for the Bench," *The Miami Times*, March 1, 2022, www.miamitimesonline.com/news/local /ketanji-brown-jackson-born-for-the-bench/article_2e544688-99b8 -11ec-aeaf-8f2f47dd9eb5.html.

10 "professional role model": Robert C. Jones Jr., "Ketanji Brown Jackson, President Biden's Nominee for the High Court, Was Inspired by Her Father, Johnny Brown, a University of Miami School of Law Alumnus," University of Miami School of Law News and Events, February 28, 2022, news.miami.edu/law/stories/2022/02/supreme-court-nominee,-ketanji -brown-jackson,-was-inspired-by-miami-law-alum-and-father.html.

10 "The race-based experiences of African Americans in this country through the ages": Jackson, "Commemorate and Mourn, Celebrate and Warn," 3.

10 "on December 1, 1955, Ms. Rosa Parks . . . in Montgomery": Ibid., 4.

10 "young John Lewis . . . Bloody Sunday": Ibid.

10 "not much older than myself": Ibid.

11 "never lied": Ibid.

11 "prepared for life in America": Ibid.

CHAPTER 3

22   "blessed child": Juana Summers, Ashley Brown, and Tyler Bartlam, "Ketanji Brown Jackson Gets Personal with NPR about Family and the Supreme Court," *All Things Considered*, NPR, September 3, 2024, www .npr.org/2024/09/02/nx-s1-5096102/ketanji-brown-jackson-supreme -court-book-opinion-election-memoir.

24   "simply the sweetest woman God ever made": Ketanji Brown Jackson, *Lovely One: A Memoir* (New York: Random House, 2024), 33.

27   "cultural and spiritual fulfillment to the community through classical and spiritual music": Bea L. Hines, "Prayers Won't Bring Back Loved Ones, but They Can Help Soothe the Loss," *Miami Herald*, June 20, 2017, www .miamiherald.com/news/local/community/miami-dade/community-voices /article157223064.html.

28   "For my people everywhere . . . our blood. . . .": Margaret Walker, *The Poetry of Margaret Walker Read by Margaret Walker* (Folkways Records & Service Corp., 1974), folkways-media.si.edu/docs/folkways/artwork /FW09795.pdf.

32   "Mississippi appendectomy": Allison, "Black History Month, Week 2: Fannie Lou Hamer," Department of Obstetrics & Gynecology, WashU Medicine, February 7, 2022, obgyn.wustl.edu/black-history-month-week -2-fannie-lou-hamer/.

33   "to identify and upgrade potential college students from" . . . "limited cultural opportunities": Marion M. Scully, "The Demonstration Guidance Project and Teaching of English," *College Language Association Journal* 7, no. 2 (December 1963): 153, www.jstor.org/stable/44321416.

34   "the four-year-old inner-city black youngster": Bryan Greene, "The Unmistakable Black Roots of 'Sesame Street,'" *Smithsonian Magazine*, November 7, 2019, www.smithsonianmag.com/history/unmistakable -black-roots-sesame-street-180973490/.

36   "brok sink, wate for repare": Jackson, *Lovely One*, 56.

37   "all that": Ibid., 57.

37   "I thought I raised you better than this": Ashley Brown, Juana Summers, and Tyler Bartlam, "Justice Ketanji Brown Jackson Opens Up on Family," NPR, September 4, 2024, www.iowapublicradio.org/2024-09 -03/justice-ketanji-brown-jackson-opens-up-on-family.

37 "because that would really hurt her feelings": Jackson, *Lovely One*, 57.

38 "I'm really sorry for how I acted, Grandma": Ibid., 58.

38 "blessed child": Summers, Brown, and Bartlam, "Ketanji Brown Jackson Gets Personal."

40 "I cannot remember a time where we had to say, 'Do your homework'": Charles, "Ketanji Brown Jackson Born for the Bench."

40 "She made sure that my brother and I were always learning": Ketanji Brown Jackson, "Four Lessons My Mother Taught Me," ALI Council Dinner Talk, October 19, 2017, 10; see SJQ, 808.

40 "I was raised . . . towering presence": Ibid., 2; see SJQ, 800.

40 "from an early age . . . in the legal profession": Shamonee Baker, "Uncles of Ketanji Brown Jackson Applaud Her Supreme Court Nomination from Tallahassee," *Tallahassee Democrat*, March 28, 2022, www.tallahassee.com/story/news/2022/03/28/kentaji-brown -jackson-supreme-court-tallahassee-famu-calvin-ross-uncles-family -nomination-hearing/7155513001/.

40 "whatever she did, she was going to land on her feet": Ibid.

40 "she always showed tenacity": Ibid.

40 "she was a leader—and a very studious one at that": Ibid.

41 "Ketanji had already made up her . . . mind in junior high school": Charles, "Ketanji Brown Jackson Born for the Bench."

41 "That was her goal and she never wavered from it one iota": Ibid.

41 "an instrument of change": Roxanne Roberts, "Ketanji Brown Jackson on Being a 'First' and Why She Loves 'Survivor,'" *Washington Post*, May 16, 2022, www.washingtonpost.com/lifestyle/2022/05/16/ketanji -brown-jackson-interview/.

41 "experienced firsthand . . . in South Florida": Ketanji Brown Jackson, "Remarks for the Empowering Women of Color Sixth Annual Constance Baker Motley Gala, Columbia Law School," March 12, 2021, 3; see SJQ, 553.

42 "If I worked hard . . . I wanted to be": Marc Fisher, Ann E. Marimow, and Lori Rozsa, "How Ketanji Brown Jackson Found a Path Between Confrontation and Compromise," *Washington Post*, February 22, 2022, www.washingtonpost.com/politics/2022/02/25/ketanji-brown-jackson -miami-family-parents/.

43 "Foxy Roxy": Stephen Rosenthal, interview with authors, May 28, 2023.

44   "that educational base from Roxanne Lombroia": Ibid.

45   "We'd go to pool parties. . . . now and then": Fisher, Marimow, and Rozsa, "How Ketanji Brown Jackson Found a Path."

46   "We as parents could never . . . the debate team": Charles, "Ketanji Brown Jackson Born for the Bench."

CHAPTER 4

49   "star in the making": Aaron Leibowitz, Jay Weaver, and Bryan Lowry, "Supreme Court Prospect Brown Jackson Was 'Star in the Making' at Her Florida High School," *Miami Herald*, January 27, 2022, www.miamiherald.com/news/local/community/miami-dade/article 257749578.html.

49   "could write and give a speech . . . outstanding in all those things." Nia Prater, "Meet Ketanji Brown Jackson: The Debate Star, Theater Kid, Public Defender, and Judge Who Would Join the Supreme Court," *New York Magazine*, February 25, 2022, nymag.com/intelligencer/2022/02 /supreme-court-nominee-ketanji-brown-jacksons-rise.html.

49   "literally . . . crying . . . because she was so good": Ibid.

49   "people dying with laughter when she did the humorous ones": Ibid.

49   "the same person today . . . both thirteen": Ibid.

49   "incredibly polished speaker": Fisher, Marimow, and Rozsa, "How Ketanji Brown Jackson Found a Path."

49   "the most morally centered person": Prater, "Meet Ketanji Brown Jackson."

49   "You look at this gold-plated . . . kind of person": Ibid.

49   "incredibly humble . . . very generous, giving, self-deprecating . . . I've ever met": Ibid.

50   "She would always just articulate it really clearly": Stephen Rosenthal, interview with authors, February 17, 2023.

50   "It was a simple, 'Hello, my name is Ketanji Brown, K-e-t-a-n-j-i'": Ibid.

50   "Black young woman . . . off the bat": Ibid.

51   "She was very poised . . . entered a room": Ibid.

51   "Whether it was running . . . to push forward nonetheless": Ketanji Brown Jackson, "Three Qualities for Success in Law and Life," James E. Parsons Award Dinner Remarks, University of Chicago, BSLA, February 24, 2020, 10; see SJQ, 575.

52 "fulfill my fantasy . . . Broadway stage": Andres Gans, "Supreme Court Justice Ketanji Brown Jackson to Have Walk-On Role in Broadway's *& Juliet*," *Playbill*, December 9, 2024, playbill.com/article/supreme-court -justice-ketanji-brown-jackson-to-have-walk-on-role-in-broadways -juliet; Jackson, *Lovely One*, 103.

52 "despite the obstacles . . . high school experience as a competitive speaker": Leibowitz, Weaver, and Lowry, "Supreme Court Prospect Brown Jackson Was 'Star in the Making.'"

52 "the one activity that best prepared me for future success in law and in life": Patricia Mazzei, "How a High School Debate Team Shaped Ketanji Brown Jackson," *New York Times*, February 26, 2022, www.nytimes .com/2022/02/26/us/ketanji-brown-jackson-high-school-debate.html.

52 "gained the self-confidence . . . at an early age": Prater, "Meet Ketanji Brown Jackson."

53 "If you don't talk about it, you never deal with it": Mazzei, "How a High School Debate Team Shaped Ketanji Brown Jackson."

55 "I cannot recall a single time . . . came my way": Erica L. Green, "At Harvard, a Confederate Flag Spurred Ketanji Brown Jackson to Act," *New York Times*, March 20, 2022, www.nytimes.com/2022/03/20/us /politics/ketanji-brown-jackson-harvard.html.

55 "What I do remember is often thinking, 'Hmm, well, I'll show them'": Fisher, Marimow, and Rozsa, "How Ketanji Brown Jackson Found a Path."

55 "oil and water don't mix": Leibowitz, Weaver, and Lowry, "Supreme Court Prospect Brown Jackson Was 'Star in the Making.'"

55 "He didn't really answer the question": Teresa Smith, "Secretary Is Grilled on Policies," *Miami Herald*, October 4, 1987; see SJQ, 1525.

56 "do not frequently mix": Jonathan Karp, "Palmetto Students Examine Their Values," *Miami Herald*, April 17, 1988; see SJQ, 1524.

56 "We were in different spaces from a lot of our classmates": Fisher, Marimow, and Rozsa, "How Ketanji Brown Jackson Found a Path."

56 "I was driving a 12-year-old . . . new Camaros": Ibid.

57 "guard your spirit": Jackson, *Lovely One*, 83.

57 "legendary" . . . "the way she pauses . . . at seventeen": Nigel Roberts, "Ketanji Brown Jackson's Harvard Classmates Talk about the Joy Her Supreme Court Confirmation Has Brought Them," BET, April 8,

2022, www.bet.com/article/negiyj/judge-ketanji-jackson-had-circle-of
-support-from-classmates.

57 "smart, friendly, engaging, [and] dynamic": Mazzei, "How a High
School Debate Team Shaped Ketanji Brown Jackson."

57 "She is the absolute best": Leibowitz, Weaver, and Lowry, "Supreme
Court Prospect Brown Jackson Was 'Star in the Making.'"

58 "It's not just what you say . . . how you say it" . . . "and how you get your
message . . . to convince": Ketanji Brown Jackson, "Commencement
Address at Boston University School of Law," Archives of Women's
Political Communication, Iowa State University, May 21, 2023, awpc
.cattcenter.iastate.edu/2023/05/30/commencement-address-at-boston
-university-school-of-law-may-21-2023/.

58 "while other kids were . . . wake-up call": Fisher, Marimow, and Rozsa,
"How Ketanji Brown Jackson Found a Path."

58 "carried through at every stage . . . even dreamed about": Jackson,
"Three Qualities for Success in Law and Life," 10; see SJQ, 569.

58 "She'd do the thing over and over . . . working on": Rosenthal, interview, February 17, 2023.

59 *The heights by great men reached . . . in the night*": Henry Wadsworth
Longfellow, "The Ladder of St. Augustine," Poetry Foundation, quoted
by Jackson, "Three Qualities for Success in Law and Life," 6.

60 "bagel baskets, Mother's Day presents . . . sell at a good profit": Elinor J.
Brecher, "Fran Berger—Dedicated Debate Legend Called 'Unforgetta-
ble Hero,'" *The Miami Times*, August 7, 2008; see SJQ 1513–15.

60 "Stephen, put that down! Don't eat that. That's salt!": Rosenthal, interview, May 28, 2023.

61 "like a living legend in the speech and debate community": Fisher,
Marimow, and Rozsa, "How Ketanji Brown Jackson Found a Path."

61 "pee-in-your-pants": Jackson, *Lovely One*, 74.

61 "had this beaming, energetic, friendly personality and natural charisma": Fisher, Marimow, and Rozsa, "How Ketanji Brown Jackson
Found a Path."

62 "I, for one, am a classic example of wasting time due to my lack of organization": Ketanji O. Brown, "It's about Time," William Faulkner Invitational, Oratory Winner, *Progressive Forensics* 4, no. 1 (Fall 1987): 2;
see SJQ, 257.

62 "I wind up struggling . . . my time went": Ibid.

62 "I worry that if peanut oil . . . come from?": "Ketanji Brown Jackson, 'Search for Signs of Intelligent Life in the Universe'—1988 Humorous Interpretation," National Speech & Debate Association (1988), You-Tube, www.youtube.com/watch?v=l_wpT4hgu1w.

64 "Both Denise and I . . . romantic sense": Jackson, *Lovely One*, 78.

64 "the peculiar loneliness . . . in high school": Ibid., 79.

65 "incredibly smart, hardworking . . . nicest people": Leibowitz, Weaver, and Lowry, "Supreme Court Prospect Brown Jackson Was 'Star in the Making.'"

65 "Why don't we go together?": Jackson, *Lovely One*, 78.

65 "We can't pick that song. . . . gonna get old": David Kujawa, interview with authors, February 14, 2023.

65 "she was like one of those leaders . . . they were": Ibid.

66 "She likes to get people to smile . . . her wit": Ibid.

66 "You know, not everybody's gonna be happy . . . too upset": Ibid.

66 "always count on her . . . good about": Ibid.

66 "I was a sophomore . . . chair was empty": Richard B. Rosenthal, "Statement of Richard B. Rosenthal, Esq.," March 22, 2022, www.judiciary .senate.gov/imo/media/doc/Rosenthal%20Testimony.pdf.

66 "came on the PA system . . . public high school": Ibid.

67 "The entire class immediately . . . she was Ketanji": Ibid.

67 "I'm sure Harvard is a perfectly good school too": Jackson, *Lovely One*, 100.

67 "to go into law and eventually have a judicial appointment": Stephen F. Rosenthal, "Ketanji Brown Jackson Was a Hall of Famer Even in My High School," CNN, March 1, 2022, www.cnn.com/2022/03/01 /opinions/ketanji-brown-jackson-classmate-yearbook-rosenthal/index .html.

67 "sights so high": Jackson, "Three Qualities for Success in Law and Life," 10; see SJQ, 575.

CHAPTER 5

68 "After God had carried . . . Harvard College": "Harvard's Founding," *The Harvard Crimson*, October 6, 1884, www.thecrimson.com/article /1884/10/6/harvards-founding-this-quaint-account-of/.

73 "*When I think of home . . . With the things I been knowing*": Charles Emmanuel Smalls, "Home," *The Wiz* (1975).

80 "Persevere": "Persevere," C-SPAN, March 23, 2022, YouTube, www .youtube.com/watch?v=w6gUP3XxbjA&t=2s.

81 "noble gift to learning" . . . "comes to us . . . sorrow resting on it": Corydon Ireland, "Widener Library Rises from Titanic Tragedy," *The Harvard Gazette*, April 5, 2012, news.harvard.edu/gazette/story/2012/04 /as-result-of-titanics-sinking-widener-library-rose/.

82 "I was in a strange place . . . no one cared": Fisher, Marimow, and Rozsa, "How Ketanji Brown Jackson Found a Path."

82 "*Why do I feel like I'm drowning . . . different they find me*": Charles Emmanuel Smalls, "Soon as I Get Home," *The Wiz* (1975).

83 "remembered me, believed in me . . . be successful": Fisher, Marimow, and Rozsa, "How Ketanji Brown Jackson Found a Path."

84 "to torture a suspect to get the information" . . . "to steal a drug that your child needs to survive": Green, "At Harvard, a Confederate Flag Spurred Ketanji Brown Jackson to Act."

84 "The kinds of questions . . . philosophy and law": Colleen Walsh, "Eight Current Overseers Share Their Unique Stories," *Harvard Gazette*, June 16, 2020, news.harvard.edu/gazette/story/2020/06/eight-current -overseers-share-their-unique-stories/.

84 "just really, really formative, and I think it set a path for me": Ibid.

CHAPTER 6

86 "Oh my God. It's the best show. You gotta watch this show": Rosenthal, interview, May 28, 2023.

90 "very good with language" . . . "funny to be delicate . . . explosive": "Seinfeld | 60 Minutes Archive" *60 Minutes*, 1997, posted on YouTube, May 12, 2023, 10:03, youtu.be/2togFepved8.

90 "We would do rehearsals . . . student audiences": Prater, "Meet Ketanji Brown Jackson."

91 "And that was a really challenging . . . quickly on your feet": Ibid.

91 "always very outgoing . . . interested in people": Roberts, "Ketanji Brown Jackson's Harvard Classmates Talk."

91 "Ketanji wasn't the person . . . She had diverse interests": Ibid.

92 "extremely powerful" . . . "very humble . . . impresses people": Elaine McArdle, "'One Generation . . . from Segregation to the Supreme Court,'" *Harvard Law Bulletin*, July 15, 2022, hls.harvard.edu/today /one-generation-from-segregation-to-the-supreme-court/.

92 "an unprecedented Harvard production. . . . possibilities of jazz": Alexander E. Marashian, "Yesterday's the Way for Holiday," *The Harvard Crimson*, April 11, 1991, www.thecrimson.com/article/1991/4/11 /yesterdays-the-way-for-holiday-piyesterdays/.

93 "a fresh interpretation . . . at Harvard": Ibid.

CHAPTER 7

94 "I'm so sorry": Jackson, *Lovely One*, 120.

96 "very intelligent": Nathan Cooper, "A Call for Reconciliation: Lincoln's Final Speech," Abraham Lincoln Presidential Library and Museum, July 29, 2020, presidentlincoln.illinois.gov/Blog/Posts/20 /Abraham-Lincoln/2020/7/A-Call-for-Reconciliation-Lincolns-Final -Speech/blog-post/.

96 "That is the last speech he will ever make": "Why Booth Shot Lincoln," Indiana State Museum, April 14, 2023, www.indianamuseum.org /blog-post/why-booth-shot-lincoln/.

97 "show any respect": Cheryl Lederle, "Frederick Douglass on Abraham Lincoln: The Writer and Abolitionist Remembers the President in Library of Congress Primary Sources," Library of Congress Blogs, February 7, 2013, blogs.loc.gov/teachers/2013/02/frederick-douglass-on -abraham-lincoln-the-writer-and-abolitionist-remembers-the-president -in-library-of-congress-primary-sources/.

98 "the full and equal enjoyment . . . every race and color": *Plessy v. Ferguson* (1896), Milestone Documents, National Archives, www.archives .gov/milestone-documents/plessy-v-ferguson.

99 "South shall rise again": "Jefferson Davis Hopes the 'Oppressed South' Shall 'Rise Again,'" October 9, 1868, Raab Collection, www.raab collection.com/jefferson-davis-autograph/oppressed-south-shall-rise -again.

101 "in many places, Black people . . . white society was concerned": Ketanji Brown Jackson, "Courage, Purpose, Authenticity: Black Women Leaders in the Civil Rights Movement Era and Beyond," MLK Day 2020 at University of Michigan Law School, 6, www.scribd.com /document/565127840/1-20-20-UM-Law-MLK-Day-Lecture?secret _password=FPnMVYgBIOVxKgEZFL56; see SJQ, 601.

102 "I think we just delivered . . . long time to come": Becky Little, "How the 'Party of Lincoln' Won Over the Once Democratic South," History.com, August 18, 2017, www.history.com/news/how-the-party-of -lincoln-won-over-the-once-democratic-south.

103 "knew what she was getting herself into": Ira E. Stoll, ". . . Who Is Bridget Kerrigan?," The Harvard Crimson, March 19, 1991, www.thecrimson .com/article/1991/3/19/who-is-bridget-kerrigan-plots/.

104 "of home. That's all": Carlos Lozada, "When the Confederate Flag Flew at Harvard," Washington Post, June 23, 2015, www.washingtonpost .com/news/book-party/wp/2015/06/23/when-the-confederate-flag -flew-at-harvard/.

104 "just the average blond girl from Virginia": Stoll, ". . . Who Is Bridget Kerrigan?"

104 "If they talk about diversity . . . ready to have it": Lozada, "When the Confederate Flag Flew at Harvard."

104 "Just because you can stick a flag . . . should do it": Annie E. Schugart and Samuel Vasquez, "Political Correctness Debate Shook Harvard," The Harvard Crimson, May 27, 2015, www.thecrimson.com/article /2015/5/27/political-correctness-debate-harvard/.

105 "This is a signifier of white supremacy" . . . "The official flag . . . financed by inhumanity": Lozada, "When the Confederate Flag Flew at Harvard."

106 "If you're calling me . . . take my flag down": Carol Stocker, "Student's Response to Confederate Flag Touches Off Free Speech Dispute at Harvard," Baltimore Sun, April 21, 1991, www.baltimoresun.com/news /bs-xpm-1991-04-21-1991111001-story.html.

106 "That wasn't the intent": Ibid.

106 "insensitive and unwise": Ibid.

107   "censure, not censor": "Censure, Not Censor," *The Harvard Crimson*, March 4, 1991, www.thecrimson.com/article/1991/3/4/censure-not -censor-pbjbust-how-insensitive/.

107   "take more account of the feelings and sensibilities of others": Green, "At Harvard, a Confederate Flag Spurred Ketanji Brown Jackson to Act."

107   "As a community . . . noxious ideas": Schugart and Vasquez, "Political Correctness Debate Shook Harvard."

108   "*Wait a minute . . . going to be failing*": Green, "At Harvard, a Confederate Flag Spurred Ketanji Brown Jackson to Act."

108   "While we [are] busy . . . library studying": Fisher, Marimow, and Rozsa, "How Ketanji Brown Jackson Found a Path."

108   "unacceptably lax": Green, "At Harvard, a Confederate Flag Spurred Ketanji Brown Jackson to Act."

108   "for us to be so distracted . . . like Harvard": Fisher, Marimow, and Rozsa, "How Ketanji Brown Jackson Found a Path."

109   "the very serious function of racism . . . is distraction": Jackson, *Lovely One*, 130.

112   "So what does it take to rise . . . than indulging them": Green, "At Harvard, a Confederate Flag Spurred Ketanji Brown Jackson to Act."

112   "You may write me down in history . . . I'll rise": Maya Angelou, "Still, I Rise," quoted in Jackson, "Three Qualities for Success in Law and Life," 13; see SJQ, 578.

CHAPTER 8

113   "My mother told me . . . can do it'": Green, "At Harvard, a Confederate Flag Spurred Ketanji Brown Jackson to Act."

114   "bopping" . . . "Who is this person?": Madeleine Carlisle, "What Ketanji Brown Jackson Could Bring to the Supreme Court," *Time*, February 25, 2022, time.com/6151590/ketanji-brown-jackson-supreme -court-profile/.

114   "she spelled out her name . . . where she came from": Errin Haines, "Four Black Women Became Classmates, Roommates and Lifelong Sisters. One of Them Is Now a Historic Nominee for the Supreme Court,"

The 19th, February 25, 2022, 19thnews.org/2022/02/ketanji-brown
-jackson-analysis-lifelong-friendships-sisterhood/.

114 "Through her eyes . . . can be supportive": Green, "At Harvard, a Confederate Flag Spurred Ketanji Brown Jackson to Act."

115 "that the best learners are those who hear different perspectives": Ibid.

115 "I was feeling a little lost and like I didn't belong": Haines, "Four Black
Women Became Classmates, Roommates and Lifelong Sisters."

115 "It was the first time that . . . in Ketanji's room": Ibid.

116 "It was the first time that I was like, 'I can make it here'": Ibid.

116 "her very diverse group of friends" . . . "'You have to talk to different
people'": Fisher, Marimow, and Rozsa, "How Ketanji Brown Jackson
Found a Path."

116 "She's extremely intelligent, probably one of the smartest people I know":
McArdle, "'One Generation . . . from Segregation to the Supreme Court.'"

117 "Her parents really took us in . . . loved us up": Ibid.

117 "We got some of the strong support that she had her whole life": Ibid.

117 "the ladies": Suzanne Yeo, "Lifelong Friends Open Up about Supreme
Court Nominee Ketanji Brown Jackson," *GMA*, ABC News, March 9, 2022,
abcnews.go.com/GMA/Living/lifelong-friends-open-supreme-court
-nominee-ketanji-brown/story?id=83337328.

118 "You are going to be the first Black woman . . . going to be one": Haines,
"Four Black Women Became Classmates, Roommates and Lifelong
Sisters."

118 "I could see it. . . . the absolute best": Ibid.

118 "piercing intellect": Green, "At Harvard, a Confederate Flag Spurred
Ketanji Brown Jackson to Act."

118 "silly things": Tonya Mosley, "Justice Ketanji Brown Jackson Shares the
Poem She's Kept in Every One of Her Offices." *Fresh Air*, NPR, September 4, 2024, www.npr.org/2024/09/04/nx-s1-5095923/ketanji-brown
-jackson-supreme-court-lovely-one.

119 "quintessential Boston Brahmin": Nina Totenberg, "Ketanji Brown
Jackson, a Supreme Court Prospect, Is Confirmed to a Key Appeals
Court," *All Things Considered*, NPR, June 14, 2021, www.npr.org
/2021/03/30/977919229/ketanji-brown-jackson-bidens-pick-is-viewed
-as-potential-supreme-court-justice.

121 "Why are you doing this?": Jackson, *Lovely One*, 134.

122 "all the advantages" . . . "help level the playing field": Ibid., 135.

123 "I love you": Ibid., 139.

124 "walked into history class": Ibid.

124 "He's coming over": Fisher, Marimow, and Rozsa, "How Ketanji Brown Jackson Found a Path."

124 "What do they have in common?": Ibid.

124 "side-eye" and "once-over": Green, "At Harvard, a Confederate Flag Spurred Ketanji Brown Jackson to Act."

125 "I did not realize that . . . so unassuming": Emma Platoff, "Beside the Nation's First Black Woman Supreme Court Justice Is Her Husband, a 'Quintessential Boston Brahmin,'" *The Boston Globe*, July 9, 2022, www.bostonglobe.com/2022/07/09/nation/beside-nations-first-black -woman-supreme-court-justice-is-her-husband-quintessential-boston -brahmin/.

125 "If we had an image of a quintessential prep school boy" . . . "he was not it. . . . That was not his personality at all": Ibid.

126 "this is not a color-blind society . . . Brown children": Fisher, Marimow, and Rozsa, "How Ketanji Brown Jackson Found a Path."

126 "Patrick really demonstrated . . . sweet to her": Ibid.

127 "We are out here because . . . sick of it": "Harvard Students End Sit-in Protest, Demand More Afro-American Faculty," *The Boston Globe*, November 17, 1990, 34; see SJQ, 1521.

128 "Young Black professionals . . . can be overcome": Fisher, Marimow, and Rozsa, "How Ketanji Brown Jackson Found a Path."

128 "She was always the person trying to find the middle ground": Ibid.

129 "They're not going to listen to us if we're screaming at them": Ibid.

129 "Ketanji moves the crowd, and it's a very diverse crowd": Ibid.

129 "If they knew her . . . I'd take it as it came": Ibid.

129 "She knows who she is . . . with her to school": Haines, "Four Black Women Became Classmates, Roommates and Lifelong Sisters."

130 "We can embarrass the university in front of the alumni": "Harvard Students End Sit-in Protest," 34; see SJQ, 1521.

132 "There is a chance that . . . creating injustices": Green, "At Harvard, a Confederate Flag Spurred Ketanji Brown Jackson to Act."

132 "Black people are the magical faces . . . gazing down on us": Marcellus C. Barksdale, review of Derrick Bell, *Faces at the Bottom of the Well:*

The Permanence of Racism, The Journal of Negro History 78, no. 2 (1993), www.journals.uchicago.edu/doi/abs/10.2307/2717451?journal Code=jnh.

133 "As a dark-skinned Black girl . . . about my abilities": Fisher, Marimow, and Rozsa, "How Ketanji Brown Jackson Found a Path."

CHAPTER 9

136 "a woman of character and integrity": Anne E. Bromley, "Professor Hails Classmate's Historic Confirmation," *UVA Today*, April 8, 2022, www.law.virginia.edu/news/202204/professor-hails-classmates -historic-confirmation.

137 "remarkable combination of gifts: charisma, [and] penetrating intelligence": Prater, "Meet Ketanji Brown Jackson."

138 "tiny but mighty" . . . "always saying thoughtful, knowledgeable things": Green, "At Harvard, a Confederate Flag Spurred Ketanji Brown Jackson to Act."

138 "We were all focused on . . . different level": Roberts, "Ketanji Brown Jackson's Harvard Classmates Talk."

138 "[Ketanji] was a very strong law student. . . . very kind": Angi Gonzales, "Justice Ketanji Brown Jackson's Harvard Classmate Reveals What She Was Like in Law School," *Spectrum News*, July 7, 2022, spectrumnews1 .com/ma/worcester/politics/2022/07/07/justice-ketanji-brown-jackson -s-harvard-classmate-reveals-what-she-was-like-in-law-school.

138 "brave, poised, and outspoken in classroom discussions on legal issues": Rosenthal, "Ketanji Brown Jackson Was a Hall of Famer Even in My High School."

138 "insightful remarks . . . valuable new direction": Ibid.

138 "essentially an honor society": "Questions for Judge Jackson at the Burke School Academy," March 23, 2018, 3; see SJQ, 795.

139 "a considerate roommate and a supportive friend": Bromley, "Professor Hails Classmate's Historic Confirmation."

139 "But when she spoke . . . insightful and valuable": Kimberly Jenkins Robinson, "The Hope of Ketanji Brown Jackson's Nomination," *Richmond Times-Dispatch*, March 24, 2022, richmond.com/opinion/column /kimberly-jenkins-robinson-column-the-hope-of-ketanji-brown-jacksons -nomination/article_443b678b-2196-546b-9e36-b0b09c87b11c.html.

139 "brilliant legal mind that could critique any legal argument" . . . "humility and tenacity": Ibid.

139 "proof that she had a brilliant legal mind" . . . "humble and easy to work with": Fisher, Marimow, and Rozsa, "How Ketanji Brown Jackson Found a Path."

139 "There are lots of smart people . . . down to earth": Gonzales, "Justice Ketanji Brown Jackson's Harvard Classmate Reveals What She Was Like in Law School."

140 "especially significant" . . . "opened doors to other opportunities": "Questions for Judge Jackson at the Burke School Academy," 3; see SJQ, 795.

140 "a wonderful experience for a law nerd like me!": Ibid.

140 "She always kept a sense . . . into the night": Robinson, "The Hope of Ketanji Brown Jackson's Nomination."

140 "who encouraged me . . . quiet perseverance": Ibid.

140 "she stood out for her brilliance": "Penn Law Reacts to the Nomination of Judge Ketanji Brown Jackson," University of Pennsylvania Penn Carey Law, February 22, 2022, www.law.upenn.edu/live/news/14510 -penn-law-reacts-to-the-nomination-of-judge-ketanji.

141 "She was a great person . . . to answer a question": Keith Edwards, "Kennebec-Somerset County District Attorney Was Mentored as a Student by Ketanji Brown Jackson," *Kennebec Journal*, April 7, 2022, www.centralmaine.com/2022/04/07/kennebec-somerset-county-da -mentored-by-new-supreme-court-justice/.

141 "participation by minority groups . . . monopoly": Ketanji O. Brown, "Guinier: 'The First Lesson of Democracy Is Dialogue,'" *Harvard Law Record* 98, no. 10 (April 22, 1994): 1; see SJQ, 102.

141 "cannot be achieved in a system . . . of the power": Ibid., 11; see SJQ, 103.

141 "we are facing the problems . . . vote but no voice": Ibid.

142 "only Blacks can properly represent Blacks": George Will, "Sympathy For Guinier," *Newsweek*, June 13, 1993, www.newsweek.com/sympathy -guinier-194016.

142 "quota queen": Clinton Bolick, "Clinton's Quota Queens," Op-Ed, *Wall Street Journal*, April 30, 1993. "welfare queen": Gene Demby, "The Truth Behind the Lies of the Original 'Welfare Queen,'" *All Things Considered*, NPR, December 20, 2013, www.npr.org/sections

/codeswitch/2013/12/20/255819681/the-truth-behind-the-lies-of-the
-original-welfare-queen.

143 "While I remained silent . . . looking for a person": Brown, "Guinier: 'The First Lesson of Democracy Is Dialogue,'" 1.

143 "The loss of Lani Guinier . . . and the country": William T. Coleman Jr., "Three's Company: Guinier, Reagan, Bush," Op-Ed, *New York Times*, June 4, 1993, www.nytimes.com/1993/06/04/opinion/three-s-company -guinier-reagan-bush.html.

143 "[It] was not only unfair but . . . different jurisdictions": Ibid.

143 "I would ask the country . . . years of segregation": Ibid.

144 "a giant step backward. . . . Fairness and due process were abandoned for political expediency": Michael Tackett, "Guinier Defends Her Views, Denies She Backs Quotas," *Chicago Tribune*, June 5, 1993, www .chicagotribune.com/news/ct-xpm-1993-06-05-9306050143-story.html.

144 "a principled person": Green, "At Harvard, a Confederate Flag Spurred Ketanji Brown Jackson to Act."

144 "stood out for her consideration of others . . . and her kind words to lots of people": Fisher, Marimow, and Rozsa, "How Ketanji Brown Jackson Found a Path."

144 "she was always well-liked . . . differing views": Rosenthal, "Ketanji Brown Jackson Was a Hall of Famer Even in My High School."

145 "We were an unlikely pair . . . found each other": Sally H. Jacobs, "Ketanji Brown Jackson's Ancestors Were Enslaved. Her Husband's Were Enslavers," *Washington Post*, June 19, 2023, www.washingtonpost.com /history/2023/05/30/ketanji-brown-jackson-harvard-supreme-court/.

145 "I love you, Ketanji" . . . "so sweet": McArdle, "'One Generation . . . from Segregation to the Supreme Court.'"

145 "Do you love my daughter?" . . . "Do you believe in God?": Jackson, *Lovely One*, 179.

CHAPTER 10

148 "She has become a lifelong friend and mentor of mine in the real world": Roberts, "Ketanji Brown Jackson on Being a 'First.'"

148 "Hearing cases . . . talking to the teacher": Ibid.

150 "Happy Loving Day! . . . Richard and Mildred Loving": Nicole Briese, "Who Is Ketanji Brown Jackson's Husband Patrick Graves Jackson?"

Brides, May 2, 2022, www.brides.com/who-is-ketanji-brown-jackson
-husband-5270582.

150 "Judge, would you like me to remove the homeless man in the back
row?": Totenberg, "Ketanji Brown Jackson, a Supreme Court Prospect,
Is Confirmed to a Key Appeals Court."

151 "liberals intent on sowing division and race-hustlers": Don Feder,
"Despite Liberals Race Does Matter," *Boston Herald*, March 31, 1997,
23; see SJQ, 75.

151 "Feder's as racist as . . . irredeemably evil": Ketanji Brown Jackson, *Boston Herald*, April 10, 1997, 36; see SJQ, 74.

152 "I learned writing skills in a different way with him" . . . "the attention
to detail . . . up until that point": Roberts, "Ketanji Brown Jackson on
Being a 'First.'"

153 "Tell me, Ms. Jackson . . . law clerk at the Supreme Court?": Jackson,
Lovely One, 213.

153 "eternal optimist": Jenny S. Martinez, Jennifer Nou, Andrew Manuel Crespo, John G. Roberts Jr., Ketanji Brown Jackson, and Charles R. Breyer,
"In Tribute: Justice Stephen G. Breyer," *Harvard Law Review* 136, no. 1
(November 2022), harvardlawreview.org/print/vol-136/tribute-breyer/.

153 "It's hard to even describe the degree of influence" . . . "in terms of just
his character. . . . all agree on": Roberts, "Ketanji Brown Jackson on
Being a 'First.'"

154 "was someone who was . . . thought it required": Prater, "Meet Ketanji
Brown Jackson."

154 "very calm under fire": Ibid.

154 "natural leader": Ibid.

154 "the world with openness . . . good will in others": Ibid.

154 "She will always listen carefully . . . she believes to be right": Ibid.

154 "just extraordinary in his thought . . . can't really be replicated": Ibid.

155 "I don't know anybody . . . didn't get along with Ketanji" . . . "incredibly
good at her job": Associated Press, "Jackson, in High Court Mix, Traces
Law Interest to Preschool," *Tampa Bay Times*, February 6, 2022, www
.tampabay.com/news/nation-world/2022/02/06/jackson-in-high
-court-mix-traces-law-interest-to-preschool/.

155 "Welcome home": Jackson, *Lovely One*, 229.

156 "white healer": Ibid., 237.

157 "goat who was stolen": Ibid., 23.

157 "friend of the court": Amy Howe, "Profile of a Potential Nominee: Ketanji Brown Jackson," *SCOTUSblog*, February 1, 2022, www.scotusblog.com /2022/02/profile-of-a-potential-nominee-ketanji-brown-jackson/.

157 "making every effort . . . deleterious secondary effects": Ibid.

157 "something of a professional vagabond": Candace Norwood, "How Ketanji Brown Jackson's Pursuit of Success as a Lawyer and Parent Got Her a Supreme Court Nomination," *The 19th*, February 22, 2022, 19thnews.org/2022/02/ketanji-brown-jackson-speech-law-career/.

CHAPTER 11

160 "a very careful reader of text" . . . "cares about the original meaning . . . Constitution": McArdle, "'One Generation . . . from Segregation to the Supreme Court.'"

160 "autopsy on a case": Ketanji Brown Jackson, "Disparity, Discretion, and Debate: Understanding the Federal Sentencing Dilemma," HLR Keynote, April 2017; see SJQ, 869.

160 "enemy combatants": Ketanji Brown Jackson, "Responses to Questions for the Record from Senator Ben Sasse to Judge Jackson, Nominee to the United States Court of Appeals for the D.C. Circuit" (2012), 6; see SJQ, 465.

161 "There is a direct line . . . I think it's beneficial": Ann E. Marimow and Aaron C. Davis, "Potential Pick Ketanji Brown Jackson Would Make History as First Federal Public Defender on Supreme Court," *Washington Post*, February 11, 2022, www.washingtonpost.com /politics/2022/02/11/ketanji-brown-jackson-supreme-court-defender/.

162 "a duty to represent her clients zealously" . . . "contradicting her client's legal . . . crimes I found offensive": Kevin McCoy and Nick Penzenstadler, "We Binge-Watched 14 Hours of Ketanji Brown Jackson's Speeches. Here's What We Learned," *USA Today*, March 18, 2022, www .usatoday.com/story/news/nation/2022/03/18/ketanji-brown-jackson -supreme-court-pick-stress-senate-hearing/9419571002/?gnt-cfr=1.

162 ". . . it's like a social experiment. . . . I love it": Roberts, "Ketanji Brown Jackson on Being a 'First.'"

163　"Season after season . . . and conflict": Ketanji Brown Jackson, "Commencement Address at American University Washington College of Law, May 20, 2023," Archives of Women's Political Communication, Iowa State University, awpc.cattcenter.iastate.edu/2023/05/24/commencement-address-at-american-university-washington-college-of-law-may-20-2023/.

163　"choose optimism . . . no matter what happens": Ibid.

163　"enormously impressive . . . compelling charisma": Green, "At Harvard, a Confederate Flag Spurred Ketanji Brown Jackson to Act."

167　"slave class": "Africans in French America," African-American Heritage and Ethnography, National Park Service, www.nps.gov/ethnography/aah/aaheritage/FrenchAmA.htm.

168　"Boys and girls: Only the student's natural hair is permitted. . . . are not allowed": Julia Jacobs and Dan Levin, "Black Girl Sent Home from School Over Hair Extensions," *New York Times*, August 21, 2018, www.nytimes.com/2018/08/21/us/black-student-extensions-louisiana.html.

169　"expression of cultural pride": Jonathan Franklin, "A Black Texas Student Suspended for His Hairstyle Is Shifted to an Alternative School," NPR, October 12, 2023, www.npr.org/2023/10/12/1205502505/black-student-crown-act-texas-hairstyles-alternative-school.

170　"channel my nervous energy . . . If anybody wants a scarf, I'm your source": Norwood, "How Ketanji Brown Jackson's Pursuit of Success as a Lawyer and Parent Got Her a Supreme Court Nomination."

170　"cast a long and persistent shadow": Fisher, Marimow, and Rozsa, "How Ketanji Brown Jackson Found a Path."

170　"It has spawned clouds of controversy . . . [illegal drug] sentence": Ibid.

170　"I believe that the commission . . . make this right": Carlisle, "What Ketanji Brown Jackson Could Bring to the Supreme Court."

171　"The decision we make today . . . Dr. Martin Luther King, Jr.": Transcript, "Before the United States Sentencing Commission, Public Meeting," June 30, 2011, https://www.ussc.gov/sites/default/files/Meeting_Transcript_0.pdf.

171　"He said: 'the arc of the moral universe . . . demands this result'": Ibid.

171　"And when you add to that . . . like for me": Totenberg, "Ketanji Brown Jackson, a Supreme Court Prospect, Is Confirmed to a Key Appeals Court."

172 "fifteen years from now, the use of racial preferences will no longer be necessary": Ketanji Jackson, "Written Questions of Senator Ted Cruz," Nominee, United States District Judge for the District of Columbia, U.S. Senate Committee on the Judiciary, January 25, 2013; see SJQ, 501.

172 "race-conscious admissions policies must be limited in time": Ibid.

172 "I have no particular insight . . . race in admissions": Ibid.

172 "One day I woke up and Ketanji and Lisa are at my door": Yeo, "Lifelong Friends Open Up."

172 "She just appeared . . . going through": McArdle, "'One Generation . . . from Segregation to the Supreme Court.'"

172 "That was a time where I . . . she just showed up": Yeo, "Lifelong Friends Open Up."

172 "Ketanji can organize something . . . your strengths as well": Ibid.

173 "Judge Jackson will be . . . sense of justice": Fisher, Marimow, and Rozsa, "How Ketanji Brown Jackson Found a Path."

173 "my judge": Ketanji Brown Jackson, Federal Bar Association Panel, "USSC Update," United States Sentencing Commission, 1; also see SJQ, 1272.

173 "baby judge school": Jackson, Lovely One, 341.

174 "I'm methodically and intentionally . . . considerations": Monica Dunn, "Who Is Ketanji Brown Jackson, the Incoming Supreme Court Justice? And the Inside Story Behind Her Name," ABC News, June 29, 2022, abcnews.go.com/Politics/ketanji-brown-jackson-incoming-supreme -court-justice-inside/story?id=82509753.

174 "Part of the frustration . . . Black woman": Haines, "Four Black Women Became Classmates, Roommates and Lifelong Sisters."

174 "is the idea that because she . . . presiding over cases": Ibid.

175 "I now use this photo . . . meet along the way": Jackson, "Four Lessons My Mother Taught Me," 12; see SJQ, 810.

175 "judge is a very active process . . . responding to new stimuli": Ibid., 4; see SJQ, 815.

175 "Because she did . . . as the appellant": McArdle, "'One Generation . . . from Segregation to the Supreme Court.'"

175 "I lost the appeal, as I knew I would": Ibid.

176 "One of my proudest moments . . . Supreme Court vacancy'": Ron Elving, "What Happened with Merrick Garland in 2016 and Why It Matters Now," NPR, June 29, 2018, www.npr.org/2018/06/29/6244

67256/what-happened-with-merrick-garland-in-2016-and-why-it
-matters-now.

176   "the single most consequential . . . majority leader of the Senate": Alison Durkee, "McConnell: Biden Won't Get Supreme Court Pick in 2024 If GOP Wins Back Senate," *Forbes*, June 14, 2021, www.forbes.com/sites /alisondurkee/2021/06/14/mcconnell-biden-wont-get-supreme-court -pick-in-2024-if-gop-wins-back-senate/.

177   "I hear the tax benefits . . . married in 2018": McCoy and Penzenstadler, "We Binge-Watched 14 Hours of Ketanji Brown Jackson's Speeches."

177   "She'd help plan . . . always went well": Kujawa, interview, February 14, 2023.

177   "She was on the organizing . . . food and the DJ" . . . "They were always a lot of fun": Ibid.

177   "Go, Panthers!": Ketanji Brown Jackson, "Rising Through the Ranks: A Tale of Hard Work, Big Breaks, & Tough Skin," Husch Blackwell Retreat Keynote Speech, Washington, DC, October 10, 2019, 5; see SJQ, 698.

177   "I'm a Florida girl": Ibid., 3; see SJQ, 696.

177   "It is impossible to overstate . . . given me so much." Ketanji Brown Jackson, "Chief Marshal 2017," Harvard Alumni, 2017, alumni.harvard.edu /college/reunions-events/chief-marshal-2017#ketanji.

178   "sure to emphasize how difficult . . . that first semester." Ibid.

178   "the enduring friendships that . . . other walks of life": Ibid.

180   "to always start by asking *why* when you confront a new situation": Jackson, "Commencement Address at Boston University School of Law."

180   "if [Aaron Burr] really wants to . . . make a change": Molly Glass, "Supreme Court Justice Ketanji Brown Jackson to 2023 BU Graduates: 'Anything Is Possible,'" *Boston University Today*, May 21, 2023, www .bu.edu/articles/2023/supreme-court-justice-ketanji-brown-jackson -speaks-to-2023-bu-law-graduates/.

180   "Find something you care about . . . room where it happens": Jackson, "Commencement Address at Boston University School of Law."

180   "It's not just what you say that leaves an impact . . . it's also how you say it": Ibid.

181   "The lawyers of color . . . justice for all": Jackson, "Remarks for the Empowering Women of Color Sixth Annual Constance Baker Motley Gala, Columbia Law School," 4; see SJQ, 554.

CHAPTER 12

183 "Kay! How are you? This is your uncle Thomas. . . . look at my case": Jackson, *Lovely One*, 282.

183 "Your dad tells me you're a public defender": Ibid., 281

185 "You may have seen it in person . . . Equal Justice Under Law": "Judge Ketanji Brown Jackson's Remarks at the 2021 Virtual Commencement," University of Pennsylvania Penn Carey Law Commencement, February 25, 2022, YouTube, www.youtube.com/watch?v=-Bb-iLaBYBA.

185 "That is a stark reminder . . . our justice system": Ibid.

185 "Practicing lawyers are also obligated . . . access to justice": Ibid.

185 "There will come a time . . . and open to all": Ibid.

186 "Our justice system can only . . . paying clients": Ibid.

188 "my passion in the law": Ketanji Brown Jackson, "Fairness in Federal Sentencing: An Examination," 1; see SJQ, 919.

188 "ultimate exercise of the power . . . will of the people": Ibid., 1; see SJQ, 941.

188 "I chose to become . . . in my family": Jackson, "Responses to Questions for the Record from Senator Ben Sasse," 5; see SJQ, 464.

188 "And after becoming a lawyer . . . my time and talents": Ibid.

190 "Stated simply . . . presidents are not kings": Ketanji Brown Jackson, "House Judiciary Committee v. McGahn, United States District Court for the District of Columbia," November 25, 2019, 114; see SJQ, 411.

190 "This means they do not . . . entitled to control": Ibid.

190 "In this land of liberty . . . People of the United States": Ibid.; see SJQ, 412.

CHAPTER 13

192 "Dear Mr. President" . . . "While you are considering judges . . . to the list": Ketanji Brown Jackson, "Musings at the Midway Point: My Reflections on My Journey as a Mother and a Judge," University of Georgia School of Law, Athens, GA, March 3, 2017, 19; see SJQ, 791.

192 "I, her daughter Leila Jackson . . . for the position": Ibid.

193 "She is determined, honest . . . for the job": Ibid.

193 "Thank you for listening!" . . . "Leila Jackson": Ibid.

193 "oblivious to Supreme Court politics and the process of nominating justices": Ibid.; see SJQ, 916.

193 "'You know, your mom's a judge . . . Supreme Court seat'": "35th Edith House Lecture: Ketanji Brown Jackson, U.S. District Court for the District of Columbia," University of Georgia School of Law, March 2, 2017, YouTube, www.youtube.com/watch?v=jXFerWhSckA.

193 "that getting to be on the Supreme Court . . . want to do that job": Ibid.

194 "Well, if the President has to find you, . . . who you are!": Ibid.

194 "My parents actively . . . raise my own daughters": Jackson, "Three Qualities for Success in Law and Life," 10; see SJQ, 575.

194 "a brief, shining moment": Jackson, "Musings at the Midway Point," 20; see SJQ 792.

194 "It is difficult to put into words . . . my daughters feel": Ibid., 19; SJQ, 791.

195 "I realized not only that I'm raising . . . and our entire family": Ibid.

195 "It has been a lot . . . as if I'm failing": Ibid.

195 "I was, in fact, terrified . . . and family": Ketanji Brown Jackson, "Remarks for Saris USSC Portrait Unveiling," February 21, 2020, 3; see SJQ, 975.

195 "feelings of not-enoughedness": Michelle Obama, "'Is Everyone Doing This Perfectly But Me?,'" *The Guardian*, November 12, 2022, www .theguardian.com/us-news/2022/nov/12/michelle-obama-golden -rules-of-parenting-the-light-we-carry.

195 "The images of maternal . . . female bodies": Ibid.

196 "But still, we are conditioned . . . *perfectly but me?*": Ibid.

196 "Self-scrutiny is something women . . . kids ourselves": Ibid.

196 "None of us—truly none—ever live up": Ibid.

196 "And so began the delicate balancing . . . needs of your family?": Jackson, "Rising Through the Ranks," 8; see SJQ, 701.

196 "Like many young women . . . and new mother": Ibid.

197 "In my case, it was . . . the deal-breaker": Ibid., 12; see SJQ, 705.

197 "That period of my life taught me . . . working environment": Ibid., 13; see SJQ, 706–7.

197 "Armed with that realization . . . epic proportions": Ibid., 13; see SJQ, 706.

198 ". . . to help people in need, and to promote . . . assistance of counsel": Jackson, "Responses to Questions for the Record from Senator Ben Sasse," 5; see SJQ, 464.

198 "rigorous progressive education . . . social justice": Debra Cassens Weiss, "Sen. Cruz Asks Jackson about Critical Race Theory at Georgetown Day School, Where She Is a Board Member," *ABA Journal*, March 22, 2022, www.abajournal.com/web/article/cruz-asks-jackson-about-critical-race-theory-at-georgetown-day-school-where-she-is-a-board-member.

199 "mothered me in my first job . . . work and family": Jackson, "Remarks for Saris USSC Portrait Unveiling," 5; see SJQ, 593.

199 "What would Patti Saris do?": Ibid., 3; see SJQ, 591.

199 "One thing I learned is . . . have misbehaved": Ketanji Brown Jackson, "Healthcare Best Compliance Practices Forum," Alexandria, VA, October 23, 2012, 13; see SJQ, 1075.

199 "Push Me, Pull You: Understanding and Diffusing Power Struggles at Home," Ketanji Jackson and Rachael Fleurence, "Push Me, Pull You: Understanding and Diffusing Power Struggles at Home" November 10, 2009; available at SJQ, 1425–38.

199 "a judge in the federal trial . . . two daughters": Jackson, "Musings at the Midway Point," 2; see SJQ, 774.

199 "One moment, you have this beautiful . . . About everything": Ibid., 3; see SJQ, 775.

200 "near daily whiplash . . . on the other": Ibid.

200 "had an exquisite singing voice": Jackson, *Lovely One*, 306.

201 "would have to fight harder . . . autistic person": Ibid., 310.

201 "Talia was autistic . . . especially anime": Ibid.

202 "But . . . when I leave the courthouse and go home . . . at all": Jackson, "Musings at the Midway Point," 3; see SJQ, 775.

202 "the indomitable spirit of hard work" . . . "those long-suffering . . . most circumstances": Ibid., 16; see SJQ, 788.

203 "do what you need to do before what you want to do": Ibid.

203 "My mother" . . . "would be very proud": Jackson, "Four Lessons My Mother Taught Me," 7; see SJQ, 805.

CHAPTER 14

204 "I'm looking forward to . . . get every representation": Joseph Biden, "Democratic Debate," Charleston, South Carolina, February 25, 2020.

205 "Someone extremely qualified . . . equally as important": Joseph Biden,

"Remarks by President Biden on His Nomination of Judge Ketanji Brown Jackson to Serve as Associate Justice of the U.S. Supreme Court," The White House, February 25, 2022, bidenwhitehouse.archives.gov /briefing-room/speeches-remarks/2022/02/25/remarks-by-president -biden-on-his-nomination-of-judge-ketanji-brown-jackson-to-serve -as-associate-justice-of-the-u-s-supreme-court/.

205 "Someone with extraordinary character . . . she thinks is right": Ibid.

205 "For too long, our government, our courts, haven't looked like America": Ibid.

205 "the court is equally as important . . . It's co-equal": Ibid.

206 "best qualified by training . . . the right place": Lyndon B. Johnson, "Remarks to the Press Announcing the Nomination of Thurgood Marshall as Associate Justice of the Supreme Court," June 13, 1967.

208 "love of country" . . . "distinguished service in the American Revolution": Martin Kelly, "What Are the Requirements to Become a Supreme Court Justice," ThoughtCo, May 9, 2025, www.thoughtco.com/what -are-the-requirements-to-become-a-supreme-court-justice-104780.

208 "support and advocacy of the U.S. Constitution": Ibid.

210 "strong, persistent, and disturbing . . . civil rights": "Oppose the Confirmation of Janice Rogers Brown," The Leadership Conference on Civil and Human Rights, May 17, 2005, civilrights.org/resource/oppose-the -confirmation-of-janice-rogers-brown/.

212 "It is the beauty and . . . this nomination": Ann E. Marimow, "Biden's Court Pick Ketanji Brown Jackson Has Navigated a Path Few Black Women Have," *Washington Post*, April 30, 2021, www.washingtonpost.com /local/legal-issues/ketanji-brown-jackson-biden-dc-circuit/2021/04/29 /c0bd2f0c-a761-11eb-8d25-7b30e74923ea_story.html.

212 "interpret the law wisely and fairly . . . whom it serves": Kelsey Reichmann, "US Marks Ascension of Jackson to Supreme Court," *Courthouse News Service*, June 30, 2022, www.courthousenews.com/us-marks -ascension-of-jackson-to-supreme-court/.

213 "Her opinions are always . . . everyday people": Biden, "Remarks by President Biden on His Nomination of Judge Ketanji Brown Jackson."

213 "It doesn't mean . . . her decisions": Ibid.

213 "She listens. . . . to do justice": Ibid.

214 "I . . . believe in transparency . . . my decision": Associated Press, "Read

the Full Text of Supreme Court Nominee Ketanji Brown Jackson's Opening Remarks."

214 "And all of my professional . . . prevail in court": Ibid.

214 "Like so many women . . . US Sentencing Commission": Biden, "Remarks by President Biden on His Nomination of Judge Ketanji Brown Jackson."

214 "a distinguished American . . . her family": Ibid.

CHAPTER 15

219 "No matter what happens, always act the part!": Ketanji Brown Jackson, "Remarks for Dinner at the Supreme Court: Phase II Orientation for Newly Appointed District Judges," Federal Judicial Center, February 26, 2014, 2; see SJQ, 984.

221 "my trusted sherpa": "Remarks by President Biden, Vice President Harris, and Judge Ketanji Brown Jackson on the Senate's Historic, Bipartisan Confirmation of Judge Jackson to Be an Associate Justice of the Supreme Court," The White House, April 8, 2022, bidenwhitehouse .archives.gov/briefing-room/speeches-remarks/2022/04/08/remarks -by-president-biden-vice-president-harris-and-judge-ketanji-brown -jackson-on-the-senates-historic-bipartisan-confirmation-of-judge -jackson-to-be-an-associate-justice-of-the-supreme-court/.

221 "The reception I got . . . feel good": Greg Garrison, "High Court 'Sherpa' Doug Jones Reflects on Helping Guide Ketanji Jackson to Supreme Court Seat," AL.com, April 8, 2022, www.al.com/news/2022/04/high -court-sherpa-doug-jones-reflects-on-helping-guide-ketanji-jackson -to-supreme-court-seat.html.

222 "You walk in there and . . . really well": Ibid.

223 "I have no doubt that . . . been possible": "Confirmation Hearing on the Nomination of Hon. Ketanji Brown Jackson to Be an Associate Justice of the Supreme Court of the United States," US Government Publishing Office, March 21–24, 2022, www.govinfo.gov/content/pkg/CHRG -117shrg47858/html/CHRG-117shrg47858.htm.

223 "the best husband, father . . . Patrick, I love you": Ibid.

223 "Girls, I know it has not been . . . I love you so much": Ibid.

223 "You got this!": Alia E. Dastagir, "Ketanji Brown Jackson's Comments on Motherhood, Her Husband's Tears and What They Mean for a Historic Moment," *USA Today*, March 22, 2022, www.usatoday.com/story

/life/health-wellness/2022/03/22/ketanji-brown-jackson-motherhood
-comments-husbands-tears-importance/7131789001/.

225 "fear or favor": "Confirmation Hearing on the Nomination of Hon. Ketanji Brown Jackson to Be an Associate Justice of the Supreme Court of the United States."

225 "My North Star . . . our constitutional scheme": Ibid.

225 "And in my view, judges should not be speaking to political issues": Ibid.

225 "can't make law": Ibid.

225 "stay in my lane": Ibid.

226 "affectionately by a term of medieval justice, known as the 'trial by ordeal'": Ibid.

226 "soft on crime": Ibid.

226 "a proud day for America": Ibid.

227 "There was no equal justice . . . living in America": Ibid.

227 "In its more than 230 years . . . can be the first": Ibid.

227 "It's not easy being the first. . . . the national spotlight": Dick Durbin, "Durbin Delivers Opening Remarks at First Day of Confirmation Hearings for Supreme Court Nominee Judge Jackson," March 21, 2022, www.durbin.senate.gov/newsroom/press-releases/durbin-delivers-opening-remarks-at-first-day-of-confirmation-hearings-for-supreme-court-nominee-judge-jackson.

227 "But your presence here . . . themselves in you": Ibid.

227 "It's not necessarily easy . . . what's possible": "Confirmation Hearing on the Nomination of Hon. Ketanji Brown Jackson to Be an Associate Justice of the Supreme Court of the United States."

228 "For the last three days . . . achievement and accomplishment": Alex Padilla, "Sen. Padilla | Day 2: SCOTUS Confirmation Hearing—Padilla Questioning Judge Jackson | Judiciary," March 23, 2022, YouTube, www.youtube.com/watch?v=QkkIvKuzJZw.

228 "What would you say . . . same great heights that you have?": Ibid.

229 "I hope to inspire people . . . and be anything": Ibid.

229 "persevere": Alex Padilla, "Following Questioning from Padilla, Judge Jackson Shares Her Advice to Young Americans on Perseverance," Alex Padilla, U.S. Senator for California, March 23, 2022, www.padilla.senate.gov/newsroom/press-releases/following-questioning

-from-padilla-judge-jackson-shares-her-advice-to-young-americans-on
-perseverance.

229 "I would tell them to persevere": Ibid.

229 "disappoint[ing]" ... "grit and grace": Christina Carrega and Chauncey Alcorn, "'Nobody's Going to Steal That Joy': Cory Booker's Full Speech to Ketanji Brown Jackson, Annotated," *Capital B News*, March 25, 2022, capitalbnews.org/booker-ketanji-brown-jackson-full-speech/.

230 "meritless to the point of demagoguery": Ibid.

230 "the largest organization of rank-and-file police officers": Ibid.

230 "uncles that are officers . . . after 9/11!": Ibid.

230 "Let the work I've done speak for me": Ibid.

231 "Your family speaks to service, service, service": Ibid.

231 "You got here how every . . . backwards in heels'": Ibid.

231 "Nobody's going to steal [my] joy [today]": Ibid.

232 "I see my ancestors, and yours": Ibid.

232 "You have earned this spot. . . . a great American": Ibid.

232 "They didn't stop loving this country . . . them back": Ibid.

232 "O, let America be America again . . . America will be!": Ibid.

232 "No Irish or dogs need apply": Ibid.

232 "Chinese Americans . . . ugliest of America": "Senator Cory Booker Talks Historic Nature of Supreme Court Nominee Judge Ketanji Brown Jackson," Booker on Trailblazing SCOTUS Nominee, March 23, 2022, www.booker .senate.gov/news/videos/watch/senator-cory-booker-talks-historic-nature -of-supreme-court-nominee-judge-ketanji-brown-jackson.

233 "make this nation live up to its promise and hope": Ibid.

233 "Don't worry, my sister. . . . God has got you": Ibid.

233 "She kept looking up": Ibid.

233 "That star—it was a harbinger of hope": Ibid.

233 "Today, you're my star. You are my harbinger of hope": Ibid.

233 "This country is getting better and better and better": Ibid.

233 "When that final vote happens . . . because of you": Ibid.

234 "It is our opinion that her direct . . . to the Supreme Court": Frederick L., Thomas, "Nomination of Ketanji Brown Jackson to be an Associate Justice of the Supreme Court of the United States," National

Organization of Black Law Enforcement Executives (NOBLE) Before U.S. Senate Committee on the Judiciary, March 24, 2022.

234 "a stellar nominee": Ibid.

234 "From the very first day . . . anyone like her": Rosenthal, "Statement of Richard B. Rosenthal, Esq."

234 "Ketanji's incandescent brilliance . . . was destined for greatness": Ibid.

236 "I told her that I felt . . . for her future": Aaron Morrison, "Jackson's Speech Highlights US Race Struggles, Progress," Associated Press, April 9, 2022, apnews.com/article/ketanji-brown-jackson-us-supreme-court-united -states-race-and-ethnicity-a3d76f3c3823df59eb949b995ca5de6d.

236 "Dear Chloé . . . with hair like yours": Guilia Carbonaro, "'Deeply Moved' Kamala Harris Reacts to Ketanji Brown Jackson's Confirmation," *Newsweek*, April 8, 2022, www.newsweek.com/deeply-moved-kamala-harris -reacts-ketanji-brown-jackson-confirmation-supreme-court-1696274.

237 "turn to our children and grandchildren . . . so many minorities": Joseph R. Biden, "Remarks on Senate Confirmation of Ketanji Brown Jackson as a Supreme Court Associate Justice," Administration of Joseph R. Biden, Jr., April 8, 2022, www.govinfo.gov/content/pkg /DCPD-202200266/html/DCPD-202200266.htm.

237 "We're going to look back . . . American history": Ibid.

237 "It is exciting to see . . . and dedication": Danielle Campoamour, "Black Moms React to Judge Ketanji Brown Jackson: 'Representation Matters,'" *Today*, April 7, 2022, www.today.com/parents/moms/black -moms-react-judge-ketanji-brown-jacksons-nomination-rcna20885.

237 "I am happy for my girls and . . . our country": Ibid.

237 "Representation matters . . . shifts career ambitions": Ibid.

238 "Being represented on . . . court in the land": Ibid.

238 "All through the . . . '*You* are possible'": Oprah Winfrey, "Oprah on the Historic Confirmation of Judge Ketanji Brown Jackson to the Supreme Court," *Oprah Daily*, April 7, 2022, www.oprahdaily.com/entertainment /a39666848/oprah-on-confirmation-of-judge-ketanji-brown-jackson-to -the-supreme-court/.

238 "And congratulations to Johnny and Ellery Brown: Your daughter did good": Ibid.

238 "To my daughters . . . I love you very much": "Remarks by President Biden, Vice President Harris, and Judge Ketanji Brown Jackson on the Senate's Historic, Bipartisan Confirmation of Judge Jackson to be an Associate Justice of the Supreme Court."

239 "for everything you've done . . . but now I do": Ibid.

239 "They also tell me . . . Judge Constance Baker Motley": Ibid.

240 "The marches, the boycotts, the sit-ins, the arrests": Jackson, "Three Qualities for Success in Law and Life," 2; see SJQ, 567.

240 "Think about that for a moment . . . table of brotherhood": Ibid., 3; see SJQ, 568.

240 "And less than a decade . . . have felt invincible!": Ibid.

241 "an honor of a lifetime": "Remarks by President Biden, Vice President Harris, and Judge Ketanji Brown Jackson on the Senate's Historic, Bipartisan Confirmation of Judge Jackson to be an Associate Justice of the Supreme Court."

241 "To be sure . . . possibly ever imagined": Ibid.

241 "But no one does this . . . to this occasion": Ibid.

241 "And in the poetic words . . . 'bringing the gifts my ancestors gave . . .'": Ibid.

241 "I, 'I am the dream and the hope of the slave.' . . . We have come a long way to perfecting our union": Ibid.

CHAPTER 16

244 "hard-won freedoms are under attack": Kamala Harris, "Remarks by the Vice President at the Delta Sigma Theta Sorority, Inc. National Convention in Indianapolis, Indiana," The American Presidency Project, July 20, 2023, www.presidency.ucsb.edu/documents/remarks-the-vice-president-the-delta-sigma-theta-sorority-inc-national-convention.

248 "For far too long . . . in history combined . . . including, of course": Ibid.

248 "the first Black woman . . . Justice Ketanji Brown Jackson!": Ibid.

248 "It's a good day": Ibid.

249 "fueled by the love . . . when we fight, we win": Ibid.

251 "They are a cohort . . . Black existence in America": Haniyah Philogene, "Delta Sigma Theta Sorority, Inc. Welcomes Justice Ketanji Brown Jackson and More to Its Sisterhood," The Grio, July 21, 2023, thegrio.com/2023/07/21/delta-sigma-theta-sorority-inc-welcomes-justice

-ketanji-brown-jackson-and-more-to-its-sisterhood/.

251 "Because Delta Sigma Theta . . . extraordinary group of inductees": Ketanji Brown Jackson, Statement to CNN, July 21, 2023, Abby D. Phillips, Reporting for CNN, x.com/abbydphillip/status/168238812451557 3760?lang=en.

CHAPTER 17

254 "the historic John Marshall Bench Chair": Mark Sherman, "Jackson Set to Make Supreme Court Debut in Brief Ceremony," Associated Press, September 30, 2022, www.wxyz.com/news/jackson-set-to-make -supreme-court-debut-in-brief-ceremony.

255 "humbled by the fanfare": Ariane de Vogue, "'We See You, and We Are with You': Justice Jackson Says She Is Humbled by Reactions Since Her Appointment to Supreme Court," CNN, September 30, 2022, www.cnn.com/2022/09/30/politics/justice-ketanji-brown-jackson -investitutre.

255 "The people who approach . . . this great country": Ibid.

255 "all walks of life": Ibid.

255 "I can see it in their eyes": Ibid.

255 "They say this . . . and we are with you'": Ibid.

256 "She came to play": Adam Liptak, "In Her First Term, Justice Ketanji Brown Jackson 'Came to Play,'" *New York Times*, July 7, 2023, www.nytimes .com/2023/07/07/us/supreme-court-ketanji-brown-jackson.html.

259 "I don't think that . . . being treated unequally": Ketanji Brown Jackson, "Merrill v. Milligan, U.S. Supreme Court Oral Arguments," October 4, 2022, www.supremecourt.gov/oral_arguments/argument _transcripts/2022/21-1086_1pd4.pdf.

259 "She was confident, and she was idealistic about the law": Evan Milligan, interview by authors, November 27, 2023.

259 "She really seemed to believe . . . didn't shrink from that": Ibid.

260 "Just on a personal level . . . shot of hope": Ibid.

260 "She's an inspiration": Ibid.

260 "that all men are created equal . . . equally before the law": Nina Totenberg, "Supreme Court Guts Affirmative Action, Effectively Ending Race-Conscious Admissions," NPR, June 29, 2023, www.npr.org /2023/06/29/1181138066/affirmative-action-supreme-court-decision.

261 "is color-blind": "Students for Fair Admissions Inc. v. President and Fellows of Harvard College," Supreme Court, June 29, 2023, www.supremecourt.gov/opinions/22pdf/20-1199_hgdj.pdf.

261 "I just sat there . . . I grew up with'": Lucien Bruggeman and Briana Stewart, "Ketanji Brown Jackson's Candid 2007 Take on Justice Clarence Thomas: 'I don't understand you,'" GMA, February 23, 2022, www.goodmorningamerica.com/news/story/ketanji-brown-jacksons-candid-2007-justice-clarence-thomas-83026032.

261 "But the lessons he tended to draw . . . everybody I know": Ibid.

262 "articulating her black and white world (literally)": "Students for Fair Admissions Inc. v. President and Fellows of Harvard College."

262 "Gulf-sized race-based gaps . . . American citizens," Ibid.

262 "They were created in the distant past . . . created equal": Jackson, "Commemorate and Mourn, Celebrate and Warn," 10.

263 "Oppressors of every stripe . . . frees them": Ibid.

263 "But history is also our best teacher . . . lest we lose it all": Ibid., 12.

264 "The court majority's dereliction . . . original public meaning": George F. Will, "The Supreme Court Should Have Heeded Ketanji Brown Jackson's Wisdom," *Washington Post*, November 17, 2023, www.washingtonpost.com/opinions/2023/11/17/supreme-court-mistake-solitary-confinement/.

265 "deeply rooted in the county": "Resolution R-892–22 Codesignating, by a Three-Fifths Vote of Board Members Present, That Portion of Southwest 184th Street (Eureka Drive) Between Old Cutler Road and Caribbean Boulevard as 'Justice Ketanji Brown Jackson Street,'" October 6, 2022, www.miamidade.gov/govaction/legistarfiles/MinMatters/Y2022/222159min.pdf.

265 "Her father, Johnny Brown . . . from 1991–1994": Ibid.

265 "Justice Jackson has credited . . . this community" Ibid.

266 "It was surprisingly emotional": CBS Miami Team, "Supreme Court Justice Ketanji Brown Jackson Honored with Street Renaming in Miami-Dade: 'This Is Where I Got My Start,'" CBS News Miami, 00:32–00:33, March 6, 2023, www.cbsnews.com/miami/news/supreme-court-justice-ketanji-brown-jackson-honored-with-street-renaming-in-miami-dade-this-is-where-i-got-my-start/.

266 "I hope that this street naming . . . great state of Florida": Ibid., 04:18–05:13.

266 "It was while I was studying . . . love this place": Ibid., 03:37–04:08.

267 "I have faith in our great nation": Jackson, "Commemorate and Mourn, Celebrate and Warn," 13.

267 "The people of this country . . . justice and equality": Ibid.

267 "entrusted with the solemn responsibility of serving our great nation": Ibid., 6.

267 "a service that I hope will inspire people . . . and equality": Ibid.

APPENDIX: JUSTICE KETANJI BROWN JACKSON'S EIGHT KEYS FOR A SUCCESSFUL LIFE

269 "My mother was (and still is) . . . rest on my laurels": Jackson, "Four Lessons My Mother Taught Me," 7; see SJQ, 805.

269 "Yes, I was an accomplished competitive orator . . . boy did I learn": Ibid.

270 "We have a mantra . . . would testify": Jackson, "Musings at the Midway Point," 16; see SJQ, 788.

270 "'Do what you need . . . our house'": Ibid.

270 ". . . self-discipline and sacrifice has carried . . . even dreamed about": Jackson, "Three Qualities for Success in Law and Life," 4; see SJQ, 569.

270 "She was unflappable. She is unflappable": A. J. Kramer, "Investiture Ceremony of the Honorable Ketanji Brown Jackson, United States District Court for the District of Columbia," May 9, 2013; see SJQ, 1034.

270 "When one of the secretaries . . . to do that": Ibid.

271 "look for mentors . . . to go into": Jackson, "Musings at the Midway Point," 17; see SJQ, 789.

271 "As a dark-skinned black girl . . . about my abilities": Jackson, "Three Qualities for Success in Law and Life," 10; see SJQ, 575.

271 "Don't get mired down . . . get in your way!" Ibid., 12; see SJQ, 577.

272 "I am the first to say that . . . along my professional journey": Jackson, "Rising Through the Ranks," 20; see SJQ, 713.

272 "Nothing I've done . . . they've done before": Ketanji Brown Jackson, "Morrison and Foerster Reflections and Remarks," Attorneys of Color Workshop, May 23, 2011, 12–13; see SJQ, 1257–58.

272 "It is crucial . . . opportunities are created!" Ibid., 9; see SJQ, 1254.

273 "I have seen every episode . . . priorities, people": Jackson, "Commencement Address at American University Washington College of Law."

273 "And that's exactly the first lesson . . . and I love that show": Ibid.

APPENDIX: JUSTICE KETANJI BROWN JACKSON'S TEN SUPERHEROINES

274 "I stand on the shoulders . . . not just an ideal": Associated Press, "Read the Full Text of Supreme Court Nominee Ketanji Brown Jackson's Opening Remarks."

275 "birthday twin": Jackson, "Commemorate and Mourn, Celebrate and Warn," 9.

275 "For me, many of the women . . . every day": Jackson, "Musings at the Midway Point," 20; see SJQ, 915.

275 "the invisible leaders of the Civil Rights Movement": Jackson, "Courage, Purpose, Authenticity," 1; see SJQ, 599.

276 "You know, friends . . . made me mad": Alisha Norwood, "Josephine Baker (1906–1975)," National Women's History Museum, www.womens history.org/education-resources/biographies/josephine-baker.

AFTERWORD

280 "the entire point of our democratic experiment . . . not exclusion": Jackson, *Lovely One*, 384.

281 "near-riot": Phillip Bump, "In 1927, Donald Trump's Father Was Arrested After a Klan Riot in Queens," *Washington Post*, February 29, 2016, www .washingtonpost.com/news/the-fix/wp/2016/02/28/in-1927-donald -trumps-father-was-arrested-after-a-klan-riot-in-queens/.

283 "Whoever would . . . publick Traytors": Cato, "Free Speech Is the Great Bulwark of Liberty," Encyclopedia.com, www.encyclopedia.com/law /legal-and-political-magazines/free-speech-great-bulwark-liberty.

283 "divisive, race-centered ideology": Zolan Kanno-Youngs, "In Trump's Ideal Picture of America, Diversity Is Taboo," *New York Times*, August 21, 2025, www.nytimes.com/2025/08/21/us/politics/trump -diversity-black-americans.html.

283 "up to its steps . . . academic exploration": Jennifer Schuessler, "Trump and Harvard Both Want 'Viewpoint Diversity.' What Does It Mean?," *New York Times*, May 5, 2025, www.nytimes.com/2025/05/05/arts /harvard-trump-viewpoint-diversity.html.

284 "truly bizarre" . . . "I worry . . . damages our institutional

credibility": Joan Biskupic, "Ketanji Brown Jackson Is Not Holding Back Against Trump or Her Fellow Justices," CNN, April 11, 2025, www .cnn.com/2025/04/11/politics/ketanji-brown-jackson-trump-analysis /index.html.

285 "The President of the United States . . . foreign-run prison": Edith Olmsted, "Ketanji Brown Jackson Torches Supreme Court Shadow Docket in Dissent," *New Republic*, April 8, 2025, newrepublic.com /post/193724/ketanji-brown-jackson-supreme-court-shadow-docket -immigration.

285 "For lovers of liberty, this should be quite concerning": Ibid.

285 "At least when the Court . . . how it went wrong": Ibid.

285 "morally repugnant": Josh Gerstein, "Supreme Court Repudiates Infamous Korematsu Ruling," *Politico*, June 26, 2018, www.politico.com /story/2018/06/26/supreme-court-overturns-korematsu-673846.

285 "With more and more . . . willing to face it": Olmsted, "Ketanji Brown Jackson Torches Supreme Court Shadow Docket in Dissent."

286 "I write separately . . . of the United States": Ketanji Brown Jackson, "Read the Supreme Court's Ruling on Immunity," *New York Times*, July 1, 2024, www.nytimes.com/interactive/2024/07/01/us/scotus-immunity.html.

286 "In its purest form . . . '[t]he King can do no wrong'" . . . "rejected at the birth of [our] Republic": Ibid.

287 "In short, America has . . . rule of judges . . .": Ibid.

287 "The majority of my colleagues . . . I dissent": Ibid.

288 "Across the nation . . . doing our jobs." Ketanji Brown Jackson, "Preserving Judicial Independence and the Rule of Law: Remarks by Justice Ketanji Brown Jackson," First Circuit Judicial Conference, Rio Grande, Puerto Rico, May 1, 2025, 2, www.supremecourt.gov/publicinfo /speeches/1st%20Cir.%20Judicial%20Conference%20in%20Puerto%20 Rico%20Remarks%20AS%20DELIVERED.pdf.

288 "it can sometimes take . . . the law requires": Ibid., 4.

288 "The attacks are not random. . . . critical capacity": Ibid., 2.

288 "I urge you to keep going . . . your service": Ibid., 8.

288 "have faced challenges like the ones we face today, and have prevailed": Josh Gerstein, "Ketanji Brown Jackson Sharply Condemns Trump's Attacks on Judges," *Politico*, May 1, 2025, www.politico.com

/news/2025/05/01/ketanji-brown-jackson-sharply-condemns-trumps
-attacks-on-judges-00323010.

289   "I like it too . . . it must be brilliant": "Justice in Juliet. Ketanji Brown
Jackson on Broadway," *New York Theater*, December 16, 2024, www
.youtube.com/watch?v=llPUlLznKpY.

289   "Female empowerment. Sick!": Ibid.

BIBLIOGRAPHY

To reference the bibliography, please visit
www.harpercollins.com/products/the-dream-the-hope-garen
-thomaslori-rozsa?variant=43793446666274

ACKNOWLEDGMENTS

WE WOULD LIKE TO EXPRESS our sincerest gratitude to Alyson Day for her care and guidance through smooth and choppy waters while getting this project in shape. Thank you also to Eva Lynch-Comer and Karina Williams for their belief in this work, and to the design team, copyeditors, and managing editor who got this to the finish line. Todd Shuster, Jack Haug, Lauren Liebow, Anna Shumay, thank you for being such involved stewards.

Very special recognition goes to William R. Thomas and all of Junior High School 43, class of 1958—we hope you've reached the horizon. We are also indebted to Stephen Rosenthal for helping us fill in the blanks and add necessary shading to the justice's backstory.

Lori would like to especially thank her stellar colleagues at the *Washington Post* and reporters at other publications who continue to do the hard and necessary work of keeping the public informed about issues large and small, some of which will end up before the Supreme Court.

We're incredibly grateful to historian Sharah Thomas for the access she provided and her diligent genealogy research. Garen would also like to send thanks to Niku and Zachary Thomas for their counsel and encouragement and love of the *Titanic*, respectively. We'd also like to offer so much credit to Michelle Lesley Johnson for the leads and fellowship she shared.

Most of all, we want to show our highest appreciation to the justice herself, whose childhood habit of self-discipline and natural affinity for writing and speaking created a rich record to mine for facts, going back to her days as a second grader.

And to our parents—for their support, and for the moral compasses and north stars they modeled for us. May we continue along those paths, always following the light.